SS & Jaguar Cars
1936–1951

SS & Jaguar Cars
1936–1951

by Allan Crouch

JAGUAR HERITAGE

Herridge & Sons

Published in 2013 by
Herridge & Sons Ltd
Lower Forda
Shebbear
Beaworthy
Devon
England
EX21 5SY

in association with the Jaguar Daimler Heritage Trust

Edited by Anders Ditlev Clausager
Designed by Chris Fayers
Special photography by Allan Crouch

ISBN 978-1-906133-49-8
Printed in Hong Kong

Picture Acknowledgments
The author and the publisher are grateful to the
following for supplying the photographs for exclusive
use in this book:
Australia: Ed and Doug Nantes, Bill Coombs, Terry
McGrath, Bob Kretschmer, Eldon Smith, Colin Galey
and Warwick Carter
Belgium: Frank Van Reybroeck
Canada: R & M Auctions
Denmark: Niels Kruger
Germany: Gunther Weber and Uwe Schreiber
Hungary: Henrik Szoke
India: T Raghunathan
Netherlands: Tom Zwakman, Bert Ziengs, Roberto
Verboon and Frank Ruppert
New Zealand: Beulah Farland, John Endean, Monty
Claxton and Alan Blundell
Poland: Mateusz Krajewski
South Africa: John Bird
Switzerland: Christian Jenny and Urs Ramseier for the
Swiss Car Register
UK: Jaguar Heritage Archive at Gaydon, Alan Gibbins,
David Davenport, Peter Morel, Martin Redmond, Alex
Aldous, William Salmon, Richard Kitchen, Michael
Turner, Geoff Ironside, Duncan Roland, Lawrence
Hopkins, Gary Johnson, David Howe, Ed Abbott,
Michael Martin, Geoff Dawe, Denis Foxley, Ken Page,
Peter Scott, Wayne Blackburn, Richard Burns, Owen
Wynn, Brian Gibbins, David Potter, Mike Harvey, Nigel
Smith, Robet Crawford, Neville Hamilton, Nick
Williams, LAT Photo Archives and Jim Patten
of *Classic Jaguar World* magazine
USA: Dick Strever, Michael Mueller and William Robson

Contents

Introduction

We rightly honour William Lyons as the father of Jaguar. He was, in modern parlance, a go-getter, highly goal-driven. As early as 1935 when he had been in the car business effectively for only four seasons, he spoke of his ambition to make one of the finest luxury cars in the world. He then set about achieving this, step by carefully planned step.

From 1931 to 1935, his early S.S. cars had established two important brand values: they were stylish, and they were affordable. With the new Jaguar models of 1935, Lyons added a third ingredient to the recipe – performance. While the S.S.I and S.S.II cars had established a following and had carved out their own niche in the market, they were always a trifle off-beat, even downright bizarre. The SS Jaguar was by contrast much more mainstream, and infinitely more respectable. An early S.S. car might have been the choice of some extrovert "bright young thing" of the period, but an SS Jaguar was a car that a provincial bank manager or solicitor could drive to the golf club without shame.

The SS Jaguars brought Lyons and his young company success. Lyons was fortunate in that he owned the largest shareholding, and therefore could – and did – run SS Cars Limited as his personal fiefdom, acting almost as a despot, if at least sometimes a benevolent one. His parsimony was incidentally legendary. Among many talents, he usually had the knack of choosing the right people to assist him, in those areas where he realised his personal limitations, particularly in engineering where William Heynes and Walter Hassan made an enormous contribution.

However, Lyons reserved for himself the prerogative of styling his cars, an art for which he had a considerable talent. Never perhaps the most innovative of designers, and allegedly unable to express himself in sketches or drawings, he had an extraordinary eye for line, and working with a select small band of craftsmen, produced bodywork of remarkable elegance. If at first he did not quite succeed, he would tirelessly work on the development of a shape, even on minute details, until he got a result which satisfied him – and the Jaguar customer.

The period covered in this book lasted for about fifteen years, a period during which the Jaguars came to establish themselves not only in the UK but also in many export markets, particularly after 1945, as very fine luxury cars indeed, with style and performance at reasonable prices. Even in the 1930s, there had been exclamations in the press along the lines of "I can't think how they do it" at the prices asked, and such remarks were to be repeated almost *ad nauseam* over the next thirty or more years.

As we know, from 1948 onwards Jaguar went on to even greater things, but the period from 1935 to say 1950 represented the formative years for the company, and for the cars, and as such are a tremendously important part in the history of Jaguar. Allan Crouch previously wrote an outstanding book about the S.S. Cars from 1931 to 1935, and he has made an equally excellent job of this follow-up volume. Having owned and restored his own Jaguar Mark IV drophead coupé since 1979, and having been for many years the Jaguar Drivers' Club Registrar for the cars discussed in his two books, he is undoubtedly the leading expert in the world on the minutiae of these early Jaguars. It has been a privilege and a pleasure to offer him some assistance during the years of research that have gone into writing the present book, and I wish him every success with it.

Anders Ditlev Clausager

Author's Foreword

This book continues the story of the cars made by William Lyons after the side-valve-engined S.S.I and S.S.II went out of production in 1935. Lyons now adopted the name of SS Jaguar for his new cars and introduced overhead-valve engines, first on the 1936 model 2½ litre, and two years later on the 1½ litre model, when the new 3½ litre engine was also brought into the range. These pushrod engines, with small modifications, were then used to power all the pre- and post-war cars up to and including the Mark V model until 1951, from 1948-49 made in parallel with the XK 120 sports car and later the Mark VII, both of which had the new twin-cam XK engine.

These were crucial and formative years for the SS Company, or, as it was renamed in 1945, Jaguar Cars Limited. During this period William Lyons' company moved from being a small volume producer of coachbuilt ash-framed cars, to a mass manufacturer of all-steel bodied luxury high performance Saloons and Drophead Coupés which enjoyed considerable success throughout the world.

All the pushrod cars made between 1936 and 1951, including the SS 100, are covered in this book, with a great deal of hitherto unknown detailed information, in part gleaned from the archive of the Jaguar Daimler Heritage Trust (JDHT), now also known informally as Jaguar Heritage, which published my first book on the S.S.I and S.S.II cars in 2006, and whose close co-operation has been invaluable also for the present follow-up volume.

Jaguar Heritage gave me full access to its archive of documents, sales ledgers, technical information and photographs, and these served as a solid base for the historical aspects of this book. I am indebted to the help given to me by the Jaguar Heritage archivist emeritus Anders Ditlev Clausager, who not only gave me support in computerising all the sales records but also performed the invaluable task of editing my final draft. I am equally grateful to photographic archivist Karam Ram for his generous assistance and support on the pictorial side. Thanks are also due to the Swiss Car Register for the information supplied on the destinations of most of the "chassis only" units sent to Switzerland for onward delivery to the country's coachbuilders.

For the history of the factory and its products I have drawn heavily on two books, Paul Skilleter's *Jaguar Saloon Cars* and Andrew Whyte's *Jaguar, the Definitive History of a Great British Car*. A third useful source of information was Donald Cowbourne's *British Rally Drivers – Their Cars and Awards 1925–1939*.

The SS Jaguar Company operated pre-war on the basis of the minimum of documentation for its cars, so there were significant gaps in the detailed information available for these early cars. With the impending war, the company was selected as a supplier of equipment for the war effort and as such was required to produce detailed drawings and specifications for all its products. This had the beneficial effect of changing the culture in the company, to producing most of the necessary drawings for assemblies, sub-assemblies and individual parts, but this change of approach seems however to have been partially skin-deep, as many of these drawings were discarded or destroyed in later years during the moves of the factory to other premises.

In order to put together the information and photos for this book I had therefore to rely heavily on a great many people around the world, and I am extremely grateful for their patience in sharing their knowledge and providing photos of their cars over the five years it has taken me to put this book together.

With so many contributors, I took the decision not to try to credit individual photos to the donors, but instead to list the countries of those who have in some way contributed to this book. Contributions came from Australia, New Zealand, South Africa, Switzerland, The Netherlands, USA and the UK, and all have helped make this book as accurate and comprehensive as possible, thus making a detailed history available to the large number of devotees of these cars. Whilst owners of the cars photographed are not named, the cars in the photos are each identified by chassis number, where known.

Allan Crouch, April 2013

Chapter One

From the SS Jaguars to the Mark V

A step towards mass production for William Lyons and his team – the 1936-model 1½ litre four-door Saloon, here wearing a wing-mounted spare wheel and optional cover for the spare.

From Swallow to SS

William Lyons and William Walmsley had set up the original Swallow Sidecar Company at Blackpool in 1922, making the Walmsley-designed streamlined sidecars. Their partnership had flourished and the business had progressed from sidecars to coachbuilt bodies on chassis from other car makers, at first the Austin Seven. By 1928 the company had become the Swallow Sidecar and Coachbuilding Company, and moved to Coventry at the end of that year. Swallow now expanded their activities to make bodies on other chassis, including Standard and Wolseley Hornet. In 1931, they began to make the S.S. cars using their own design of chassis, with mechanical components supplied by the Standard Motor Company. The S.S. cars were successful and the company later became SS Cars Limited.

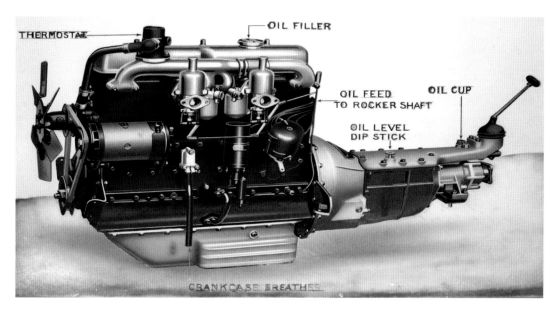

THERMOSTAT — OIL FILLER — OIL FEED TO ROCKER SHAFT — OIL CUP — OIL LEVEL DIP STICK — CRANKCASE BREATHER

Harry Weslake earned his reputation as an engine transformer – he developed this 1936 2½ litre overhead-valve powerplant (displaying two-piece water manifold and vertical thermostat) to produce more than 100bhp.

In 1934 the S.S. factory at Holbrook Lane, Foleshill, still had neither an engineering department nor an engine making capability of its own. These aspects of design and manufacture were carried out by the Standard Motor Company under Captain John Black, with whom William Lyons had a good relationship. This arrangement relieved Lyons of the need to raise a lot of capital, but it also restricted his ability to advance the design of his cars to achieve his ambition of making elegant, fast, and luxurious cars at modest prices, and eventually to undertake the majority of the manufacturing process. Already then, his aim was to make one of the finest luxury cars in the world.

It was at this stage that the less ambitious Walmsley decided to leave the company to join Coventry Steel Caravans, where he pioneered the introduction of lightweight aluminium panels for the caravan bodies. Lyons had always been the front man of the company, with Walmsley keeping in the background. This arrangement had suited both parties and their parting when it happened was apparently amicable.

When Walmsley left, Lyons floated the company on the London stock exchange, and this might have been what had prompted Walmsley's departure. Lyons kept a controlling shareholding and was left in sole charge. As a legal requirement he did have a board of directors, but the board had little or no say in the actual running of the company, a very satisfactory arrangement for the authoritarian Lyons, who ran the firm with only a few senior

managers in his inner circle. Arthur Whittaker was the general manager and Ernest Huckvale was the company secretary who also looked after the finances. Another influential person was Alice Fenton, who had joined the company as a typist in the 1920s and had Lyons' complete confidence, eventually becoming the home sales director in the 1950s.

Birth of the Jaguar

Lyons wanted to develop a new range of cars to replace the now ageing S.S.I and S.S.II cars that he had been making so successfully since 1931. These cars had all been fitted with Standard sidevalve engines, with various two-door body styles from Coupés through four-light Saloons, and two open versions, the Tourer and the Drophead Coupé. The S.S.I six-cylinder sidevalve engine of 2.1 or 2.7 litres, essentially the same units as Standard put in its own 16 and 20hp cars, needed to be improved to achieve more power output to consolidate the position of the S.S. models as fast touring cars.

Harry Weslake had a reputation as an engine transformer and had already assisted Lyons with improvements to the later S.S. engines. Lyons now wanted to increase power output from the current 70bhp of the 20hp 2½ litre sidevalve engine which was fitted to the S.S.I cars to a minimum of 90bhp, and Weslake accepted a contract to achieve an output of at least 95hp. His solution was to convert the Standard engine from side to overhead valves (OHV), and the new engine eventually developed more than

The new SS Jaguar chassis of 1936, with widened rear section and inboard rear springs, vane-type hydraulic shock absorbers and rod brakes.

100bhp. Lyons' other masterstroke was to get the Standard company to invest in the tooling and equipment to produce the OHV engine, thus allowing his own company to produce the new car with a particularly low capital investment on his part.

With an engine underway which would produce more than the required power, Lyons still needed the ability in-house to complete the design of the proposed new cars. In early 1935 he headhunted William Heynes to set up and lead an engineering department. Heynes was working at Humber, where he had been for ten years, and though he was only 32 years old at the time Lyons hired him for the job. Heynes joined in April 1935 and immediately started designing the chassis for the new car with its more powerful engine. There was very little time since the car needed to be ready in time for the Olympia Motor Show in October of that year.

Heynes took the S.S.I chassis and stiffened it by boxing-in the side members and strengthening the cruciform section in the centre. It was also widened by 4in (102mm) at the rear but the track was only increased by 3/8in (10mm), as the rear springs were moved inboard of the chassis side members, thus providing a wider base for the passenger compartment. The wheelbase was left unchanged at 9ft 11in (3023mm). The wider

chassis enabled a four-door saloon body to be accommodated which would give rear passengers more space and easier access to the cabin. This was the first four-door car the company had produced and it determined the nature of the cars that the company would be producing in the future. Lyons himself directed the body styling, aided by Fred Holland and his team of craftsmen. The cars were still coachbuilt, with an ash-framed, steel-skinned body assembled on a separate chassis, and despite the obvious difficulties in producing coachbuilt cars, Lyons was determined to increase the company's production volumes.

Lyons was gearing his products for mass production and getting away from the virtually bespoke S.S.I and S.S.II cars. The range and variety of the 1935 cars that the factory offered had been wide for mass production, as there were six body styles on the S.S.I chassis, the Coupé, Saloon, Airline, Drophead Coupé, Tourer, and the low-volume SS 90 two-seater sports car. There were another three styles for the S.S.II, Coupé, Saloon and Tourer. As each model was offered with two engine sizes, 16hp and 20hp for the S.S.I and 10hp and 12hp for the S.S.II, this amounted to an unsustainable diversity for a factory whose ambition lay in mass production.

For the 1936 models Lyons standardised on two engine sizes, a four-cylinder 1½ litre 12hp sidevalve engine for the smaller car and the new six-cylinder 2½ litre 20hp OHV engine for the larger model, with only one four-door saloon body for each of the two engine sizes. The body for the smaller 1½ litre car was similar in shape and size to the 2½ litre car but its chassis had a shorter wheelbase, although at 9ft (2743mm), it was 4in (102mm) longer than the S.S.II chassis. The engine was the 1.6 litre 12hp sidevalve Standard unit that had powered the S.S.II cars. Production of the four-cylinder car started in February 1936. It was only converted to an over-head-valve engine for the 1938 model year when the new all-steel models were introduced.

Lyons had concentrated his efforts on producing and launching his flagship car, the four-door 2½ litre Saloon. This he did with considerable flair at a reception on 23 September 1935 at the Mayfair Hotel in London. When the car was unveiled it caused a considerable stir among the assembled dealers and journalists. Each was asked by Lyons to write

The Mayfair Hotel, central London, September 1935: the launch of the 1936-model four-door 2½ litre Saloon caused a stir among dealers and journalists.

down on a card what he thought the selling price of the car would be. The cards were collected and the various estimates averaged at £632, which reflected the perception of the value of the car, so there was general excitement when Lyons triumphantly announced the actual price of £385. The launch was spectacularly successful and extremely well managed by Lyons, and the new model was already in production by October.

With the new car came a new model name, "Jaguar", selected by Lyons personally from a list of possible names drawn up by his advertising people. The SS Jaguar 2½ litre Saloon was much faster and £10 cheaper than the side-valve

engined Standard Twenty, although around this time Standard relaunched the Twenty in the Flying Standard range at only £315. The Jaguar had a significant advantage in price and performance compared with other cars of its class: Humber whose Eighteen cost £445, Armstrong Siddeley whose Twenty cost £550, and Daimler whose Light Twenty cost £675. On the other hand, the closest Jaguar rival was the new MG SA 2.3-litre 18hp saloon which was £10 cheaper at £375, while a Wolseley Super Six of 21 or 25hp cost just £340.

In addition to the two Saloon cars, the company brought out two other new, low-volume cars, to offer a total of four models. The

An early mock-up for the 1936 model Saloon with rear-opening back doors. This car probably became the 2½ litre machine shown at the Mayfair launch in 1935.

A 1936-model 2½ litre Saloon featuring separate sidelights used only on 1936 models, side-mounted spare wheel with no cover and the early P100S headlamps.

four-seater Tourer was very similar in looks to the S.S.I Tourer, but was now called the SS Jaguar Tourer as it was built on the new chassis with the 2½ litre OHV engine. The fixing brackets had to be redesigned to accommodate the wider rear end of the new chassis with the largely unchanged body tub. There was no 1½ litre Tourer. This revamped Tourer was some-

what of a stop-gap with a short production run of 105 cars from May 1936 to August 1937, when the company replaced it with five-seater Drop-head Coupé versions of the Saloons.

In 1935 the company had made a small number, only 24, of the short-chassis S.S.I 90 open two-seater sports car with the 20hp side-valve engine. Lyons now went into full production of a

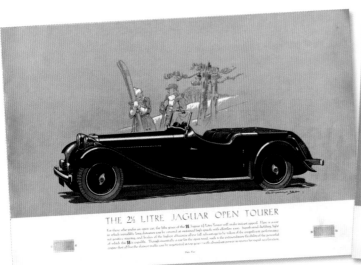

The 1936-model OHV 2½ litre SS Jaguar Tourer, similar to the sidevalve S.S.I Tourer it replaced, but built on the new chassis. Just 105 examples were produced.

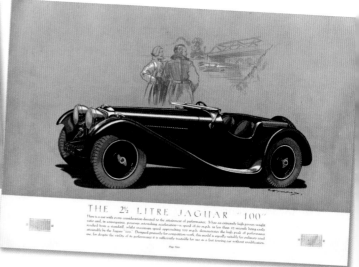

The successor to the sidevalve S.S.I 90 was the 1936 2½ litre OHV SS Jaguar 100, pictured here in the brochure for the new Open Two-Seater (OTS) car.

The 1937-model OHV 2½ litre Saloon owned from new by Lady Lyons, photographed outside Lyons' house Wappenbury Hall. The car now lives in the Jaguar Heritage collection.

new version of this car, the SS Jaguar 100, commonly known as the SS 100. This had the benefit of the improvements of the new Saloon and Tourer chassis, as well as the OHV engine, and was destined to become very successful in all manner of competitions. There were two SS 100 pre-production cars made in October 1935, but full production only started in April 1936.

The company was not only faced with increasing the volume of output, but it also had moved into assembling the rolling chassis that it had previously received complete from Standard. The SS Jaguar engines and transmissions were still supplied by Standard, but the other chassis components such as the frame itself, the brakes, and the suspension, etc, were purchased direct from the suppliers. The factory was reorganised to accommodate the chassis build, and the body parts were designed to keep the individual panels small enough to be made on the presses the company already had, again keeping the investment required to an absolute minimum.

For these coachbuilt cars there was still a considerable amount of manufacture and hand assembly of the ash frame and welding of the steel panels to be done by SS Cars, but Lyons used his accumulated expertise in coachbuilding to ensure that all the parts were accurately made for ease and speed of assembly. He also

arranged the assembly line fixtures so that the body and the wings were painted together at the same time, thus guaranteeing a perfect colour match. These processes set the basis for the increase in production volume that Lyons was looking for, and which he achieved for the 1936 and 1937 models.

As a measure of the success of the new Jaguar range, the factory had made 1750 of the 1935 model S.S.I and S.S.II cars, but 2241 were made of the 1936 Jaguars, an increase of nearly 30 per cent over the previous year. The following year, still making the coachbuilt cars, the output increased a further 60 per cent to 3628 cars. These volumes were remarkable for a specialised coachbuilt car, and the company was only finally able to improve on the figures in 1938-39 when the all-steel cars that replaced the coachbuilt design were in their second year of production.

The 2½ litre Saloon that was the company's main model was very well received by the motoring press, which praised its comfort, quality of design and build, and its undoubtedly class-leading performance. The 1½ litre Saloon with its side-valve engine of course had a relatively poor performance, markedly so when compared with the bigger car, with a top speed of 70mph (113 km/h) rather than 85mph (137 km/h), but was

Lovely colour poster supposedly illustrating a 1937-model 2½ litre Saloon with quarterlights. To be correct it should have had sidelights inset into the wings and not the separate units depicted.

appreciated for its other qualities, especially as it cost only £285. The SS 100 was quite simply sensational, offering 95mph (153 km/h) at £395, just £10 more than the 2½ litre Saloon.

In September 1936 Lyons launched the 1937 range. The Saloons were basically unchanged but a substantial number of relatively small improvements had been introduced. The Tourer and SS 100 models also continued in production. Characteristically, Lyons was not resting on his laurels and was preparing for his next major step, the introduction of the all-steel bodied

cars, to allow him finally to move away from the constraints to his ambition inherent in making coachbuilt cars.

The 1938 Models

Lyons took a bold and almost unprecedented step by deciding to introduce all-steel bodywork for his 1938 models. All-steel bodies had only arrived in Britain from the USA about ten years earlier when the Pressed Steel Company was established at Cowley, followed in 1931 by the American Briggs company which set up a plant

New 1938 3½ litre rolling chassis with cross-members eliminating the cruciform layout, and widened for the front occupants. The 3½ litre engine was introduced into the range for 1938-model cars.

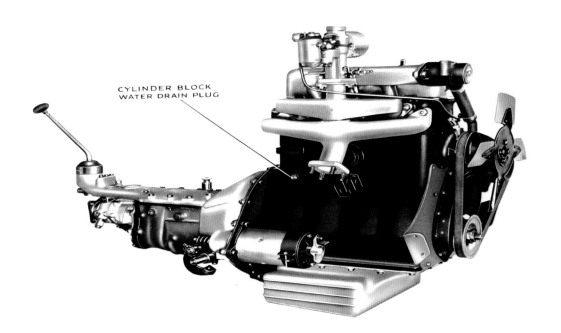

CYLINDER BLOCK
WATER DRAIN PLUG

The long-awaited 1½ litre OHV engine of 1776cc capacity for 1938-model cars. This engine had the inlet and exhaust on the same side, unlike the six-cylinder crossflow engines.

at Dagenham to supply Ford, and even in 1937 not all of the mass-producers had fully adopted this method of construction. SS was probably the first small specialist company to introduce all-steel coachwork and certainly the first small company to assemble their own bodies from individual panels, rather than buying in complete bodies from a single supplier.

For the 1938 models, Lyons continued with his determination to keep ahead of his rivals by bringing out two new OHV engines to complement the well-established 2½ litre unit. Firstly, a new 1½ litre engine which was essentially a Weslake overhead-valve version of the Standard engine, which had been enlarged to 1776cc for Standard's own Fourteen. This engine was in effect a four-cylinder version of the six-cylinder 2½ litre unit, with the same bore and stroke, but had only three main bearings compared with the seven of the larger engine. It produced 65bhp, at least 25 per cent more than the side-valve Standard Twelve engine on which it had been based, and considerably improved the performance of the 1½ litre Saloon.

The second, a new 3½ litre engine, was brought in as an alternative to the 2½ litre unit for the large Saloon, and was also available in the SS 100. This engine caused a lot of excitement when it first appeared as both the Saloon and the SS 100 became more competitive, which was especially appreciated by the SS 100 owners and drivers who had already achieved a number

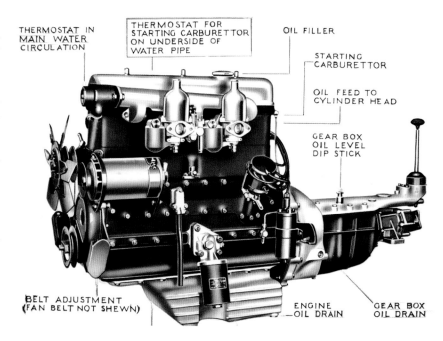

THERMOSTAT IN MAIN WATER CIRCULATION

THERMOSTAT FOR STARTING CARBURETTOR ON UNDERSIDE OF WATER PIPE

OIL FILLER

STARTING CARBURETTOR

OIL FEED TO CYLINDER HEAD

GEAR BOX OIL LEVEL DIP STICK

BELT ADJUSTMENT (FAN BELT NOT SHEWN)

ENGINE OIL DRAIN

GEAR BOX OIL DRAIN

of notable successes with the 2½ litre cars. The big-engined SS 100 was capable of the magic 100mph (161km/h); at £445 it was the cheapest British car capable of doing the "ton". The 3½ litre version differed externally from the smaller-engined car mainly in the engine size and background colour on the winged radiator badge. The 2½ litre SS 100 was continued essentially unchanged into 1938 and 1939.

Prices for the new all steel Saloons were kept impressively low, the 1½ litre cars selling at £298,

The OHV 3½ litre engine appeared to be similar to the existing 2½ litre unit but was in fact a new design. It caused great excitement when launched in 1938.

The new all-steel 3½ litre OHV Saloon, registration A1, owned by George Pettyt, manager of Maude's Motor Mart of Exeter, who bought the car new in January 1939. It was equipped with P100L headlamps with fluted glasses in place of the normally-seen P100Rs.

and the 2½ litre and 3½ litre models at £395 and £445 respectively. SS Jaguar cars continued to lead the field in performance for the price, and the 3½ litre Saloon in particular, capable of speeds in excess of 90mph (145km/h), was virtually equal in performance to cars which were twice the price, such as the Alvis Speed 25, which could reach 97mph (156km/h) but was selling for £885. Other high-speed touring cars such as the Bentley and Lagonda were priced at around £900 for the chassis alone. Perhaps the closest rival for the big SS Jaguar was the MG WA, which though equal in price only had a 2.6-litre engine and was correspondingly slower. It was discontinued at the outbreak of the war after

only 369 cars had been made, and marked the end of the big-engined MG cars.

Production of the Tourer ended in the spring of 1937. It had to make way for the introduction of the model it had been filling-in for, the Drophead Coupé version of the Saloon, which would become available with all three engine sizes. These started appearing off the production lines in April 1938 and all three were part of the model range until the last SS Jaguars were made in 1940. After the war only the 2½ litre and 3½ litre Drophead Coupés were made for a short period in 1948, but the 1½ litre version did not come back.

Unfortunately, as will be recounted in a following chapter, the introduction of the all-

Period poster illustrating side profiles of the 1938-model six-cylinder Saloon and DHC against suitably iconic British backdrops.

steel Saloon bodies was beset with many teething troubles, and it was well into the calendar year of 1938 before production reached the expected level. This was a very trying and costly time for Lyons and SS Cars Limited, though characteristically he was able to weather the difficult period and even managed to announce a profit for the company at the ordinary general meeting in November 1938, a real credit to his ability to control costs under very adverse conditions. This is how he reported on the year to the shareholders:

"The past year has been a very anxious one for your Directors, owing to the failure of certain material suppliers to deliver by the dates stipulated in their contracts, and subsequently to maintain satisfactory supplies, in consequence of which, until the last three months of the year only a very limited production was obtained. As late as April it appeared that the year's trading must inevitably show a substantial loss, but after that date we were able to overcome the major part of our difficulties, and have since arranged an amicable settlement with the suppliers concerned."

The dividend was down to 5 per cent from the 12 per cent of previous years and Henlys, the main dealer, suffered a drop in their income from £56,700 to £38,000 as a direct consequence of the reduced output from the SS Company. The 1937-38 model year was indeed nearly disastrous as only 2162 cars had been made. The 1938-39 model year ,which saw an unchanged range of models, was in marked contrast, as output had stabilized at around 600 cars per month by September 1938 and production for the fiscal year ending 31 July 1939 rose to 5436 units, the company's best figure before the war.

This success allowed Lyons to press on with his expansion plans. He made a sizeable purchase of the Motor Panels (Coventry) Company, so as to be able to make his panels in-house. This company had the advantage of being on the same estate, Whitmore Park, as the SS factory. Apart from this acquisition he was also expanding his own factory, and these calls on his finances extended him to the point where at one time Lyons had to guarantee the bank loans personally. This didn't stop him, however, and he was able to see in the impending war opportunities for diversifying and expanding into the production of equipment for the war effort.

As the company expanded, there was a need for more experienced staff in the technical areas. Bill Heynes, the engineering director, recruited Wally Hassan as senior engineer for his department; he joined soon after being approached in September 1938. Hassan became the chief experimental engineer, and brought into the company the experience he had gained from his time working on racing Bentleys, both with that company and on specials for Woolf Barnato and Bill Pacey, while he was also associated with John Cobb's Railton Land Speed Record car. Hassan was instrumental in preparing the 3½ litre Saloon with which Jack Harrop was so successful in the 1939 Monte Carlo Rally, coming tenth overall, and winning the Barclays Bank Silver Cup for the highest placed British car.

The elegant 1940-model Saloon, which looked superficially similar to outgoing versions but with a redesigned boot and spare wheel compartment. These cars were fitted with the pre-war P100L headlamps.

Inside a 1940 six-cylinder Saloon – this mock-up of the interior showed the unpleated upholstery and front seats that were adjustable for reach.

Rare photo of a 1940-model DHC, showing its short-lived quarterlights.

The 1940 Models

In the run up to the war the threat of hostilities was increasing daily, but the car makers had to go ahead with their preparations for the following year's models as if there was not going to be a war. The 1940 model cars were announced in July 1939 as usual, for production to start in August. They were superficially very similar to the 1938 and 1939 models, but the

boot and spare wheel compartment were redesigned. The upholstery was changed, picnic tables were fitted to the rear of the front seats, and the so-called "air conditioning" – in reality, a simple heating system – was fitted. These interior improvements were standard on six-cylinder models but in the 1½ litre range were restricted to a new Special Equipment (SE) version which cost an extra £20.

Heynes had taken the opportunity to introduce the Salisbury hypoid back axle on the last 393 examples of the 1940 model 1½ litre cars made from the end of August 1939 to July 1940. These axles, which had a lower profile than the ENV unit, allowed the transmission tunnel to be less intrusive in the cabin, and after the war they were fitted to all Jaguars. The 1940 models were clearly new in many ways and complete models in themselves, but so few of them were made, only 892 across the range, that they ended up as in effect interim models between the pre- and the post-war cars.

In 1939 the company had returned a record profit of £60,641, putting it back to the level reached in 1937, before the costly introduction of the all-steel body. Lyons presented the

Outbreak of World War II saw car production rapidly reduced; during the war, SS Jaguar Company repaired the wings of damaged Whitley bombers.

A Whitley bomber overshadowing a six-cylinder SS Jaguar Saloon.

accounts to the shareholders on 22 November 1939 but did not recommend that a dividend be paid, as provision had to be made for the "financing of the reorganisation and the preliminary work prior to full (war) production, the provision of further plant and machinery, the increased taxation now in force and the air raid protection for our employees". At this meeting a resolution was passed to increase the ordinary capital of the company by £100,000, should the need arise. This was only taken up some time after the war had ended.

The War Years

With the outbreak of war the production of cars was rapidly reduced. There were 367 cars made in August 1939, but only 112 in each of the months of September and October, and this fell to 60 in November. There were 3 of the 1½ litre cars made in January 1940, then none until the final burst of production of the 1½ litre model, with 34 each in April and May, 31 in June and finally 10 in July 1940, together with 8 2½ litre cars. The impact of the war on people's buying habits soon became evident as all of the last 112 1½ litre cars built in 1940 were the standard model, whereas the more expensive Special Equipment version that had been introduced for the 1940 model year had accounted at first for over 30 per cent of sales.

Initially it seemed as if Lyons would play a significant role in the manufacture of the Manchester bomber, but this twin-engined aeroplane was soon cancelled in favour of the longer-range four-engined Lancaster. Lyons was however able to get his company appointed as

the main repairer of the Whitley bomber, a significant contract from the Government requiring larger premises, and therefore helping to justify and finance the new factory that Lyons had been planning. In addition he won Ministry contracts to supply spare parts for the Stirling, Mosquito and Spitfire.

This work required improved and more up-to-date machinery, and Lyons was able to upgrade his facilities and pay for this work financed by the Ministry contracts, without having to call on any of the £100,000 contingency that had been put in place at the shareholders' meeting in November 1939. Coventry suffered extensive bombing during the war, but SS Cars, being a little outside the city centre, was less damaged than for instance the

Swallow sidecars continued to be produced in volume for the RAF throughout World War II, amounting to 9308 in all.

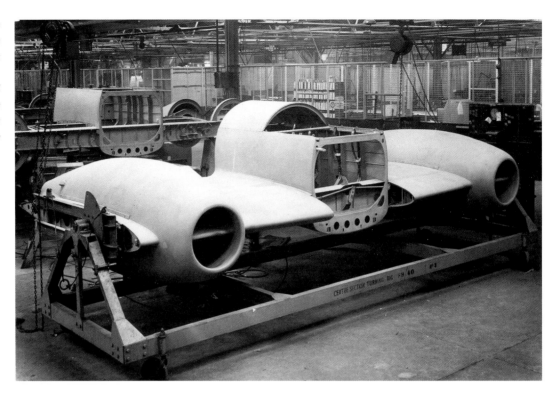

more central Daimler factory. Lyons and his wife Greta had moved out of Coventry into the country before the war, to Wappenbury Hall some 7 miles (11km) distant. This kept the family away from the immediate danger of being bombed, and they were able to offer lodging to some twenty people who had become homeless due to the bombing of the city.

The company still supplied Swallow sidecars to the armed forces, with 9308 made during the war, until this business was eventually sold off in 1944 to the Helliwell Group, who used the Swallow name occasionally and briefly in 1946 for the 125cc Villiers-powered Swallow Gadabout scooter and then in 1954 for the Triumph TR2 engined Swallow Doretti 100mph (161km/h) Sports Tourer. With this diversification of manufacturing, Lyons needed an experienced production engineer and found John Silver, who joined the company in 1942. He was immediately given the task of setting up for the manufacture of the main section of the fuselage for the Gloster Meteor III fighter. This was very secret and went into operation in mid-1944, closely following the appearance of the German jet engined Messerschmitt 262; the Meteor I and II had both been non-operational prototypes.

The war work had a lasting effect on Lyons' method of design and bringing a product to manufacture. Before the contracts for supply to the Ministry there had been few, if any, detailed drawings of parts and assemblies made by the factory, which had relied on reproducing parts from full-size models. The Ministry naturally required that all parts had to be able to be made by other manufacturers at short notice, so they needed to be thoroughly and accurately documented. This applied immediately to the Swallow sidecars, for which the drawings had to be made through measurement of the parts from dismantled completed sidecars. From that time on and through into the design of later models there were technical drawings made for the constituent parts, though only a few of these drawings have survived to this day.

It is worth noting some of the highlights both in size and volume from the company's wartime output. For the Whitley bomber the company repaired and flight tested 134 aircraft and dismantled a further 339 for salvage of parts. Also made for the Whitley bomber were 1399 cockpit roofs and 100 pairs of bomb doors, as well as fireproofing 1223 fuel tanks. For the Mosquito bomber the work was limited to fireproofing 19,562 fuel tanks and 500 oil tanks. In the last year of the war the company made 98 complete centre sections for the Meteor III jet aircraft. Apart from aircraft work and sidecars,

Alex Henshaw in the driving seat of his father's SS Jaguar saloon beside his own private aeroplane. Alex was the top test pilot of Spitfires and the Seafire naval version, which were made at Castle Bromwich.

Lyons was a major supplier to the War Department of various types of trailers, and nearly 50,000 trailers were made. The factory was also involved in a number of other development projects that did not reach production, including lightweight utility vehicles designed to be parachuted from aircraft.

The photograph taken in 1938 of the SS Jaguar beside a Percival Vega Gull light aeroplane nicely brings together three attributes of the SS Jaguar Company's activities during the war. The first is the car itself, a 1938 3½ litre Saloon owned by G Alfred Henshaw, whose son Alex owned the aeroplane and was sitting in his father's car for the photo. Alex was for most of the war the chief test pilot of the Supermarine Spitfires, working for Vickers-Armstrong at its Castle Bromwich factory. He personally tested some 10 per cent of the 27,000 Spitfires and the naval version the Seafire made during the war. As we have seen, at that time the SS Company was also involved in aircraft work for the war effort.

The Castle Bromwich factory had been built in 1939 for the purpose of producing high volumes of the Spitfire and the Avro Lancaster bomber. After the war the factory was bought by the Fisher and Ludlow body making company, which first became part of the British Motor Corporation (BMC) and later part of British Leyland (BL). Jaguar had been bought by BMC in 1966 so production of bodies for the XJ-S and the XJ saloon was moved to Castle Bromwich in the 1970s. In 1980 Jaguar took full control of the Castle Bromwich site where it is centred to this day. In a document for the Engineering and Allied Employers' National Federation in 1943 there is a statement of the numbers of workers employed and wages paid by the factory during the period 1939-43. The return covers: "all classes of male and female workpeople – skilled, semi-skilled and unskilled – employed in federated departments specified below, whether in or away from employers' premises or taken on locally at site in connection with the carrying out of a contract or work away from the home establishment" and "Foremen and shop staff (including progress clerks and rate fixers) rated under £250 per annum inclusive of war bonus". From this return the growth in the size of the company can be seen.

Year ending 31 July	Number of employees
1939	1005
1940	543
1941	1273
1942	2403
1943	2563

Towards the end of the war, Lyons took the opportunity of selling Motor Panels to Rubery Owen, having decided that he did not want an in-house panel-making facility as it was not giving him the results he had hoped for. During the war, Sir John Black had reassessed the future of the Standard Motor Company, and decided to make only one model, the 2 litre four-cylinder Standard Vanguard, and so felt unable to continue supplying the six-cylinder engines to SS Cars. He offered to sell the engine-making facility for these cars to Lyons, who accepted

October 1945 witnessed Jaguar restart manufacture of cars. These 1½ litre Mark IV Saloons were first off the production line.

immediately, sent a cheque, and set about transferring the machine tools to his factory, which was now much better equipped after the war effort. When Black wanted to change his mind, Lyons insisted that he keep to the deal, and also flatly rejected Black's suggestion that the two of them might join forces. The manufacture of the four-cylinder 1776cc engines was kept by Black, who continued to supply them to Lyons, while also using them to power the post-war cars made by his newly acquired Triumph company.

The Post-War Period and the Mark IV

When work for the War Department was coming to an end, the priority for Lyons was to get the factory back into producing cars. The name of the company needed immediate attention, since "SS" could no longer be part of it. The company was therefore renamed Jaguar Cars Limited in March 1945. The dropping of the SS brand name also served to reinforce the company's move away from the coachbuilding company to Jaguar, the mass producer of the all-steel bodied cars. The name change was reported in *The Autocar* in a rather sensitive manner, part of

which read "whilst it is recognized that it is a bold step to change the name of so well established a firm it is felt that the advantages of adopting a name which is distinctive and cannot be connected or confused with any similar foreign name make the alteration desirable – reasons which become all the more important in view of the increased export business expected from the utilisation of the company's war factories".

Lyons had to face up to the dramatic shortage of steel after the war, with priority of supply being given to those companies producing goods that earned foreign currency, preferably US Dollars. To get an adequate quota of steel for his factory Lyons had to prepare a detailed export programme, which he did and personally submitted to Sir George Turner, the Permanent Secretary to the Ministry of Supply. He had a track record, albeit limited, for exporting cars before the war and this no doubt helped in getting acceptance of his plan and with it all the steel he needed for his factory. There were no worries about markets and customers for the cars, as the world had been starved of new cars

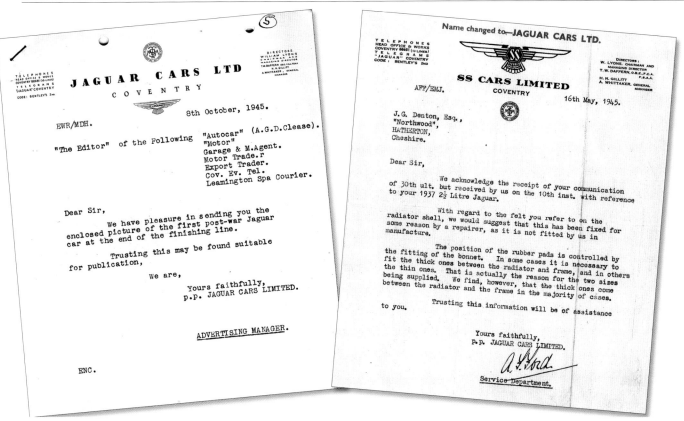

An October 1945 press release, notifying editors of the restart of Jaguar car production.

After World War II the pre-war SS Jaguar-headed stationery was used up, albeit overstamped with the new Jaguar Cars Ltd company name.

during the war.

Lyons was therefore able to launch into full-scale production of the three Saloons; the 1½ litre cars were first off the line some four months before production started of the two six-cylinder cars. This might have been due to initial short supply of the larger engines that Jaguar now had to start to make for itself. As the company name had changed, the post-war cars were officially designated Jaguar 1½, 2½, and 3½ litre. This bland identification of models was clearly unsatisfactory to later owners and possibly the company itself, for after the launch of the Mark V, these first post-war cars became known as the Mark IV, a name which has persisted to this day. For the sake of convenience and clarity I will refer to the early post-war cars as Mark IV, whilst recognising that Jaguar never called them by that name.

The SS 100 had been abandoned altogether and the low-volume Drophead Coupé models had to wait another two years before being revived. The post-war cars were essentially to the same design as those made in 1940, with some of the changes made for that model year

reversed, particularly the style of the upholstery. Girling brakes of twin leading shoe (2LS) type were introduced on all models, and all the cars were now fitted with the Salisbury hypoid differential.

As the six-cylinder engines were now being made by Jaguar themselves, the cylinder block castings carried the Jaguar name in place of the pre-war SS letters. The 1½ litre engine was still supplied by Standard and its power output was claimed to have been improved by 10 per cent by fitting it with a water-heated inlet manifold.

In common with other British specialist car manufacturers keen to join the export drive, for the first time Jaguar introduced left-hand drive (LHD) cars after the war. Once the LHD cars came on stream in the last quarter of 1947, the company was able to look across the Atlantic to the major prize, the US market. Exports of LHD cars to the USA started in October 1947 and continued for a year, during which time 309 of the Mark IV cars were shipped, the largest number of LHD cars exported to a single country. There was then to be a three-month pause in US exports until the new Mark V

One of the first left-hand-drive 3½ litre Mark IV cars, ready for export in 1947. Jaguar was yet to establish its strong position in the American market.

Line-up of Mark IV Saloons for export to distributor Goodwin Coccoza in Rio, Brazil in late 1947.

model became established, and it was this car that together with the XK 120 really consolidated Jaguar's place in the US market, with 936 Mark V cars exported over a period of two-and-a-half years.

The entry into the US market was not without incident, the inadequate supply of spares and the poor service and repair facilities available in that country causing distress to the new owners, as well as grief to the Jaguar management. Jaguar was not alone in having these problems, but Lyons himself travelled to the USA to help set up a parts distribution network to complement that already provided by the two main agents, Max Hoffman in New York and Charles Hornburg in Los Angeles. This was not straight-

Shipment of 3½ litre Saloons to the USA aboard the liner Queen Elizabeth, which sailed from Southampton.

Clark Gable taking delivery of his 1948 Mark IV 3½ litre DHC from Roger Barlow of the Los Angeles distributor International Motors.

forward as all the large stockists were contractually tied to US car makers and so could not be used. The absence of good after-sales support in the USA was to dog Jaguar and other exporters to the USA for many more years.

Production output had started to go well in late 1946, but suffered various interruptions such as a factory fire at the end of January 1947, various stoppages due to shortages of steel or coal, and power cuts in the 1947 winter. The fire virtually brought the factory to a standstill in February 1947, reducing the output by about 60 per cent to 163 units for the month, but by March the production had been substantially improved, resulting in the loss of only 40 cars in that month. The shortages of materials and power later in the year had a less dramatic but more prolonged effect on production, reducing output by some 12 per cent for each month from September 1947 to March 1948. From then on output hovered around the 400 per month mark but went into decline as the ageing model found fewer buyers both in the UK and in overseas markets. Exports had halved by September 1948 and came to a halt in November. This situation was only to be reversed in the second quarter of 1949 when the new Mark V came on stream.

April 1949, the last Mark IV delivered to Jaguar Car distributors in Brussels. It had been made in July 1948 but shipped out nine months later.

Illustration of the new independent front suspension (IFS) on the Mark V displaying its torsion-bar springing and Newton telescopic shock absorbers.

The Mark V

The Mark IV had been very well received in post-war export markets, with 32 per cent of the total output going overseas, and had allowed Lyons to become a significant exporter of cars. The basic design of the Mark IV had first appeared in 1938 as the SS Jaguar, and whilst changes and improvements had been made, it remained in 1948 essentially the same car as first made. With the war now well in the past, Lyons was able to devote time to pursuing his goal of producing a modern 100mph (161km/h) family saloon with handling, comfort, and looks to match.

In the mid-1930s Citroën had brought out their revolutionary *Traction Avant* model with its independent front suspension (IFS), using torsion bars. This car impressed the two Jaguar

A Mark V's all-steel bodyshell in early stages of the car's production.

engineering bosses, Bill Heynes and Walter Hassan, who set about designing their own IFS to be introduced on the new Jaguar cars. Before the war, they had designed and installed IFS with torsion bars on an SS Jaguar and were using it as a test bed. The replacement model for the SS Jaguar was therefore predestined to have independent front suspension.

During the early post-war period Jaguar went ahead with the design and development of a new car based on a new chassis with the IFS, powered by an all-new six-cylinder twin overhead camshaft engine, and with a body that was to be made by the Pressed Steel Company at Cowley near Oxford and shipped complete to Jaguar, ready to be dropped on to the chassis. Of the three main constituents of the new car, the chassis was the most advanced in terms of being ready for production. It was needed because the IFS required a stiff chassis, since any flexing would detract from its effectiveness. The wheelbase was the only aspect of the Mark IV that was retained; all the rest was new for the Mark V.

The twin-cam engine, which became the very successful and long-lived XK power unit, was also advanced in its development, and whilst it would soon be capable of being produced in the factory there was concern that there could be difficulties in achieving the increased volumes planned for the new car.

The all-new body had been designed to be made and assembled complete by a supplier so as to eliminate the time and space consuming body assembly operations that the Jaguar factory was then performing for the Mark IV. Pressed Steel was the only company capable of producing such a large body shell, but it would take up to eighteen months for them to prepare the tooling to be able to start making the first shells. This would effectively push the availability of the new car for production into 1950. But the old Mark IV was dying on its feet, and compared badly with more modern post-war cars from Jaguar's competitors. The overriding need was to have a new car ready and launched at the latest by the end of 1948, preferably to be introduced in time for the first post-war Motor Show at Earls Court, which had been scheduled for October 1948.

Faced with these constraints, Lyons adopted a compromise solution. He knew that the chassis could reliably be made on time, but the twin OHC engine was doubtful for the volumes required, and the new body shell was a non-

An early mock-up of the Mark V with a single front bumper blade, similar to that of the Mark IV.

starter, so Lyons set about designing and making ready for production an interim new car with the new IFS chassis, the existing pushrod OHV engine, and a new style body to be made in parts by external suppliers and assembled by Jaguar in line with current practices.

In designing a new body, Lyons took his usual approach, which was to get Fred Gardner to prepare a series of full-size complete or half section models for consideration and design improvements. Lyons himself played an important part in this process, both in defining the overall profile of the car and in the details that contributed to its final appearance. There are numerous photos of the several stages that the design went through, with Lyons himself appearing in some of them.

This compromise car was to be called the Mark V, for no better reason apparently than that the adopted design was that of the fifth prototype that the company had put together. There has been some speculation that because the Mark V was followed by the Mark VII, there had at some time been a Jaguar Mark VI created by

Hands-on styling by Fred Gardner and Lyons, working out where to best position the spot lights on the wings of the Mark V mock-up.

the factory. This was not the case, as at the time Bentley already had a Mark VI saloon, so the name could not have been adopted for a Jaguar. The Company simply jumped straight to the Mark VII for its next model and continued with Marks VIII, IX and X.

In late 1937 when SS Jaguar started production of the all-steel body, unexpected difficulties had occurred in the supply of accurate and usable body panels and Lyons, having turned the factory completely over to the production of the new model, had faced a virtual shutdown of production until several months later in April 1938. This time however Lyons was able to assess the situation in advance and plan for the

delayed start of production of the Mark V by extending the production of the Mark IV to February 1949, when the Mark V could be brought on stream.

The Mark V was only made with the two six-cylinder engines, the 1½ litre having been dropped from the range. As the horsepower tax had been replaced by a flat-rate tax from the start of 1948, there was less need for a small car in the UK, and export markets also preferred the bigger engines. The Mark V would have been totally underpowered with the four-cylinder engine, and there was the additional factor that the tooling for this engine was still owned by the Standard Motor Company which used it for its own Triumph cars.

The finally-designed Mark V Saloon outside Lyons' house Wappenbury Hall. Note the bumpers had doubled in height.

The easy-to-get-at instruments and wiring in a left-hand-drive 1949 Mark V Saloon. The not-very-effective umbrella-handle handbrake is just visible ahead of the driver's door.

As we have seen, Lyons wanted all the major elements of his cars to be under his control, so it is not surprising that he discarded the 1½ litre engined car from the company's portfolio. The decision proved to be absolutely correct, as the majority of Mark V cars made were fitted with the largest of the engines, the 3½ litre.

The Mark V was to be launched at the Earls Court Motor Show in October 1948 but Lyons prepared a pre-Motor Show unveiling of the car on the last day of September. Invitations were sent out by the company to its major dealers worldwide; those who attended were greatly impressed by the car and started spreading the word through advance reviews, and more importantly placed orders for their dealerships.

At the Motor Show, Lyons displayed the 2½ and 3½ litre Mark V Saloons, but he had also managed under wraps to bring onto the stand the brand-new aluminium bodied two-seater XK 120 sports car. This car had exceptionally attractive, smooth lines, and with the XK engine and its polished twin cam covers drew most of the attention of the crowds, but though it stole the show, the orders taken for the Mark V soon outstripped the predicted supply.

Lyons priced the 2½ litre car at £930 and the 3½ litre at £988, to which was added Purchase Tax of £259 and £275 respectively (see also table at the end of this chapter). By keeping the basic price below £1000 for both models, the

company was able to avoid the double Purchase Tax imposed on more expensive cars.

The public flocked to this the first London Motor Show since 1938, and was thrilled to see so many new British cars on show. It was at the same show that the Issigonis-designed Morris Minor, also with independent torsion bar front suspension, made its first appearance. This car was notable for the long time it stayed in production and for being in 1961 the first British car to reach a production figure of one million. In 1948 there was however a realisation that the greatest number of cars was destined for the export market, as the country desperately needed the foreign exchange, particularly US Dollars. There-

The Mark V rear compartment's flat floor was made possible by the use of a two-piece propshaft.

An early Mark V DHC, identifiable by the pointed front corner of its quarterlight.

fore production of the RHD and LHD versions of the Mark V started at the same time.

The Mark V Saloon was to be joined later by the Drophead Coupé, which Lyons decided to sell for the same price as the Saloon, despite being more expensive to produce. The Purchase Tax threshold no doubt governed this decision, for if priced over £1000 the differential in price to buyers caused by the higher tax would have been unacceptable. The design and construction of the Drophead Coupé was similar to that of the Mark IV, continuing with the considerable use of ash for the frames, but the resulting car was arguably the most elegant Drophead Coupé that the company has made.

To coincide with the launch of the Mark V cars at the London Motor Show in 1948, Jaguar sent out a letter to all its UK dealers advising them of the prices for the new cars and warning them of delays in the availability of the cars for the home market. It stated:

"When deliveries of the JAGUAR Mark V commence, they must, as you will appreciate, be confined in the first place to our Export Markets, but release of the new models to the Home Market will, it is hoped, commence in the New Year. In the meantime the current range of models at present in production will continue until expiration of existing schedules. The balance of orders which cannot be satisfied by

delivery of the existing models will be fulfilled by the allocation of the new models, when they are available for home delivery".

This was something of a masterly letter as it managed to avoid referring to or admitting to the six-month delay in starting up volume production of the Mark V, blaming any shortage of cars for the home market on the priority given to exports. Presumably something equally well crafted was sent to the overseas dealers to buy time and maintain faith with them. Production of the Mark IV range did indeed continue to the end of February 1949.

The Mark V may have had a very successful launch into the motoring world in October 1948 but even overseas buyers would have had to wait until March 1949 before they had any chance of getting one of these cars and the home market until May of that year. First off the line was the 3½ litre, which proved to be the most sought-after model; in fact not one 2½ litre Mark V was ever shipped to the USA and at the end of the run 83 per cent of all Mark V cars were 3½ litre models. Those wanting the Drophead Coupé would have to wait another year until March 1950 before these became available in any numbers, and before production of the Mark V ended only 1000 in total were made, of which 370 went to the USA, while only 143 stayed at home.

The Mark V was listed together with other high-performance cars at the 1948 Earls Court Motor Show, indicating how the cars were classed in post-war Britain.

Despite the car being an interim and compromise model, the Mark V enjoyed eager acceptance by customers worldwide and established the company's reputation in the motor trade as the maker of luxurious, fast, reliable, and comfortable cars at affordable prices. The car was considered by the motoring press to be amongst the best sports saloons on the market and was included in a line-up of British high performance cars at Earls Court in 1948, in the company of such cars as Allard, Aston Martin, Bristol, Healey, and Lagonda, all of which were rather more expensive. In fact the closest competitor for the Mark V was the Riley 2½ litre, a product of the Nuffield Organisation. It may have had a smaller engine and only a four-cylinder unit at that, but it was as quick as a 3½ litre Mark V, both would do just over 90mph (145 km/h), and prices were competitive, as in 1949-50 the Riley cost £1225 including Purchase

Jaguar cars were fast, reliable and popular with police forces. This is the fleet of Mark V Saloons supplied to the Glasgow police force in August 1950.

Another promotional shot of a 1950 Mark V, this time with a Quantas Empire Airways Lockheed Constellation.

Tax, less than a 2½ litre Mark V. However, despite its longer production run from 1946 to 1953, fewer than 9000 of the Rileys would be made, as against 10,500 Mark Vs over only two and a half years.

The Mark V was taken up by a number of celebrities and regularly featured in promotional photos. One such photo in 1949 for the Rank Organisation shows the teenage actress Glynis Johns posing by a Mark V Drophead Coupé together with another Rank actor, getting ready for a game of golf. The light-coloured Mark V looks comfortable in this setting.

Another publicity photo shows a young lady with a British bulldog in front of a Mark V Saloon standing by a Lockheed Constellation aircraft. The

Lockheed belonged to the Australian Quantas Empire Airways and was piloted, as shown on the fuselage, named after Australian aeronautical pioneer Lawrence Hargrave. This was probably a promotional photo taken for the Jaguar Company.

In the twenty years that had passed since Lyons first started making his own cars, the company had grown from a small-time specialist builder making 775 cars in a year to an internationally renowned supplier of high quality sports saloons at a rate of nearly 6000 in 1950 alone. This was by any measure an impressive and very creditable achievement.

In the post-war period in which the Mark IV and the Mark V cars were being made, owing to inflation there was a rapid increase in the selling prices of the cars, this following a period pre-war in which the prices had remained unchanged for five years. The price escalation was due in part to increased material costs but more significantly due to the introduction of Purchase Tax in 1940. Initially Purchase Tax was one-third of the wholesale value of a car but in 1947 it was increased to two-thirds on cars with a factory retail price of £1000 or over. The Jaguars all fell below the £1000 mark, but from 10 April 1951 all cars were subject to the higher tax rate.

Purchase Tax was calculated on the whole-sale factory price to distributors. For example, for the 2½ litre car in 1945 the selling price with

TABLE 1 – PRICES OF SS JAGUAR PRE-WAR MODELS

	1935-36	1936-37	1937-38	1938-39	Aug 1939	Feb 1940
1½ litre saloon	£285	£295	£298	£298	£298	£325
1½ litre SE saloon					£318	
1½ litre DHC			£318	£318	£318	
1½ litre SE DHC					£338	
2½ litre saloon	£385	£385	£395	£395	£395	£435
2½ litre tourer	£375	£375				
2½ litre DHC			£415	£415	£415	
3½ litre saloon			£445	£445	£445	£490
3½ litre DHC			£465	£465	£465	
SS 100 2½ litre	£395	£395	£395	£395	£395	
SS 100 3½ litre			£445	£445	£445	

TABLE 2 – PRICES OF MARK IV MODELS

	Nov 1945		Jun 1946		Mar 1947		Feb 1948	
	Basic	Incl. PT	Basic	Incl. PT	Basic	Incl. PT	Basic	Incl. PT
1½ litre	£535	£685	£615	£787	£676	£865	£745	£953
1½ litre SE model	£570	£729	£655	£838	£720	£921	£789	£1009
2½ litre	£695	£889	£775	£991	£852	£1089	£930	£1189
3½ litre	£775	£991	£860	£1100	£938	£1199	£988	£1263

(The Mark IV Drophead Coupé was never included in UK price lists)

TABLE 3 – PRICES OF MARK V MODELS (SAME FOR SALOON AND DROPHEAD *COUPÉ*)

	Oct 1948		Aug 1949		Apr 1951	
	Basic	Incl. PT	Basic	Incl. PT	Basic	Incl. PT
2½ litre	£930	£1189	£975	£1246	£975	£1518
3½ litre	£988	£1263	£988	£1263	£988	£1538

PT was £888 and the basic price before PT was £695, so the tax was £193. Since this was one-third of the wholesale price, then that was £579. The distributor's discount on the car was therefore £695 less £579 or £116, just under 17 per cent. When in April 1951, the two-thirds rate was applied to all cars, this effectively increased the price of the 2½ litre Mark V by £272, from £1246 to £1518. It is little wonder that Purchase Tax exemption schemes were so popular with those UK citizens able to take advantage of them by moving abroad temporarily. The tables above show the steep rise in the selling prices of the Jaguar cars ("Basic" is the factory price, and "Incl. PT." is the retail price including the Purchase Tax when applicable).

The factory price differential between the 2½ litre and the 3½ litre cars up to 1948 was no doubt based on a marketing decision rather than a true reflection of the difference in the costs of making them, as can be deduced from the fact that when the margins and selling prices were under increased pressure in late 1948, rather than increase the price of the 3½ litre cars and push them into the much higher Purchase Tax bracket, the company instead only increased the price of the 2½ litre model to almost that of the larger-engined car by August 1949. This move was only of benefit to the company for a limited period before the rules changed and all the cars were subject to the higher tax rate, but by then the company had consolidated its position as supplier in volume of high quality, high performance cars at a reasonable price.

Chapter Two

The 1936 and 1937 Coachbuilt SS Jaguars

The SS Jaguar 2½ litre

With the S.S.I and S.S.II cars, Lyons had shown that he was able to design and produce good looking and sporty cars. These were able to seat four people but had nevertheless essentially been comfortable two-seaters, with the option to carry two more passengers occasionally. They were handicapped by having only two doors, and the width and headroom in the rear passenger compartment were other constraints. Lyons wanted to move to mass production of his cars and therefore had to address the larger market of families wanting a four-door car, with its ease of access and increased comfort for the rear passengers. This had to be achieved without sacrificing the hard-won reputation for the production of fast, comfortable and affordable cars.

A rare surviving 1936 OHV 2½ litre Saloon, chassis 10256, fitted with the early QK596 headlamps and separate Lucas 1180 sidelights.

1936 2½ litre Saloon

A full four-seater, four-door car would inevitably be heavier than a two-door one, so it was imperative that the car should have a more powerful engine than its predecessor. In fact the four-door car at 29 cwt (1475kg) turned out to be 4 cwt (203kg) heavier than the S.S.I it replaced, and as Lyons was restricted in the amount of money he had to invest in the new car, he looked for a way to increase further the power output of the Standard 20hp side-valve engine. He had already raised the compression ratio of this engine to 7.0:1 in the last of the S.S.I cars, so Lyons now turned to the engine specialist, Harry Weslake, to work on the engine to achieve the desired improvement.

Weslake had carefully studied gas flow in cylinder heads, and then re-designed them to maximise the flow of the air/petrol mixture, thereby achieving considerably improved efficiency and power output. He had developed a method of measuring gas flow and was therefore able to undertake the design of an engine that would deliver the required power in a predictable, repeatable, and reliable manner. His skill and expertise in the management of the gases, both in and out of the engine, to measure these flows and evaluate the effect of any changes to power output, would give consistent performance from production engines.

Weslake met Lyons' expectations by converting the Standard side-valve engine to overhead valves. The bottom end of the Standard engine with its seven-bearing crankshaft was sufficiently robust to take the planned increase in power, and this kept the capital

investment required to a manageable level. The cast-iron cylinder block was of course new, and now carried the SS logo in place of the name Standard, but kept the same bore and stroke of 73mm by 106mm as its predecessor, and the capacity of 2664cc. With the same dimensions, the OHV block could be machined using Standard's existing tools, which must have helped Lyons to persuade the Standard Company to make the engine for him. Just as importantly, this engine was to be exclusive to SS Cars.

Weslake paid much attention to the engine's breathing. The cast-iron cylinder head was unusual in design in having a cast-in inlet manifold or gallery, so the twin 1¼in SU carburettors were bolted directly onto the cylinder head, each carburettor feeding three cylinders. This shortened the path of the air/petrol mixture to the lozenge-shaped combustion chambers, which were machine-finished to promote a smooth gas flow, as were the inlet ports and galleries. The centre row of head studs actually passed through the inlet gallery. The head was cross-flow with inlet and exhaust on opposite sides of the engine, unlike the side-valve engine where both were on the nearside. The exhaust side was treated in a similar fashion, with machined though slightly longer ports to take the exhaust gases to the cast-iron single exhaust manifold.

The same crankshaft was retained, but was now fitted with balance weights, and held in new Glacier white metal bearings backed by steel shells. This arrangement allowed larger diameter bearings to be used in the existing engine bearing housings, and the SS Jaguar was one of the first engines to adopt this design. The pistons were changed to a new type with Invar struts in place of skirt slots, and the connecting rods were made of Duralumin fitted with a steel lubrication pipe running from the gudgeon pin to the big-end. With the extra power the OHV engine could produce, the compression ratio could be reduced to 6.4:1 for a less stressed engine to give flexibility at low revs, and still be able to produce 95-100bhp against the 70bhp that the side-valve engine had developed. The camshaft low down on the nearside was driven by single chain. The overhead valves were operated by hollow tube pushrods and the tappets were adjusted by means of ball-ended screws with locknuts into the rods, but this was soon modified so that screws with locknuts set into one end of the rocker arms were used for the adjustment. An unusual feature was an auxiliary valve spring at the bottom of each pushrod.

The changes resulted in a dramatic increase in the developed power of the new engine, according to some sources measured on test as 103.3bhp, which was considerably higher than the target which Lyons had contracted Weslake to achieve. Lyons later told the story that Weslake had asked for a fee of around 250 Guineas to design the new engine to meet the required power of 90bhp, but Lyons considered this to be too high a price, so instead a different agreement had been reached between the two of them. This roughly consisted of a fixed basic fee of 100 Guineas and in addition, for every bhp over 75bhp of the old engine that the new engine achieved, Weslake would receive 10 Guineas. The exact numbers have been lost over time, but the net result was that Lyons got a superbly powerful engine that developed 103bhp and Weslake was paid considerably more for his efforts than if his first offer had been accepted. Both sides were delighted with the results and Lyons' closing remark on telling the story was, "money is always a good incentive you know!"

The new overhead valve, cross-flow cylinder head meant that it was necessary to relocate most of the ancillary equipment. The dynamo was moved from the offside to the nearside, to make way for the exhaust manifold, and the new larger-bodied Lucas DUH6 distributor was moved from the top of the side-valve cylinder head, to a position on the nearside of the engine, level with the camshaft where it was mounted on a new cast-iron valve tappet plate that replaced the two sheet steel blanking plates of the side-valve engine. This was however the place where the mechanical fuel pump had been on the side-valve engine, so instead an electric SU petrol pump mounted on the bulkhead was introduced. This drew fuel from a 14-gallon (64 litres) tank mounted at the rear. The mechanical pump of the side-valve engine had been driven directly off the camshaft, but the OHV engine required a totally new camshaft with the drive gear for the distributor in place of the fuel pump cam. The rev counter took its drive from the top of the cylinder head from a shaft that had previously been the drive for the distributor on the side-valve engine, and this take off point was now rather neatly recessed in the side of the new polished alloy rocker box cover.

The 1936 2½ litre Saloon OHV engine displaying its the two-piece water manifold and vertical thermostat (nearside) and single-piece exhaust manifold (offside). Note the central bulkhead recess for the battery.

An external waterway was introduced for the returning engine coolant, and this took the form of two separate alloy manifolds connected by a hose and bolted to the cylinder head a little above the line of the carburettors. A new by-pass type thermostat was introduced, mounted vertically on a flange on the water uptake manifold. The vertical thermostat housing was too tall to fit under the bonnet of either the SS 100 or the new SS Jaguar Tourer, so for these cars there was a one-piece manifold, to the end of which was bolted the same thermostat but now horizontally mounted. The two different water manifolds were available at the same time, and it is likely that the one-piece version was fitted to the later 1936 model engines. The Spare Parts Catalogue for the 1936 and 1937 cars states that the split manifold was only fitted to batches 1 and 2 of the 2½ litre engines, but how many engines this involved is not known. The one-

piece manifold later became standard on the 1937 to 1940 model engines, different only from the early ones in having a cast-in pocket for the thermostat switch that operated the electric starting carburettor which replaced the manual choke on the 1937 cars.

The effect of the changes made to the engine on the ancillary parts and equipment can best be shown by an extract from the list of parts published by the company on 25 May 1935 entitled "Standard Swallow 20 H.P. OHV conversion". The factory produced this list of parts, seemingly for the conversion of the side-valve engines to OHV, though how many S.S.I owners took advantage of this is not known. None of the surviving cars seems to have had the conversion.

Such items as the rev counter drive, thermostat, and electric fuel pump that were also needed to make the change were not apparently considered part of the engine, so do not appear on this list. More importantly, there was no mention of the new camshaft with the drive gear for the distributor, nor of a rocker shaft, so I wonder if this was a serious effort by the factory to provide full information for the engine upgrade.

The 2½ litre SS Jaguar cars used a 9in (223mm) single dry plate clutch and the same Standard double helical gearbox which had been found on the S.S.I. The box was strong enough but apparently prone to breaking teeth on the gears. It had four forward speeds with synchromesh on all except first, and a remote-control gear lever. The gearbox ratios were first 3.6:1, second 2.11:1, third 1.37:1, and top 1:1. The 1936 2½ litre Jaguar also shared the final drive ratio of 4.25:1 with the S.S.I.

The more powerful OHV engine, with some

Part no.	Name	Material	No. off
WH 1704	Cylinder head	Cast iron	1
WH 1747	Cylinder head studs	3% Ni steel	19
WH 1738/9	Valve springs	Spring steel	12 of each
WH 1718	Exhaust valve	Valkrom	6
WH 1717	Inlet valves	3% Ni steel	6
WH 1711/2	Rockers nos. 1 & 2 (inlet and exhaust)	3% Ni chrome (case hardened)	6 of each
WH 1774	Distributor bracket	Cast Iron	1
WH 1743	Distributor ext shaft	Mild steel	1
WH 1772	Exhaust manifold	Cast Iron	1
WH 1748/9	Water uptake, front and back	Aluminium casting	1 each
WH 1741	Push rod	Drawn steel tube	12
WH 1740	Ball end for push rod	24	
WH 1754	Tappet adjusting screw	Steel, 0.60 carbon	12
WH 1753	Dynamo bracket	M.S. pressing	1

40 per cent more bhp than the side-valve unit, and the four-door body required a wider and stiffer chassis. This was achieved by the use of box section side members together with a substantial centre-mounted cruciform and two sturdy cross-members, one at the front above the axle beam, and one at the rear behind the back axle. The cruciform supported the weight of the gearbox and the rear of the engine, with the weight of the front of the engine taken on two inclined brackets welded just behind the front cross-member. At the rear, the chassis side members were routed below the back axle which served to keep the centre of gravity of the car low, although it restricted the suspension movement. While the floor in the rear of the cabin could be kept low, it made the transmission tunnel seem more intrusive.

The passenger cabin was given all of the additional 4in (102mm) width by which the chassis had been widened, by fitting the rear springs inboard rather than outboard, and as this only increased the track by ⅜in (9.5mm) to 4ft 6in (1372mm) and the overall width of the car by 1½in (38mm) from 5ft 5½in (1664mm) to 5ft 7in (1702mm), the car was able to maintain a sleek appearance.

The brakes were the new Girling rod-operated brakes, with much larger 13½in by 1½in (343mm by 38mm) linings in the 15in (381mm) diameter finned brake drums made of Millenite cast-iron (although some sources call them "alloy" drums). These brakes gave powerful and reliable braking and needed considerably less frequent adjustment. The handbrake of conventional type was fitted to the left of the gear lever and operated on the rear wheels only. Centre-lock wire wheels by Dunlop were fitted, with winged hub nuts bearing the SS logo. Compared to the S.S.I, their construction was altered, with the rims now effectively in the same plane as the main bearings of the hubs and the steering pivots, giving lighter and more accurate steering. All the spokes were fixed to the outside of the wheel rim, the so-called "side-laced" type of wheel. Tyres were size 5.50x18.

Semi-elliptic leaf springs were used front and rear. The rear ends of the front springs were supported by sliding trunnions instead of shackles, to allow longitudinal movement but also to maintain the position of the springs with respect to the steering geometry. Instead of the Andre friction type shock absorbers of

the S.S.I, Luvax double-action hydraulic shock absorbers were fitted. Their location on the rear axle was apparently unusual. The steering gear was worm and nut by Burman Douglas, the column was adjustable for rake and height, and a Bluemel steering wheel with four spring spokes was fitted.

The SS Jaguar 1½ litre

The company also brought out the SS Jaguar 1½ litre as a successor to the S.S.II car, but whereas the S.S.II had been a much smaller car than the S.S.I, the new 1½ litre had been designed to have a full-sized interior. Its four-door body shared most of the features of the larger 2½ litre Saloon. The wheelbase of the 1½ litre car was shorter than the 2½ litre by 11in (279mm), being only 9ft (2743mm), the track was narrower by 6in (152mm) at 4ft (1219mm), and overall dimensions were correspondingly smaller, though it was virtually the same height, at 5ft (1524mm) just 1in (25mm) lower than the larger car. It was powered by the Standard 1608cc 12hp four-cylinder side-valve three-bearing engine as used in the last of the S.S.II cars, and as this was considerably smaller and shorter than the 2½ litre engine, the 1½ litre had a shorter engine bay and bonnet.

Unlike the 2½ litre engine block casting with its SS logo, the 1½ litre block continued with the Standard name. The engine was now fitted with a single Solex downdraught carburettor, abandoning the troublesome RAG units. With the single carburettor came redesigned inlet and exhaust manifolds, and the exhaust manifold was shaped around the inlet to heat the mixture on its way to the cylinders. These manifolds remained on the nearside, and the dynamo and ignition coil were sited on the offside. The rev counter was driven off the back end of the dynamo. An AC mechanical fuel pump was fitted. The coolant was returned to the radiator via the outlet on the front end of the cylinder head, onto which was mounted a vertical thermostat with a water temperature bulb fitted into it. The engine was fitted with a large canister type oil filter that was mounted on the engine bearing plate. The unit was made up of the outer metal cylindrical canister inside of which was a non-replaceable filter made of a folded cloth bag rolled up and sealed in the container.

This 1½ litre engine only developed 50-52bhp against the 100-102bhp claimed for the

The 1½ litre Saloon had a shorter bonnet for the length of its four-cylinder engine. This 1936 model (chassis 20415) shows the higher position of its side-mounted spare, with no optional cover.

2½ litre OHV engine so the car was underpowered in comparison with the larger car, though with the car weighing 21 cwt (1068kg) or 8cwt (407kg) lighter than the larger car, its performance was maintained at an acceptably good level. The gearing was also lower to keep the car's acceleration ahead of its rivals. Gearbox ratios were first 3.95:1, second 2.43:1, third 1.46:1, and top 1:1, with a final drive of 4.86:1.

The 1½ litre car shared the same box section chassis design as used on the 2½ litre with the inboard rear springs but the chassis was narrower, as was the passenger compartment. Detail chassis design was similar to the larger

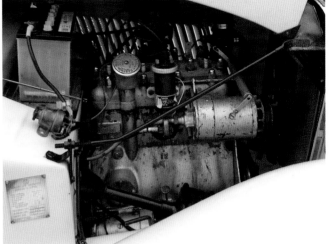

car, but the brake drums were of 14in (356mm) diameter, with linings of 12in by 1½in (305 by 38mm), and tyres were 4.75x18.

The Jaguar Saloon Body

Lyons' design for the first Jaguar Saloon may or may not have been inspired by the contemporary Bentley; certainly the radiator design had some similarity, but was also derived from the S.S. radiator. It was an example of the four-door, four-light close-coupled saloon that was becoming a popular choice, and was often called a sports saloon. With its front wings flowing into running boards and failing waistline, it was typical of the period. Remarkably, MG developed a very similar style for their new SA model launched at the same time as the Jaguar, and

between them, the two cars set the style for a generation of British cars, even into the early post-war period, and influenced Jaguar's own designs through to the Mark V. The body remained coachbuilt on an ash frame but having four doors gave much better access for the rear passengers than had been the case for the S.S.I, and of course offered them 4in (102mm) greater width, as well as more headroom.

The 2½ litre car that was on display at the launch at the Mayfair Hotel was a prototype or even a mock-up. The only existing photo of the event shows the car in the background, and it can be seen that the rear doors were hinged from the centre pillar, so they opened in the opposite direction from the front doors which were also hinged from this pillar. This is clear

The 1936 sidevalve 1½ litre engine of chassis 20415, with inlet and exhaust on the nearside, and dynamo and steering column on the opposite. The rev counter was driven through a gear from the rear of the dynamo.

Sharing a striking family resemblance but subtly different in size, the 1½ litre Saloon featured a narrower chassis and passenger compartment than the 2½ litre Saloon. This photo shows the comparative sizes of a 1937 1½ litre (left; chassis 22115) and a 1936 2½ litre (chassis 10942).

The opulent cabin of a 1936 2½ litre Saloon (chassis 10256), entered at the front via rear-hinged doors with sunburst pattern and scalloped cappings.

shows a rear three-quarter view of the car with the rear door open, partly revealing what seems to be a complete interior. On the production cars with all the doors hinged at the rear, each door had two external hinges.

The 1½ litre Saloon body was very similar to that of the 2½ litre so both can be described together. The individual front bucket seats had shaped backrests, and were adjustable for reach. The upholstery was pleated Vaumol leather and the rear backrest had a pull-down padded centre armrest, though the side armrests on the wheel arches were unpadded. The door trims had a sunburst pattern with the sun made in polished walnut to match the garnish rails and other woodwork, and there were no pockets in any of the doors, nor were there any cubby-holes in the dash and the only ashtrays were the two set into the screen rail capping. There were none in the rear compartment, but these were added on 1937 models.

There were recessed foot wells for the rear passengers offering some, though limited space for their feet. A large sliding sunroof was standard, and the channel draining ducts on each side of the roof were chrome-plated. The windscreen which had sharp pointed lower corners could be opened with a winder operating a one-way chain, and additional ventilation was provided by an opening scuttle flap, positioned in the centre of the bulkhead in front of the windscreen. The front door windows were single-pane without quarter-lights which were added on the 1937 models.

The dashboard carried a centre panel with instruments which were similar to those used on

The 1½ litre Saloon's beautifully-finished interior – this is chassis 20409, showing its sunburst-patterned door panels and standard sliding sunroof.

from the position of the rear door handle at the rear of the door, rather than at the front as on the production cars. There is a photo of a mock-up car taken in the factory at an early stage during the design process, and this seems to have the rear door handle in the same position, so this is likely to be the launch car. Photos in both *The Autocar* (27 September 1935) and *The Motor* (24 September 1935) also show the front-hinged rear door, and the photo in *The Autocar*

The 1936 2½ litre Saloon dashboard featured two 5in instruments in the centre flanked by a pair of minor dials, each with two quadrant gauges. The 1936 1½ litre Saloon (lower) was similar but lacking cubbyholes.

A 1936 1½ litre Saloon (chassis 20415) front door, featuring a sunburst-patterned panel and polished wood sun in the lower corner.

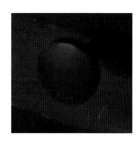

The 1936 2½ litre Saloon included a single large knob to operate both windscreen wipers together.

Chassis 10256 – a 1936 2½ litre Saloon – displaying its QK596 headlights and radiator grille with narrow slats.

the S.S.I Airline and Drophead Coupé, though now with silver rather than black dials. The two 5in (127mm) instruments positioned centrally were the 5000rpm rev counter with a small inset clock on the nearside, and the 100mph speedometer on the offside, both operating in a clockwise direction. They were flanked by two smaller instruments, each containing two quadrant dials, on the nearside the ammeter and an oil pressure gauge, on the offside a fuel gauge and the water temperature gauge.

The steering wheel manette, now with a full mushroom horn-push, still had the ignition advance lever but this was going to be less used since the cars were now fitted with distributors that had internal bob-weights to adjust the timing.

With the windscreen hinged at the top and opening at the bottom, the wipers were now positioned below the screen and needed to be parked out of the way, resting on the wind-

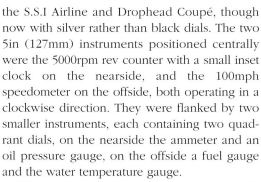

The 1936 2½ litre Saloon's separate front wing apron valance, concealing the ends of the dumb-irons.

screen only when operating. A large single brown Bakelite knob positioned on the dash between the steering column and the driver's door was pulled and turned to the right to park the wipers and to the left to activate them. The wiper motor was mounted between the dash and the scuttle on the first cars but was then

The 1936 1½ litre Saloon was fitted with an SS Jaguar Tourer-style 19-slat radiator grille and Lucas LBD150 headlights.

moved to the bulkhead under the bonnet, no doubt to make it quieter for the car's occupants.

External chrome strips which ran along the waist from front to rear enhanced the lines of the car. The radiator shell had been redesigned with nineteen elegant slim slats, giving the front of the car a wider yet more refined appearance, and the new winged badge with its dark blue hexagonal enamelled "SS" insert was bolted on the top of the radiator shell. The word "Jaguar" appeared on a blue-enamelled ribbon below the SS hexagon. A separate valance between the two front wings concealed the ends of the dumb-irons.

The 1½ litre car was fitted with the same style of radiator and grille as the SS Jaguar Tourer. With a smaller engine and shorter bonnet, the bonnet line had a greater taper from the bulkhead to the radiator and the effect on the appearance of the car from the front was to give it a larger area of grille to bodywork and together with smaller headlamps, to make the smaller car actually look more sporty and aggressive.

The spare wheel had been moved from its place on the boot lid on the S.S. cars to the nearside front wings of both Saloons. The spare was secured on the 1½ litre wing by a winged nut similar to that for the wheels, but mounted

on a spindle, and on the 2½ litre car there was a special chromed domed nut also mounted on a spindle, for which there was a special spanner in the toolkit in the 1937 car. The spare wheels for both cars could be enclosed in a pressed steel body colour cover.

This wing mounted spare wheel gained a considerable amount of space for the boot of the SS Jaguar, but its position was inconvenient if any adjustments or repairs needed to be made to the electrical and fuel units mounted under the bonnet on that side. It was however a better solution than mounting it on the offside where it would have impeded the driver's view, and made the not infrequent changing of a punctured tyre by the road side doubly hazardous.

The shorter bonnet of the 1½ litre had another knock-on effect on the appearance of the car in that the front wing was shorter, so the side-mounted spare wheel though in the same position on the wing as on the larger car, sat noticeably higher up than on the 2½ litre, with the top of the spare wheel above the level of the bonnet. The front shutline of the front door was straight all the way down, unlike the 2½ litre where it was broken at the waistline. On the 1½ litre, the cabin was further back relative to the wheelbase, with the rear wings cutting more into the rear doors, so the boot was a little shorter and had a slightly steeper rake for the rear end, nicely balancing the look of this car with its shorter bonnet.

The external boot lid could be lowered to a nearly flat position so that cases could be placed and strapped to the platform to increase the luggage carrying capacity. Inside the boot lid and held in place by a secondary lid was a full tool kit; each tool with its own recess in the tool tray, fabricated from plywood. Across the back of the boot floor there was a raised boxed area with a hatch to give access to the back axle and to the rear shock absorbers. Just below the boot lid was a recess for the number plate with circular tail/stop lamps on each side. The fuel filler was positioned very low down on the nearside, alongside the rear number plate. The front bumper of the 2½ litre model was the Wilmot Breeden harmonic stabiliser type and the rear was solidly mounted and had a hexagonal SS medallion in its centre. The bumpers on the 1½ litre model were both solidly mounted, with a considerably narrower profile and small scroll ends.

The first 2½ litre Saloons were fitted with Lucas P100S headlamps but were soon replaced by the Lucas P100R unit. The P100S lamps were undoubtedly very elegant but were also expensive so the only headlamps offered as replacements by the factory in the Spare Parts Catalogue for the 1936 and 1937 2½ litre Saloons were the simpler P100R units that were fitted to all the subsequent pre-war six-cylinder cars. Separate Lucas 1180 sidelights were fitted on 2½ litre cars. However, some early saloons appear to have the smaller QK596 headlamps (see photos on p.34 and p.41) which were standard on the SS 100 and Tourers at this time, though the Tourers soon also left the factory with the

P100S or R, but the SS 100 retained the QK596 on all the cars made. The 1½ litre had smaller Lucas LBD150 headlamps and Lucas L1130 torpedo sidelights. Both cars had chromed Lucas Alto horns mounted on the front of the car above the bumper.

Press Reception

The new Jaguar 2½ litre Saloon was very well received and reviewed by the motoring press. The lower compression ratio, made possible by the adoption of the overhead valve configuration, gave the car a particularly docile performance in top gear, as well as being smooth and quiet. Nevertheless it was capable of exceeding 85mph (137 km/h) when timed over a quarter-mile. *The Motor* (24 September 1935) even claimed to have timed the car at 90mph (145 km/h) at the Brooklands race track. Actually it may be suspected that the car used by the journalists in September 1935 was the "last year's experimental chassis in which one of the new 2½ litre Jaguar engines had been fitted for the purposes of exhaustive test" and which was in fact "an open four-seater", as specifically described in *The Autocar* (27 September 1935).

According to The Motor, at a cruising speed of 70mph (113 km/h) the car was feeling as if it was travelling at the customary 50mph (80 km/h) of its competitors, its comfort, stability and low noise levels giving the car the qualities of a thoroughbred. Top gear was very usable as the car could pull cleanly from 20mph (32 km/h), and on Stoneleigh Hill near Coventry, a favourite testing place, it would accelerate all the way up, reaching 50mph (80 km/h) at the top. The hill was a 1:9 incline and with a corner at the start to prevent building up speed on the approach, and this was considered an excellent performance by the motoring correspondent. Later on, *The Autocar* carried out a proper road test of a production Saloon, BRW 34, chassis number 10466 (3 April 1936) which weighed 30cwt 16lb (1533kg). They quoted a best timed speed of 88.24mph (142 km/h) and a mean top speed of 85.71mph (138km/h), together with acceleration from rest to 50mph (80 km/h) in 12 seconds, and to 60mph (96 km/h) in 17.4 seconds. When *The Motor* tested the production car they got up to 60mph in 16.4 seconds and an average top speed of 86.5mph (139 km/h). Fuel consumption was 19-21mpg (around 14 litres per 100km).

The rear number plate surround sat within a recess, having circular tail/stop lamps on each side.

The sixth Earl of Cottenham, who was an ex-racing driver and a leading figure in the development of the *Road Craft* manual for the training of Police drivers, wrote an article on the car for the *Sunday Pictorial* in June 1936. In this article by an undoubted expert on high-speed cars, he wrote that considering the performance of the car he advised that it be driven with wisdom and discretion, not because the car was difficult to drive, but because the acceleration was exceedingly good and the car really so fast that a driver not used to such a car could easily get into difficulty with it at speed.

The 1½ litre model also made a good impression, with lively acceleration provided by its lower gear ratios, making it quite quick off the mark and there was in fact little difference between the two cars in acceleration times up to 40mph (64 km/h), after which the performance of the 1½ litre tailed off sharply and its 0-50mph (0-80 km/h) time of 19.6secs was nearly 8 seconds more than for the 2½ litre car, while 60mph (97 km/h) came up in 33 seconds and a standing quarter-mile was covered in 24 seconds (figures from *The Motor* 23 June 1936). The car's performance compared very favourably with its competition. It was credited with a top speed of 70mph (113 km/h), and at £285 was remarkably good value; a full £100 cheaper than the 2½ litre model. It also used less fuel, at 25mpg (around 11 litres per 100km).

Changes on the 1937 Models

The production of the 1937 models began in August 1936. Still with the coachbuilt bodywork, the cars were almost identical in looks to the 1936 models and retained the same dimensions, but also incorporated a number of changes both inside the car and externally.

The most obvious external change was the use of a fifteen-slat radiator shell in which the inner lip of the shell had been eliminated. The slats were made wider to fill the same amount of space as the nineteen slats had on the previous model, considerably changing the frontal appearance of the car. Below the radiator shell was a louvered apron across the front of the

The 1937 1½ litre Saloon featured a radiator grille with 15 wider slats and Lucas LBD150 headlights. The car shown is chassis 20888.

The 1937 1½ litre
Saloon, shown with
(chassis 22099) and
without (chassis 22115)
the optional side-mount
cover. Note the sunshine
roof and the position of
the door handles.

chassis between the two wings. This apron also extended to shroud each side of the chassis along the engine bay. On the 2½ litre the side-lights were for the first time fully faired into the wings, eliminating the separately-mounted side-lights for good on the larger engined car. The 1½ litre car retained the individual torpedo light units on all the models, even post-war. The rear of the bonnet closed onto a brass extrusion,

painted body colour, fitted around the bulkhead.

The shape of the windscreen was changed, giving it rounded lower corners to improve the seal, making the car more weatherproof, and was held shut by two toggle-clamps screwed to the pillars. The ventilation for the occupants was improved by fitting quarter-lights in the front door windows, and a scuttle ventilation flap that was opened and closed by means of a hori-

The 1937 2½ litre Saloon's dashboard had its two 5in instruments moved to the outer positions and the quadrant dials placed between them. The dashboard was now fitted with cubbyholes for the driver and front passenger. This is chassis 12462.

The 1937 1½ litre Saloon's dashboard had only one cubbyhole for the passenger and two knobs on the garnish rail to park and operate the wipers individually.

The interior of 12462, showing a 1937 model's rear seats with central armrest and a rear door panel with a pocket.

zontal lever located between the dashboard fascia panel and the dash itself. The drains for the sunshine roof were now painted body colour and no longer chromed.

The 2½ litre dashboard was upgraded with lidded cubbyholes on each side. The 1937 1½ litre dashboard was provided with only one lidded cubbyhole for the passenger. On both cars, the wiper mechanism was changed to allow individual operation of the wipers, with two large Bakelite knobs located directly in front of the driver and passenger. The instruments were repositioned, with the 5in (127mm) speedometer and rev counter dials moved to the outside of the four minor instruments that retained the paired quadrant format for their dials. The rev counter on the 2½ litre now operated in an anti-clockwise direction, eliminating the need for the complex reversing gear from which the rev counter cable was driven. The 1½ litre rev counter continued to operate in the clockwise direction since the drive for this instrument had the appropriate rotation directly from the dynamo and did not need the direction reversing gear used on the early 2½ litre car.

The seats were improved by the use of Dunlopillo moulded foam rubber and the rear armrests over the wheel arches were now padded and upholstered in leather. The driver and front passenger too gained adjustable padded arm rests, mounted on the redesigned door panel that, together with the rear door panels, now had pockets. The introduction of pockets in the doors however marked the end of the sunburst pattern for the door trims, since it could not be adapted to accommodate the pockets. Ashtrays were now provided for all occupants, the additional two being recessed into the garnish rails on the rear doors that had been redesigned with thicker centre sections to house the ashtrays.

The rear passengers were given considerably more space for their feet by a number of changes. The chassis frame had been slightly widened at the rear and the chassis cross-member under the front seats had been moved 3in (76mm) further forward to increase the length and width of the rear floorboards, which now sloped downwards towards the rear. In addition, the bottom sections of the backs of the front seats were redesigned, cut away at floor level to give space for the toes of passengers' shoes to be tucked under the front seat.

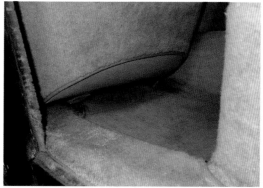

Chassis 22099, showing the 1937 1½ litre 's front door trim had swapped the sunburst pattern for a door pocket.

Rear passengers in a 1937 2½ litre Saloon had more space for their feet thanks to these cutouts in the bottoms of the front seats.

The boot opening had an internal gutter welded around the top and both sides to keep it and the toolkit weather tight. The tool compartment lid was given a light that could be switched on by turning its lamp holder. Also at the rear of the car the T-shaped boot handle was retained but the rear lights were changed to a D-shape, rather than the round ones of the previous model. This last change was I think introduced over a period of time, starting with some 1936 models, so there is no hard and fast date from which all the cars had the D lights. The Spare Parts Catalogue offers only the D lights as replacements for both the 1936 and 1937 models. The end sections of the exhaust pipes were made oval in cross-section to give this low car a bit more ground clearance over undulating or rough terrain.

The spare wheel mounting was made more rigid with a strut bolted to the bulkhead, and the wheel received a new design of painted cover, a new type of Ace wheel disc finished off with a chrome-plated centrepiece and held in place with the chromed domed nut, for which there was the special flat large ring spanner in the tool kit.

The 2½ litre headlamps were changed to the simpler Lucas P100R type that had the vertical flutes and a clear circular centre section. These were hinged at the top for access to the headlight bulb.

The four-cylinder side-valve engine on the 1½ litre car was largely unchanged on the 1937

By 1937 the 1½ litre Saloon's cabin contained passenger ashtrays in the rear door cappings.

Rear views of the 1937 2½ litre Saloon chassis 13342 and 1½ litre chassis 20888, displaying the D-shaped rear light surrounds and very low fuel filler.

model. The carburettor incorporated what was termed an "easy starting device", but this was just a manual choke operated from the dashboard. The oil filter type was changed from the large AC cylindrical canister that was mounted on a separate bearing plate on the 1936 model, to the smaller AC ZR1 unit that was piped directly onto the engine.

By contrast there were a number of modifications made to the 2½ litre engine. The height of the block had been increased by ¼in (6.4mm) probably to make it more robust, but the exact reason for the modification is not known. This increase in height required taller pistons and a longer shaft for the rev counter drive. This engine retained the single-piece cast exhaust manifold. The two-piece alloy water manifold was replaced by new single-piece alloy water manifold on which the flange for the thermostat housing was now horizontal, with the new ther-

Sidelights were faired into the front wings of the 1937 2½ litre OHV Saloon alongside Lucas P100R headlamps. The elegant machine pictured is chassis 11963.

mostat housing connected to the radiator via a right-angled hose to the repositioned entry of the radiator header tank.

The 1937 2½ litre was the first Jaguar model to have the electrically activated auxiliary starting carburettor in place of the manual choke, and its thermostat switch was mounted in a box recessed into the underside of the water manifold. The twin SU carburettors were fitted with a new cast alloy air-box on which were fixed two steel canister type air filters. This style of air box then became the standard design used for all the other pre-war and post war RHD six-cylinder cars up 1948 when the Mark V was introduced.

The 1937 model was however unique in being the only one in which the air filter canisters were angled in towards the engine to clear the bonnet and the chassis side member; and on all the subsequent cars the canisters were hung vertically.

Also new for this engine was the provision of an externally mounted oil filter on a three-bolt alloy casting and with a separate pipe to feed the oil back to the oil galley. There was a separate pressure relief valve mounted into the galley plate from which there was an oil-feed pipe for the rocker shaft. The oil filter element in the canister could be taken out and cleaned with petrol every 2000-3000 miles (3200-4800km) which was a considerable improvement over the 1936 engine in which the only filter was a mesh over the oil pump actually sited inside the sump.

Ball-ended adjusting screws on the rocker arms for valve clearance had already been introduced on the later engines fitted to the 1936 model cars, and these were continued on the 1937 engine. The Commission Plate for these cars gives the valve clearance as 0.012in for both inlet and exhaust, but in a letter from the Jaguar Service Department sent in June 1945 in response to a question raised by an owner, the valve clearances were given as 0.006in for both sets of valves on engines up to number 251233, made in September 1936, and 0.015in on the subsequent engines. The smaller clearances were presumably for the earlier engines on the 1936 model cars and the 0.015in clearance on the engines with the slightly taller block.

The steering column was noticeably larger in diameter than on the 1936 cars, having been beefed up to 2in (51mm) to eliminate whip. The windscreen wiper motor was mounted on the

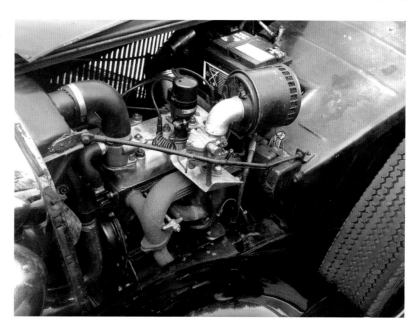

The very original 1937 1½ litre engine of chassis 22099, wearing a new air filter.

scuttle on the driver's side on a part that had been pressed out to form a vertical face on which to bolt the motor, and the battery sat in a recessed section in the centre of the bulkhead.

The Girling brakes were basically unchanged

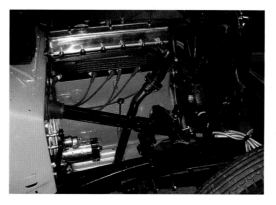

Two air filter canisters were slightly angled in towards the bottom of the 1937 2½ litre OHV engine. This is chassis 13219, which also displays its one-piece water manifold and new electric choke solenoid, which was found between the carburettors. Note the single-piece exhaust manifold on the engine's offside.

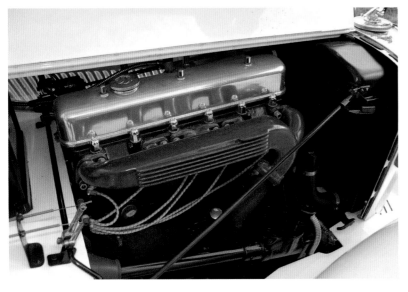

In 1936 the SS Jaguar Tourer's 2½ litre OHV engine featured pancake filters and a horizontal thermostat from a one-piece water manifold. On the offside was a one-piece exhaust manifold. The car shown is chassis 19017.

90mph" (145 km/h). Drivers always felt in control of this comfortable car and praised the excellent visibility afforded to them. The acceleration was described as lively, with 0-60mph (0-96 km/h) through the gears taking a mere 16 seconds, an improvement over the 1936 figure, possibly owing to the lower final drive ratio, but despite this, fuel consumption was a shade better at 21.3mpg (just over 13 litres per 100km).

The 1937 models were the last of the coach-built Saloons and more than upheld the reputation that Lyons had gained from producing fast, comfortable and reasonably priced sports saloons.

The 1936-37 2½ litre SS Jaguar Tourer

The third model made in 1936 and 1937 was the four-seater SS Jaguar Tourer, which was only produced with the 2½ litre engine. There were 105 of these OHV SS Jaguar Tourers made and they followed on from the similarly-bodied engined S.S.I Tourers of which 399 had been made during 1934 and 1935. The SS Jaguar Tourers were made for only two years in 1936 and 1937, and were clearly considered by the factory as a stopgap model before the Drophead Coupé versions of the all-steel Saloon cars were introduced in 1938. Nevertheless the SS Jaguar Tourers benefited from all the improvements made for the Saloons, making them faster and more driveable cars than the S.S.I versions.

The Tourer had the new chassis with the cruciform strengthening member, and the wider rear section that allowed the rear springs to be mounted inboard of the side members. Steering, brakes, suspension, wheels, and tyres, were exactly as on the 2½ litre Saloon discussed previously.

The engine was also the same as in the Saloon, though due to the lower bonnet line, it had from the start to be fitted with a horizontal thermostat mounted on a one-piece water up-take manifold that was connected by a right-angled hose to a modified radiator header tank. This was essentially the same manifold used in the similarly constricted engine bay of the SS 100, and which became the standard style for all the 2½ litre engines from 1937. The Tourers all had manual chokes even when the automatic starter carburettor was fitted to the 1937 model Saloons. The restricted space under the bonnet prevented the fitting of the new

though modifications were made to the operating mechanisms to improve the sensitivity of operation. In addition the friction surfaces of the drums were ground to improve the braking. On the 2½ litre, the final drive ratio was lowered to 4.5:1, but the gearbox ratios were not changed.

The reviewers were again ecstatic over the general finish of the 2½ bodywork and interior, and marvelled at the factory's ability to produce such a quality car for just £385, which though it was a good deal of money in those days was nevertheless less than half of what most other similarly appointed cars cost. The car was considered a delight to drive at both ends of the speed range. It was docile and flexible at low speeds, even in top gear, and quiet and smooth when running at its top speed of "nearly

Here seen with hood down (above) and hood raised (below), chassis 19017 shows the 1936 2½ litre SS Jaguar Tourer's side view and Lucas QK596 headlamps.

From the rear of chassis 19017 we can see the 1936 SS Jaguar Tourer's vertical boot lid was hinged at the bottom. The car would have had only one owl-light from new, but it's safer these days with two.

Saloon type air box and air filter canister, so the cars left the factory with slim pancake-type air filters instead.

The body was very similar to that of its predecessor, the S.S.I Tourer, and in fact was virtually the same externally, though under the body frame the fixing brackets had to be substantially changed to fit the wider rear chassis frame.

The rear section of the body and the bulkhead were basically the same for both models, but on the SS Jaguar the bulkhead was mounted further forward on the chassis. The repositioning of the bulkhead was due to the new chassis in which the engine was some 3in (76mm) further forward from the rear axle, so this in effect extended the length of the cabin by

During 1935 the S.S.I Tourer featured this small gap between the rear edge of the door and the front of the rear wing (right); the gap became larger on the 1936 SS Jaguar Tourer (far right).

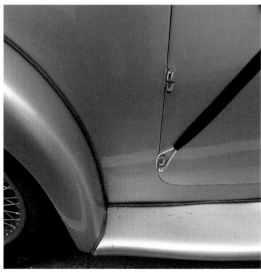

A comparison of the 1935 S.S.I Tourer (far left) and 1936 SS Jaguar Tourer (left) showing the position of the radiator grille with respect to the front axle. It was set further forward on the new SS Jaguar chassis.

that same amount. By only increasing the length of the body behind the doors, the factory was able to use the same size doors and bonnet which minimised redesign. The relative positions of the radiators with respect to the front axle can be seen in the two photos.

Internally the car also looked familiar, with upholstery and trim identical to the S.S.I Tourer, and the same dash panel, though the instruments now had silver-faced dials. The radiator grille was the new style for the 1936 cars with a lip around the nineteen slim slats inside the shell, and was the same as that fitted to the 1936 model 1½ litre cars. Like the Saloons, the 1937 model Tourer had the wider fifteen-slat radiator shell. The first Tourers were fitted with the Lucas QK596 headlamps as used on all the SS 100

cars, but quite soon and at some undetermined time the Tourers were fitted with the larger and cheaper Lucas P100R lamps as used on the 2½ litre Saloons.

At the rear of the car was the sloping boot lid, hinged along the lower edge, in which were housed the tools in a rubber insert with moulded cavities for each tool. There was also a compartment in the boot lid in which to stow the detachable side curtains when not in use. This was similar to that provided in the S.S.I Tourer but a number of the tools had been changed. In particular the jack was the slimmer "easy lift" type that could now fit in the tool compartment in place of the bottle-type screw jack that had been secured with a bracket to the top of the bulkhead in the S.S.I Tourer, and the

The 1936 SS Jaguar Tourer's black Bakelite instrument panel was glued to a steel backplate. The windscreen wipers and motor were mounted onto the top of the windscreen frame to allow the screen to be folded down forwards.

QK596 headlights flanked the radiator grille of the 1936 SS Jaguar Tourer.

Jaguar Tourer radiator badge was made up from several parts.

The 1937 SS Jaguar Tourer – including chassis 19102 seen here – wore P100R headlamps, a radiator with 15 wider slats, later one-piece winged casting and an enamel SS badge.

starting handle too could now be accommodated with the rest of the tools. The new jack fitted into the ends of the chassis to obviate the need to locate the jack under the axles to change the tyres. Also in the boot was a compartment that could take a limited amount of luggage.

The door panels retained the sunburst pattern of the earlier cars without any door pockets. There were two small drop-down semi-circular trays on the side panels for the rear passengers but these could realistically only be used when the car was stationary.

The windscreen opened forwards at the bottom or could be folded flat forwards, though if it was to be driven with the screen folded down it would probably have been wise to fit the optional aero screens that were standard on the SS 100. The side curtains when in use were secured with thumbscrews to the inside of the door, and the side panels and the driver's curtain had a hinged section to allow for hand signals.

The hood had a lightweight frame and could be easily raised or lowered, but this resulted in it being only partly weather-tight. The car was also supplied with a two-piece tonneau cover with a zip fastener down the middle so that either the rear compartment only or the whole of the interior could be kept covered.

There was not much interest taken by the motoring press in the revamped Tourer. The car seems only to have had a passing mention in the articles of the day, but I suppose that was to be expected when the spotlight had rightly been turned by the factory in late 1935 onto the new and significantly improved 2½ litre Saloon and of course the launch of the very fast SS 100 two-seater sports car. Undoubtedly however the redesigned chassis, the OHV engine, and the Girling rod brakes transformed the performance and handling of this SS Jaguar Tourer.

Since the factory seemed to have plans for production in volume of a four-seater open car it was inevitable that this SS Jaguar Tourer would be phased out at the same time as the coachbuilt Saloons, and be replaced by a Drop-head Coupé version of the new all-steel Saloon that was introduced in late 1937.

A limited selection of extras was offered for the 1936 and 1937 cars. These included Ace wheel discs in polished aluminium, black, body-colour cellulose, or chrome-plated; a selection of fog and spot lamps; a badge bar; internal sun

Chassis 19102, showing the overall roof-down view of a 1937 SS Jaguar Tourer four-seater interior.

visors in tinted safety glass; headlamp stone guards; a Philco radio, either long wave, or long and medium wave; aero screens for the Tourer; fitted suitcases for the Saloon; and Luvax shock absorbers which could be adjusted by the driver from inside the car.

Early SS Jaguar owners

Already with the S.S. cars, the company had attracted a number of celebrity owners. The names of about a dozen knights or baronets are found in the SS Jaguar records, including Sir Malcolm Campbell, the racing driver who held the World Land Speed Record for Britain, and Sir Alliott Verdon-Roe, founder of the AVRO and Saunders-Roe aircraft companies. There were a similar number of titled Ladies. They were outranked by three Lords, a Viscount, and the Earl of Northesk, as well as the fabulously wealthy Indian Prince of Baroda and Prince Suprabhat of the Thai Royal family. The name of William Lyons is recorded for no less than five 2½ litre saloons and one 1½ litre car, and his wife Greta had a 1937 2½ litre saloon chassis 12462 registered CDU 700 which is now in the collection of Jaguar Heritage. The names of William Heynes and Arthur Whittaker are also found as recorded owners, and other senior company managers had these cars, including

Messrs Huckvale, Daffern, Gill, Orr, and Howard Davies who ran the Swallow sidecar business.

Captain Black of the Standard Motor Company had two 2½ litres, as did Gordon Crosby, the motoring artist who designed the Jaguar mascot. Other well-known names from the motoring world were the rally driver Brian Lewis and the journalist Humfrey Symons. The Leicestershire Constabulary bought five 2½ litre saloons. A number of well-known companies bought these early Jaguars, and Dunlop had several of them, including one which was fitted with two spare wheels, presumably one in each front wing.

Sunburst-pattern door trims, without pockets, were found on the 1936 SS Jaguar Tourer. Chassis 19017 is shown on this photograph.

SPECIFICATIONS OF 1936 AND 1937 MODELS

	1½ litre	2½ litre
Dimensions		
Overall length	13ft 11in (4242mm)	14ft 10in (4521mm) Tourer 15ft 0in (4572mm)
Overall width	5ft 1 1/2in (1562mm)	5ft 7in (1702mm) Tourer 5ft 6in (1676mm)
Overall height	5ft (1524mm)	5ft 1in (1549mm) Tourer 4ft 7in (1397mm)
Wheelbase	9ft (2743mm)	9ft 11in (3023mm)
Track	4ft (1219mm)	4ft 6in (1372mm)
Weight	20cwt 2qrs (1042kg)	29cwt (1475kg)
	1937: 23cwt 2qrs (1195kg)	Tourer 27cwt 2qrs (1398kg)
Engine		
Type	4 cylinder side-valve	6 cylinder OHV
Capacity, RAC hp	1608.5cc, 11.98hp	2663.7cc, 19.84hp
Bore, stroke	69.5mm by 106mm	73mm by 106mm
Bhp at rpm	52 at 4300	102 at 4600
Crankshaft bearing diameters	Main journals 2.249in, big-end journals 1.749in	Main journals 2.439in big-end journals 1.824in,
Con rods	Dural, no small end bushes	Dural, no small end bushes
Compression ratio	6.1:1	7.0:1 (or 6.4:1)
Tappet clearance (inlet and exhaust)	0.004in	0.006in to eng 251333, then 0.015in
Carburettor	Single vertical Solex	Twin horizontal SU HV3 HC
Fuel pump	AC Mechanical	Single SU Electric
Transmission		
Gearbox type	Double helical	Double helical
Overall ratios	19.18, 11.80, 7.06, 4.86	15.30, 8.98, 5.83, 4.25; 1937 saloon: 16.20, 9.51, 6.18, 4.50
Rear axle	ENV spiral bevel, ratio 4.86:1	ENV spiral bevel, ratio 4.25:1; 1937 saloon 4.50:1
Electrical		
Headlamps	LBD150	P100S; tourer QK 596; then P100R on both models
Side lamps	Torpedo type 1130	Torpedo type 1180; 1937 saloon: 1185 integral in wing; Tourer: torpedo type 1130
Dynamo	C45 Y V/1 V58/0	C45/PV/L/0
Starter	M418 A/3	M418 AL V51/0
Distributor	DKH 4A/0 GC13/0	DUH 6A/0 GH14/1
Control box	RJF 50	RJF 50
Trafficators	SF45/17C	SF45/17C
Chassis		
Suspension	Semi-elliptic leaf springs; beam front axle, live rear axle	Semi-elliptic leaf springs; beam front axle, live rear axle
Shock absorbers	Luvax vane type hydraulic	Luvax vane type hydraulic
Steering box	Burman Douglas worm and nut	Burman Douglas worm and nut
Brakes	Girling rod, 12in x 1½in brake shoes, finned drums	Girling rod, 13in x 1½in brake shoes, finned drums
Wheels	18in wire spoke	18in wire spoke
Tyres	4.75x18	5.50x18
Turning circle	39ft 9in (12.1 metres)	38ft 0in (11.6 metres)
Fuel tank	9 gals (41 litres)	14 gals (64 litres)
Price	**£285**	**£385; Tourer £375**

Chapter Three

The All-Steel SS Jaguar 1938 to 1940

A Difficult Birth

In 1937 the SS Jaguar Company substantially changed its design and manufacturing philosophy, finally moving from being a coachbuilder, to a mass-producer of all-steel bodied saloons, although it continued making the low-volume ash-framed coachbuilt SS 100 sports cars. The change to an all-steel body, while initially very painful, was of fundamental importance, and it was absolutely necessary if the company was to produce cars in higher volumes.

There was great interest and excitement about the all-steel cars, and customers awaited them eagerly. The steel body would have required substantial investment in large presses if it were to be made in-house, and Lyons therefore decided to sub-contract the work, but he also needed to have finished bodies available in a matter of weeks. The most capable body-making company was the Pressed Steel Company, but on seeing the design they quoted around a year to prepare the tooling and make

Swapping to all-steel body construction was of fundamental importance to the SS Jaguar Company. This is 1938 3½ litre all-steel Saloon, chassis 30522.

the first parts. Lyons couldn't afford to wait that long, so he divided the body into smaller more manageable sections that were cut from a full-scale model made in his factory.

These sections then became the patterns and templates that were sent to the selected suppliers, including Rubery Owen (doors and roof), Sankey (quarter panels), and the Pressed Steel Company, for them to copy and to make the first prototype sets of parts for assembly and welding at the SS factory. As was Lyons' custom, to speed things up few drawings of the parts were made, which was risky at best, and inevitably when the first sets arrived some were found to be incorrect and could not be used. The problem was eventually tracked down to a set of parts from one of the suppliers made as the result of misinterpretation by him of the information supplied.

Once the separate bought-in panels had been assembled and welded on a jig in the factory, the body was lead-filled and smoothed ready for painting. Whilst liable to rust, the all-steel body was easier to repair than the ash frames of the coachbuilt cars, which often needed all the steel panels removed to gain access to the damaged wood and to remake fractured joints.

Production of the 1937 models had ceased on 1 July when the last Tourers left the assembly lines. A break in output had been normal in the past when a completely new model was introduced, with full production restarting in mid-October. With the problems in the supply of usable steel body panels, this restart was considerably delayed, and since the main assembly lines had already been converted for the assembly of the new bodies, there was no possibility of plugging the gap by making substantially more of the previous model-year cars.

It would appear that Lyons was not able even to make the coachbuilt SS 100 cars during the extended shutdown, and production of these cars also stopped from July up to the third week in November. He did manage to make 56 of the old 1937 model 1½ litre 12hp sidevalve coachbuilt cars from mid-October to the end of November, in spite of the fact that production of this model had finished at the end of June together with the other 1937 cars. I am not sure how these cars were marketed or if they were in any way different from the normal 1937 models, but given the total absence of new models, there were no doubt enough frustrated customers willing to accept an old-model SS Jaguar rather than wait months for a new one.

Very restricted production of the new all-steel cars began in December 1937, but total output at 79 cars for the month was very low, and no less than 30 were SS 100 cars. The factory had now been at a virtual standstill for the best part of four months – a third of the year gone by with nothing to show for it. This was at least two months more than Lyons would have planned for the changeover to the new models and it would be interesting to know how customers reacted to the delay, and how many cars had been back-ordered on the dealers.

Output improved in fits and starts over the next four months, helped by the all-steel 1½ litre cars with the new OHV engine coming on stream, but the average monthly production for the first four months of 1938 was still only 215, or roughly half the volume Lyons had been trying to achieve. Once, however, the 400-plus cars per month level had been reached in May 1938, it rose steadily for the next twelve months, reaching 682 at its peak in November 1938, before falling again in May 1939 and continuing to fall up to the outbreak of the war, presumably in response to reduced demand in the uncertain times.

The All-Steel 2½ litre Saloon

Little was left unchanged from the 1937 model, though the car did retain its trademark SS Jaguar appearance. The all-steel body was complemented by a completely new box-section chassis on which the cruciform of the 1937 model had been replaced by cross-members. One cross-member was at the front of the chassis, ahead of the engine, and served as a mount for the radiator, a second cross-member was positioned to support the gearbox and the rear of the engine, and a third was placed to provide the mountings for the front shackles of the semi-elliptic rear springs. There was a further cross-member at the rear of the chassis. The cross-members were riveted and welded to the chassis frame to give it the required strength and rigidity.

The frame was reshaped in its middle portion to give the body the same width for the front occupants that had previously only been available for the rear passengers. The side members ran parallel up to the bulkhead, only then tapering in before again running parallel along the engine bay. The chassis side members were still box sections, which though effective in strengthening the chassis, had the disadvantage of being liable to collect water and then to rust heavily. The wheelbase was stretched by 1in (25mm) to exactly 10ft (3048mm) and track was up 2in (51mm) at the rear to 4ft 8in (1422mm) with front track still 4ft 6in (1372mm).

The suspension was not changed. The shock absorbers were the hydraulic Luvax heavy-duty vane type that were adjusted and preset by the factory. The Instruction Book states that these were adjustable but that this should only be attempted by the owner under "exceptional circumstances". After the first year of production, all the cars pre- and post-war had the Luvax-Girling piston type hydraulic shock absorbers, though these were subsequently just called Girling. The brakes still used the Girling rod-operated single leading shoe system and the Millenite drums. The six-cylinder cars now had smaller 14in (356mm) drums and their operating mechanism was considerably redesigned for the new chassis. The handbrake was mounted further back and on the right of the tunnel, and now worked on all four wheels; on post-war cars it went back to operating just the rear wheels. Lyons did not change to hydraulic brakes, since he considered that the rod brakes were very effective and he didn't want to take any unnecessary risks with the design of the new car. In fact it would be another ten years before hydraulic brakes made their appearance in the Mark V, when they became necessary due to the independent front suspension.

The 2½ litre engine was little changed from the previous unit, but the power output had supposedly been increased by improving the engine breathing to compensate for the extra weight of the all-steel body and to keep the performance of this model ahead of its rivals. In fact, *The Autocar* (21 September 1937) quoted 102bhp at 4500rpm, but *The Motor* (20 June 1939) quoted 97bhp at the same engine speed.

These engines were given a new series of numbers with an L prefix, and the first 1050 engines made, starting with number L 1, were essentially unchanged from the 1937 version, though a two-piece exhaust manifold for a twin exhaust system was fitted for the first time, replacing the single pipe exhaust, with each pipe having two silencers. The air-box had horizontal flanges for the filters so the canisters now

hung vertically and were not angled in towards the engine as in the 1937 model.

The water pump for the 1937 engine had a long nose onto which the fan was bolted to bring the fan closer to the radiator, but on the new chassis for the 1938 model the engine and radiator were closer together so this extension was no longer needed. The pump had been redesigned without a backing plate as it was bolted straight onto the face of the engine block. This new design reduced the number of parts for the pump but created a problem for adjusting the position of the impellor with respect to the cone inside the pump when, as was inevitable, some of the face of the block had been pitted by corrosion. The back plate on the water pump was reintroduced for the post-war cars and then carried through to the end of the production of the push-rod engines.

The oil filter casting was modified and incorporated the pressure relief valve with an internal oil-feed pipe, eliminating the external location

This 1938 3½ litre wore a wider radiator grille than the previous 2½ litre car, now featuring 17 slats. New P100R headlights were added, along with standard-fit FT58 spot lights and horns mounted under the wings.

Twin fuel pumps were found on the nearside of the 1938 3½ litre Saloon engine, while the opposite side wore a two-piece exhaust manifold and battery mounted on an un-recessed bulkhead. Chassis 30522 is shown here.

of these two parts of the filter. The crankcase breather pipe was vertical and the oil feed for the rocker shaft was now taken directly from the revised oil gallery plate. From engine number L 1051 onwards, in September 1938, the 2½ litre engine received the steel con rods with thin-walled shell bearings introduced on the new 3½ litre. The crankshaft then had larger diameter surfaces for the main and big-end bearings, and though this was a relatively small increase of 0.040in (1mm) it did stiffen the shaft and reduce vibration in the engine.

Externally, the door handles were moved up and set on a redesigned chrome strip along the waistline. The front shutline of the front door was changed so that rather than kinking at the waistline it continued at the angle of the wind-screen all the way down, which made the door wider at the bottom to assist getting in and out. The rear doors were also wider. Internal drains in the windscreen pillars replaced the external drains for the sunshine roof.

The most obvious change was the elimination of the wing-mounted spare wheel as it had been relocated to a new compartment under the boot that was accessed by dropping the hinged centre section of the rear bumper and lifting the lid of the compartment. Interestingly, the press reported in September 1937 that the spare wheel had been mounted inside the boot lid of the car. "The interior arrangement (of the boot) is new, for the balanced lid carries the spare wheel completely out of sight on its inside face, and conveniently grouped around the spare wheel are rubber-filled sockets for the tool equipment." There is a photo of a prototype car (a 2½ litre registered CHP 471, chassis 12306, which later became the DHC prototype) with this arrangement for the spare wheel and another photo in *The Autocar* for 24 September 1937 that shows a 3½ litre car in side view, with a bulge visible on the boot lid which must be what the article was referring to. To accommodate the spare wheel, this boot lid was deeper, although the number plate box still fitted below it, and the lid must have been very heavy, which made it difficult to open or close, and put a great deal of strain on the hinges; hence the redesign to fit the spare under the boot.

The boot floor was partly taken up across the inside by a transverse box section that covered and gave access to the differential and shock absorbers, and the floor and the inside of the lid were protected with ribbed rubber matting. The fuel tank was above the spare wheel, below the boot floor, so the filler was moved upwards on the wing, which was also a more convenient height and made filling up faster. These cars were for the first time fitted with a reserve petrol tap sited by the filler cap, which gave access to the last 2 gallons (9 litres) of fuel.

There was the customary secondary lid inside the boot lid behind which the tools were stowed in their separate recesses. The tool tray initially had a black flock finish, though at some time during 1938 the colour appears to have been changed from black to baize green, which can be seen from some unrestored examples of the cars, though there is no record of when this happened.

A new boot and separate lidded compartment for the spare wheel was accessed by dropping down the hinged rear bumper. The car shown is chassis 36174, a 1939 3½ litre DHC.

Inside the boot there was a covered raised boxed area, which gave access to the axle and dampers (chassis 46137).

Like the boot floor, the tool kit lid was covered in tough rubber matting.

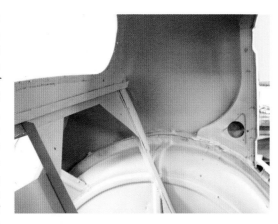

Early 1938 saloons lacked strengthening for the roof (top) and featured a very flimsy support for the back of the rear seat (second down). In contrast, later 1938 machines gained struts to make the bodyshell more stable (third down), along with a sturdy seat back support that reduced flexing in the body (bottom).

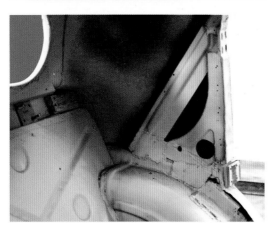

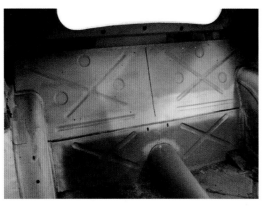

Since the all-steel body had been difficult to get into production, it is not surprising that some teething troubles remained to be resolved. In particular there had been questions about the rigidity of the body itself, and during the 1938 model year some unannounced changes were implemented which are evident on 1939 model cars. Exactly when these changes were made is anyone's guess; they were probably introduced progressively during the 1938 model year. Certainly two structural changes which increased the rigidity of the body can be seen when comparing the two models, and there was another that was probably made to eliminate or at least reduce rusting in the roof area. The first of these was the change from the open steel framework support for the backrest of the rear seat in the 1938 cars to a substantial solid sheet with pressed strengthening ribs, fitted across the whole width of the rear of the cabin. This back support for the seats was far stronger than would have been needed for the seat itself, so was designed to give more rigidity to the cabin. The second structural change, again in the rear cabin, was the introduction of additional stiffening struts just behind each of the rear windows, to give more strength to the bodywork and keep the cabin more stable.

The third change was to the construction and fixing of the sunshine roof recess on the inside of the car. The 1938 car had a formed open-top tray welded along its formed longitudinal lips to the underside of the fixed part of the roof, with a lightweight welded bracket on each side to give extra support for the tray. The welded edges and the interior of the tray would have been very difficult to rust-proof well enough to prevent corrosion, so for 1939 a self-contained open-topped tray was used with strong support and stiffening strips fore and aft of the tray that were welded to the body sides, but the tray itself was not now welded to the roof. This allowed the underside of the roof panel and the tray to be satisfactorily rust-proofed and painted before welding, and also for the tray to be replaced should it become necessary.

At the front of the car, the separate apron in front of the radiator was merged with the wings and these were bolted together with a central chromed fillet piece. The louvred apron of the 1937 model that had covered the ends of the chassis was replaced by the new extended wings with integral aprons and a recess for the bottom of the frame of the radiator shell, and the wings also covered the chassis side members along the engine bay. Around the front edge of the bulkhead there was a brass extrusion with a woven tape for the bonnet to close on to.

The radiator badge was modified and changed in colour from dark blue to a light yellow or cream for this engine size, and the hexagonal SS badge now had the Jaguar name on small extensions. The engine capacity was shown on the insert below the main badge that had previously carried the Jaguar name. These changes were no doubt prompted by the need to be able readily to tell the 2½ litre apart from the similar-looking new 3½ litre. One change that was to be of particular significance for the future occurred in December 1938, when for the first time the SS Company offered its own radiator mascot of a jaguar animal, now better known as the famous "leaper", designed by Gordon Crosby. This was an extra or accessory and was made available at a cost of 2 Guineas.

The Lucas P100R headlights were retained, as were the faired-in type 1185 side lights. The P100R headlamp front was hinged at the top, and the chrome rim was kept closed at the bottom with a sprung clip. The glass was fluted with a clear centre circle. It is possible that some late 1939 models were fitted with the P100L headlamps, still with a fluted lens, as found on the 1940 models (see below).

On the 1937 model cars the twin horns had been chrome-plated and were mounted on the bumper bar and sat above the front apron. The six-cylinder cars now had a pair of FT58 fog lights mounted where the horns had been, and the horns were changed to a pair of painted Lucas WT29 Mellotone units, mounted out of sight under the apron. According to the Spare Parts Catalogue, all the all-steel cars had these horns. There are in fact many contemporary photos of six-cylinder cars with both the fog lights and chromed Alto horns mounted above the apron, but I feel these must have been specially ordered rather than using up the stock of chromed horns, since to fit all four units on the front of the car, the mountings for the horns needed to pass through two holes drilled specially in the apron, to be able to screw the brackets onto the drilled cross tube on the chassis. This was not a trivial task.

P100R headlamps featured this blue-and-red Lucas motif set into a white circle.

Inside the car was a handsome new one-piece walnut dashboard, on which the instruments were laid out symmetrically in the centre. The early 1938 dashboard had two large cubby holes with sharp cornered lids, but these were soon replaced by a large cubby hole for the passenger and a small one on the driver's side, both with rounded corner lids. The separate instrument panel was eliminated and the instruments were mounted from behind with no chrome surrounds. The dials lost the SS logos and changed from silver to black, with white numbering and pointers, with speedometer and rev counter working in a clockwise and anti-clockwise direction respectively. The two quadrant units with the four minor dials were replaced by three round dials, with the ammeter and fuel gauges as separate units, and the oil pressure and water temperature gauges sharing the third dial.

The steering wheel boss retained three control levers, for trafficators, full and dipped headlamps, and manual ignition control. This last one had already become largely unnecessary on the 1937 model when a distributor with built-in advance and retard balance weights had been fitted. The horn push was smaller than the

Standard FT58 fog lamps and two optional chromed horns were sited on top of the apron.

An early 1938 dashboard, which housed large cubbyholes with sharp-cornered lids. The heater visible under the dash of chassis 30237 was not a Jaguar fitment.

The later 1938 3½ litre Saloon dashboard of chassis 30522, featuring rounded-corner cubbyhole lids.

two years and were eliminated on the 1940 model. There were armrests on the door panels for the front occupants, and for the rear passengers there were fixed armrests at the sides of the seat, and a pull-down central armrest. The front seats were adjustable fore and aft.

To complete the luxury fittings, there were two lights for the rear compartment, operated by a pull switch on the dashboard, and the rear window had a roller blind that could be closed by the driver by a pull-cord above his door. The early cars only had two front ashtrays, D-shaped without lids, and there were none for the rear passengers, but when the dash was changed lidded ashtrays were fitted in each of the rear door garnish rails and two, also lidded, in the windscreen rail. The omission of the ashtrays in the rear door garnish rails is odd since the 1937 models had been fitted with them.

Rear passenger footrests were provided in every 1938/39 Saloon and DHC, hinged at the front end; chassis 46137 is a 1939 2½ litre DHC.

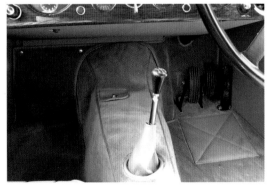

A footrest for the driver's left foot was part of the gearbox cover, with the carpet formed around it. Again, this is a 1939 2½ litre DHC, chassis 46137.

full mushroom of the 1937 model, and was set within a new separate surround on the boss. The under-dash lever to open the scuttle vent was replaced by a push-pull rod operated by a black Bakelite knob protruding through the dash just below the windscreen winder handle.

The interior was luxurious, with pleated Connolly leather upholstery and deep pile carpets. For the comfort of the rear passengers, two footrests were provided to keep their feet at a comfortable angle. These footrests lasted for

Luxuriously appointed, with pleated Connolly leather upholstery, chassis 30522 is a glorious example of a 1938 3½ litre Saloon. The front seats were adjustable for reach.

An early rear door garnish rail with no ashtrays; this is chassis 30237, an 1938 3½ litre Saloon.

The 3½ litre Model

This was the year in which the company introduced the larger 3½ litre engine to extend its range. This six-cylinder engine was new but was fundamentally similar in design and appearance to the 2½ litre unit, with the Weslake-type cross-flow head and pushrod OHV, although the valves were bigger. The bore was larger by 9mm at 82mm and the stroke marginally longer at 110mm. To accommodate the larger bores in a block of about the same length as the 2½ litre

A 1938 3½ litre Saloon (chassis 30522) shown from the front. Note the P100R headlamps and 17-slat radiator grille, which sits in a recess in the apron.

engine, there were no water passages between any of the cylinders. The compression ratio was 7.2:1 and it produced around 125bhp at 4500rpm against 97-102bhp of the smaller engine. The capacity of the engine was 3485cc, which made it 821cc larger than the 2½ litre engine with its capacity of 2664cc, a size that had been chosen many years before to get the maximum size out of the 20hp taxation category. The bigger engine was rated at 25hp.

The 3½ litre was fitted with larger 1⅛in twin SU H4 carburettors. The cylinder head still had the built-in gallery manifold. It was narrower than the head of the 2½ litre and was secured to the block with fourteen ⅞₁₆in (11mm) BSF studs arranged in two rows. These studs were slightly thinner than on the 2½ litre, whose thirteen ½in (12.7mm) BSF studs were set out in three rows. The narrower head with two rows of studs made the 3½ litre engine prone to blowing head gaskets when driven hard, but this weakness did nothing to dampen the enthusiasm for these marvellously powerful engines, neither in the saloons nor in the SS 100 sports cars.

The seven-bearing crankshaft had thin-walled shells for the main bearings and the con rods were of steel. There was a vibration damper at the front end of the crankshaft, and the rev counter drive came from the side of the head, so no recess was needed on the rocker box cover

for the drive take-off. In other respects the two Jaguar six-cylinder engines shared the same features, but very few of the parts that made up the 3½ litre engine were interchangeable with those of the 2½ litre, the principal exceptions being the dynamo, distributor, water pump assembly, and the oil pump and filter assemblies. The single dry plate clutch was 10in (254mm) in diameter, up 1in from the 2½ litre, so there was a new bellhousing. The gearbox ratios were new and they were closer than on the 2½ litre, with first 3.165:1, second 1.86:1, third 1.20:1 and top 1:1, while the final drive ratio was 4.25:1.

The new engine noticeably improved the performance of the car, since both models weighed the same. The comparative times for the two models for acceleration from 0-70mph (0-112km/h) through the gears were 20.8 and 25.8 seconds and the top speed of the 3½ litre car was quoted as 95mph (153km/h), at least 5mph (8 km/h) more than that of the smaller-engined car.

The radiator was wider than on the 2½ litre so the grille was two slats wider, with a more pronounced overhanging "beak" in the centre of the top, and this together with the black-enamelled radiator badge distinguished the 3½ litre car from the smaller-engined car. The 3½ litre car had been given the wider radiator and grille for the necessary additional cooling, and the bonnet had to be reshaped to accommodate them. The body of the all-steel car had clearly been designed around the 2½ litre engine and had the flowing lines so cherished by Lyons, running smoothly from the rear of the body along the chrome strips of the doors, bulkhead, and bonnet, up to the radiator grille.

Since the bodyshell was the same as for the 2½ litre, on close examination it can be seen that there is the same smooth line in plan along the cabin to the bulkhead, but then there is a slight deviation of the line forwards through the bonnet. The effect is pretty subtle but it does illustrate that even Lyons was willing to accept a small compromise in the lines of the car in the interests of avoiding expenditure by introducing an unnecessary variation in the design and the production of the bulkhead.

Press Reviews of the Six-Cylinder Cars

Once again the cars were very well received and reviewed by the motoring press. Their appearance and finish were judged to have bettered those of the much-praised 1937 model. Also appreciated was the spacious interior, with improved access through wider doors, and more headroom. The legroom was improved with the elimination of the sunken foot wells, giving the rear passengers a flat floor with only a low transmission tunnel intruding in the centre. The visibility for the driver was described as very fine, with both front wings visible and with few blind spots. Again the large luggage locker and the comprehensive toolkit were singled out for praise.

The motoring press tested the 3½ litre model and considered it outstanding. *The Motor* (31 May 1938) described it as "one of the fastest production cars in the world." The ride was smooth and roll free and the car "glides along in almost complete silence" without vibration. The acceleration was smooth, with no fierceness and no surging, and a response that was breathtaking if the driver desired; 50mph (80 km/h) came up in a flat 9 seconds, and the quarter-mile in 19.4 seconds. The maximum top speed was quoted as 91.8mph (147.7km/h). Fuel consumption was 18-20mpg (around 15 litres per 100km). When *The Autocar* tested a 1939 model a year later, they could not improve on any of the figures from *The Motor*.

The driving position of these cars was remarked on, being unusual in having a nearly vertical steering wheel that with the adjustable front seats allowed drivers to choose a driving position to suit them. One reviewer liked to have the seat fully back and drive with fairly straight arms. The report closed with the sentence: "Briefly then the 3½ litre SS Jaguar is a fine car with an exceptionally good performance."

There was a later road test of a 2½ litre car in *The Motor* (20 May 1939) in which the reviewer made the interesting observation that on a hot day there was considerable advantage in closing all the side windows whilst on the move and opening the windscreen some 2in as this had the effect of raising the air pressure in the cabin and thus preventing the hot air from the engine from entering the passenger compartment. The drop in temperature in the cabin was apparently immediately noticeable.

The New 1½ litre

This was the year when the specification for the 1½ litre car caught up with that of the 2½ litre model, as it was fitted with a new, larger overhead-valve engine. As part of Lyons' philosophy of streamlining production, all Saloon models regardless of size would now be fitted with the same all-steel body. To accommodate the new body, the new 1½ litre chassis was also similar in design to the bigger car, although the brake drums were smaller at 12in (305mm) in diameter. Compared to the 1936-37 1½ litre the wheelbase was lengthened by 4½in (114mm) to 9ft 4½in (2858mm). Track was up to 4ft 4in (1321mm) at the front, 4ft 7in (1397mm) at the rear, well up from the 4ft (1219mm) of the earlier 1½ litre, but still a little less than the six-cylinder cars. A penalty of the change to the all-steel body was that it was going to be heavier than the coachbuilt body it replaced. In fact it was almost 25 per cent heavier: the coachbuilt car weighed 20cwt 2qtr (1042kg) against the all-steel car at a full 25cwt (1271kg).

Therefore it was necessary to change the engine to a larger OHV unit which would compensate for the extra weight, being 25 per cent more powerful than the sidevalve engine it replaced. The OHV engine had 65bhp compared to the 52bhp of the sidevalve engine, in part due to the conversion to OHV, but also to the higher compression ratio, raised from 6:1 to 7.5:1, and the increase in size from 1608cc to 1776cc. It

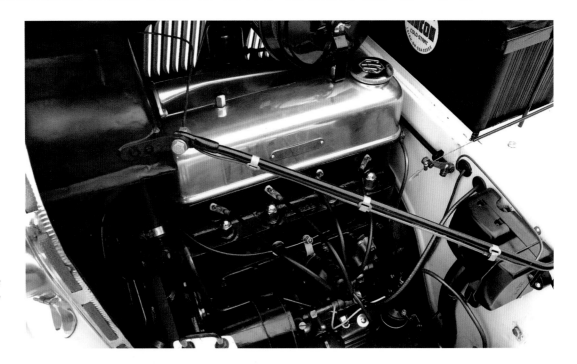

The all-new 1½ litre OHV engine, here in 1939 DHC, chassis 56197. The inlet and exhaust were on the same side as before, and the rev counter drive was off the back of the dynamo. A new air filter was mounted across the top of the engine.

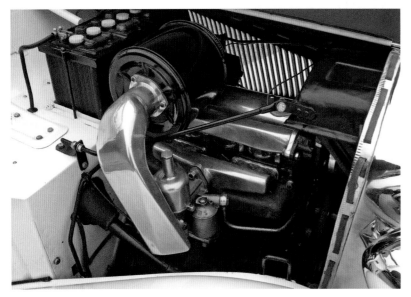

was in effect a four-cylinder version of the six-cylinder 2½ litre engine since they had the same bore and stroke, of 73mm by 106mm, but it still had a three-bearing crankshaft. The cylinder block had the SS logo cast on the offside, though it was still made by Standard alongside their Standard Fourteen sidevalve engine.

The new engine, unlike the six-cylinder units, kept the inlet and exhaust manifolds on the same side of the engine. These were moved to the offside on this engine, requiring the dynamo to be re-sited on the nearside with the rev counter still driven from the back end of it. The distributor, which had been on top of the cylinder head of the sidevalve engine, was now positioned in the middle of the engine on the nearside and driven from a gear on the new camshaft. The fuel pump was still mechanical, driven off the camshaft, and the starter motor remained on the offside. The engine was fitted with an oil filter casting and canister with a replaceable filter cartridge, and a pressure relief valve was incorporated into that housing.

Also new on this engine was an external water outlet manifold bolted to the cylinder head above the inlet manifold, with the horizontally-mounted water thermostat at the front end of this casting. The carburettor sitting high on the engine was a downdraught SU (with a horizontal dashpot bell chamber) for the first batch of engines, with just a K prefix, fitted to cars made up to September 1938. The later KA and KB engines had a normal horizontal side-draught SU carburettor (with a vertical dashpot bell chamber), with modified inlet manifolds and air cleaners and silencers, whilst retaining the same exhaust and water up-take manifolds. The air filter canister was mounted on top of and across the rocker cover and connected to the carburettor via a polished alloy air intake pipe.

The conversion of the 1½ litre to the more powerful OHV engine was well overdue, particularly as this model was destined to be

produced in the highest volumes, and to carry a substantial part of the overheads of the factory. It had to be an attractive car with the trademark lively performance to ensure that the proposed and necessary increase in sales could be realised. Once the teething troubles with its introduction had been overcome the production volumes raced ahead.

Externally, the car had the same bulkhead and body as the six-cylinder cars, but was just over a foot shorter due to the shorter bonnet. This gave the car a nicely balanced look that was further enhanced by having a smaller radiator grille and new LBD 166 Biflex headlamps. The chrome-shrouded horns were fixed to the bumper mounting supports. On this model, the radiator badge was pale lilac in colour.

There were a few differences on the instrument panel of the 1½ compared with the big cars. This model retained a manual choke pull

Chassis 53322, a handsome 1939 1½ litre OHV Saloon. LBD 166 headlamps and horns were still mounted on top of the apron as standard, but the bonnet was shorter than the six-cylinder car's. Although the body was the same, the handles had been raised in line with the chrome strips

Close-up of the 1939 1½ litre DHC radiator grille (chassis 56197), complete with lilac-coloured badge and LBD 166 headlamps.

and the rev counter worked in a clockwise direction. Otherwise, the interior, upholstery, and other fitments were now the same as on the six-cylinder models, with ashtrays, door pockets, and interior lights for all occupants.

This model had now brought the smaller car up to the same level of internal appointment as the larger cars, being comfortable and with a relatively lively performance. The up-rated engine gave the car good acceleration, in keeping with the image that the company had so carefully nurtured. The flexible mounting of the engine made the car smooth without flutter at low speeds in top gear, allowing the car to be run at around 10mph (16km/h) with the ability to accelerate briskly even from this speed. At the top end, the rev-counter was redlined at

The 1939 1½ litre DHC dashboard of chassis 56197, which was fundamentally similar to the fascia found in larger-engined models.

The 1939 1½ litre Saloon boasted ashtrays, door pockets, and interior lights for all occupants. This front door panel belongs to chassis 53322.

4500rpm, though this could be taken up to 5000rpm before the engine began feeling forced. *The Autocar* (8 July 1938) measured an average top speed of 71.71mph (115.41 km/h) and a best one-way of 74.38mph (119.70 km/h). At this sort of speed the road holding, cornering stability, steering and the braking all felt safe and the car under control.

The passengers were comfortable in the rear compartment, with ample space and with a ride free from pitching and rolling. For the driver the angle of the steering wheel was set to give a good driving position and the visibility for the driver was described as sound, with good rearward view in the mirror. The car then, albeit with only a four-cylinder engine, clearly impressed the reviewers and was very favourably compared with its two larger stable-mates.

The Drophead Coupés

The development of the all-steel Saloons opened the possibility for a higher volume four/five-seater open car to replace the now old-fashioned Tourer. Lyons had designed the

A 1939 2½ litre DHC with P100R headlamps, one of which has an incorrect replacement glass. This example – chassis 46137 - had the optional chromed horns fitted on top of the apron.

new Drophead Coupé (DHC) bodies to complement the Saloons, and to be available on all three chassis, with the three different engines. The DHC bodies used many of the same main body components as the Saloons, since this standardisation helped keep manufacturing costs as low as possible across the range of the cars. Lyons was determined to sell the DHC models at similar prices to the Saloons since he wanted to have all his cars competitively priced, though even with the use of common parts these open cars were inevitably going to be more costly to make.

The DHC was quite different from the Tourer it replaced. It had an altogether more substantial hood, which was padded and lined and could be used in three positions: fully closed, fully open and "de ville", an intermediate position in which the front part was folded back but the rear part was left closed. In this position the rear part of the hood was kept in place with landau bars, or pram irons as they are often called in the UK, and the front section was rolled up and held by two straps.

The body had a higher waistline than the Tourer, though still with only two doors, but these were full height and very wide to give easy entry for the rear passengers when the

backs of the front seats were tipped forwards. The doors had spring-loaded metal stops let into their undersides attached to restraining arms screwed to the door sills. The doors had three concealed hinges.

Wind-down door windows replaced the detachable side screens of the Tourer and these windows had two guide channels fixed to the door, to keep them secure when wound up and to provide a good weatherproof seal. The guides could be folded down flat on the top of

The letterbox sized rear window of a 1939 2½ litre DHC (chassis 46137) was necessary in order to fold the hood into the recess behind the rear seats.

A 1939 3½ litre DHC (chassis 36174) with its hood in the de Ville position, rolled up in the manner shown in the owner's handbook.

the door when the window was fully lowered and the hood down. The rear compartment had no side windows, so the rear passengers were cocooned when the hood was closed, but the sense of being enclosed was alleviated by the rear seats being higher up than the front ones, so the passengers were able to take advantage of the good forward vision. There was no tonneau cover provided for these cars, nor were there any fixings for one. The windscreen opened forward at the bottom as in the Saloons but since the DHC had no fixed roof on which

Chassis 36174 (a 1939 3½ litre DHC) with its hood open and partially folded into the recess behind the back seat.

A 1939 1½ litre DHC (chassis 56197) with its roof open, revealing the neat cover for the hood.

to mount the hinges found on the Saloon, the screen was pivoted on two simple rods fixed to brackets assembled inside the extrusion of the windscreen frame. For the same reason, the DHC cars were not fitted with sun visors.

The rear window in the DHC was made of laminated glass held in a substantial two-part chromed frame, one on the inside and one on the outside of the hood, but it was particularly narrow since its width was dictated by the need to be able to fit it into the recess for the lowered hood. This window could best be described as letter-box slot in size and shape and afforded very little rearward vision for the driver when the hood was raised. As on the saloon, the rear-view mirror was normally hung from the windscreen rail – except apparently on the 1939 DHC illustrated on this page where it is fitted on top of the winder housing in the centre of the dashboard rail. The door panels had full-width pockets and there was only one interior light, in the centre above the rear window and operated by a pull switch on the dashboard. The boot space on the DHC was a little reduced in height to accommodate the boxed section into which the hood folded behind the rear seats.

The 1940 Models

By the time war had become almost inevitable, the SS Jaguar Company had already finalised the modifications to its range. These changes were evolutionary updates to the 1938-39 models

rather than the fundamental changes that had characterised the move from the 1937 coachbuilt to the all-steel 1938 models.

The 1940 cars were similar in appearance to the previous models, with the same body and construction for the front and sides, but the rear had been noticeably modified to make the spare wheel easily accessible without having to drop down the rear bumper. The lid for the spare wheel compartment was increased in depth and its hinging position was raised, by removing the crosspiece of bodywork between it and the boot

The 1939 1½ litre DHC's interior and door panels followed the familiar theme of contemporary Saloons. Shown here is chassis 56197.

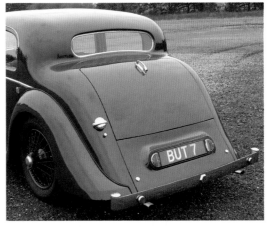

A 1940 2½ litre Saloon (chassis 80004), which featured the new P100L headlamps with fluted lenses and FT58 fog lights. Its redesigned rear end allowed the spare wheel compartment to be opened without dropping the rear bumper. Note the new boot lid handle and lock.

lid. This allowed the same spare wheel tray to be used, but its position could be raised thanks to a new fuel tank. The rear number plate and light box and its surround remained the type used in the earlier cars despite the complete re-design of the rear end.

The inside of the boot was redesigned, eliminating the raised hinged section of the boot floor that had given access to the rear axle and the shock absorbers, thus making the boot area larger and with a flat floor. The rubber lining for the boot in the previous model was thought to damage some luggage and was replaced for this

Another rear view of chassis 80004, showing that the 1940 2½ litre Saloon retained the previous number plate surround despite having a new rear end.

model by a fully painted and polished metal lining, protected by beading strips with rubber inserts. In addition, the toggle clamps for the tool compartment lid were replaced by flush catches and the lid was fitted with an automatic light. The toolkit was changed in layout and contents.

An innovative but short-lived feature of the 1940 cars was the quarter-lights in the door windows of the DHC. These were abandoned

This 1940 1½ litre DHC (chassis 70388) is the only known survivor but is in a sad condition. It shows the quarterlight that was only fitted to the 1940-model DHC, until it was reintroduced on the Mark V.

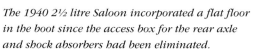

The 1940 2½ litre Saloon incorporated a flat floor in the boot since the access box for the rear axle and shock absorbers had been eliminated.

after the war on the Mark IV, and only then reappeared at the start of 1949 in the Mark V DHC. The quarter-lights, whilst providing some extra ventilation when the hood was closed, were no doubt felt to get in the way with the hood open.

The headlamps for the six-cylinder cars were changed to the P100L type with the rim hinged from the bottom rather than from the top, and these are the headlamps normally associated with the post-war cars. Initially the headlight glass was the same fluted type with a clear centre circle that was used on the previous P100R model, but it is not interchangeable with the R glass, since it is larger in diameter on the L at 285mm against the 278mm diameter of the R. At some time in the short production life of the 1940 model, it is possible that Jaguar started fitting the post-war frosted lenses, but this is speculation. The Spare Parts Catalogue for the 1938 to 1946 models lists only one Lucas part number, 506508 for the P100L headlamp glasses, which is actually for the fluted glass, supposedly stating that this was the same glass as fitted post-war, but in fact

Distinctive pre-war Lucas motif on the first P100L headlamp with fluted lens, fitted during 1940.

Chassis 70055, a 1940 1½ litre standard Saloon with LBD 166 Biflex headlamps, no fog lights, horns mounted out of sight under the apron, narrow bumpers and small scroll ends.

and the Salisbury axle was fitted as standard to the two six-cylinder cars soon after post-war production started.

The company now decided to make two versions of the 1½ litre, a basic model with the same level of equipment as in the 1938-39 cars, and a new Special Equipment (SE) version which had the same improvements in trim and fittings as the six-cylinder 1940 models, described below. Needless to say the SE was £20 more expensive than the standard model. This was the first time that Lyons had produced two versions of the same car with different levels of equipment and trim. The SE model was fairly popular when it was introduced, with around a third of the cars being made in this form.

The standard 1½ litre retained the previous model's Lucas LBD 166 Biflex headlights but the SE version was fitted with the more impressive Lucas P80 units. Except for the standard 1½ litre, all cars were equipped with the Lucas FT58 fog lamps, and all cars now had the Lucas WT29 high and low tone horns mounted under the front apron. The chrome body strips were narrower with a raised profile to give the car a lighter visual effect, and this style was continued on post-war cars. As was usual with the SS Company, some of the cars made in this period were fitted with the earlier flat profile wide strips, though the Spare Parts Catalogue states that all the 1940 model had the later slimmer type. The bonnet, whilst similar to the previous models, now sat directly on the bulkhead onto a profiled rubber surround, instead of the brass

the list should have shown that for all the post-war cars, the glass fitted was the frosted one, Lucas part number 506589. The pre-war P100L headlamps had the same design and colouring for the Lucas emblem as used on the P100R.

All the previous cars had been fitted with the ENV spiral bevel axle and this was continued for all the six-cylinder cars until after the war, but the 1940 model 1½ litre was soon fitted with the Salisbury hypoid bevel axle. This change occurred from chassis number 70296 in August 1939 and coincided with the start of the 1½ litre engines with KB prefixes that followed the KA series. The Salisbury axle had the drive shaft offset from the centre line and lower by some 2in (51mm) so the transmission tunnel became less intrusive in the rear compartment. This was naturally an advantage for the rear passengers extrusion that had been fitted previously. The 1½ litre SE cars were given a sturdier front bumper, the same size as that fitted to the six-cylinder cars but unsprung, without the weights in the scrolls, and without the three flat horizontal mounting springs of the six-cylinder cars. It had visible bolts through the bumper blade in two places, and was solidly attached to a bar, which in turn was secured to the dumb-irons in two places. The rear bumper was changed to the wider six-cylinder type.

The most useful improvement introduced to the 1940 model was the fitting of a Clayton Dewandre heater and demister unit as standard on the six-cylinder cars, and on the 1½ litre SE model. This so-called air conditioning unit was a simple fan heater which drew hot water from the cooling system and was mounted under the dashboard, with a fresh air intake from the flap on the top of the scuttle. The controls were on a small supplementary panel fitted below the centre of the main dashboard. The SS Jaguars were the first British cars to have as standard a heater that was fully controllable for fresh or re-circulated warm or cool air as needed. It also provided the much-needed built-in demister and defroster that would "clear an entire windscreen in a few seconds even when it had been exposed to the exceptionally low temperature of 30 degrees of frost".

The two separate footrests for the rear passengers under the front seats that had been provided on the 1938-39 cars were now omitted. The rev counter was the same in appearance as on the earlier model, but now housed an electric rather than a wind-up clock, though early 1940 cars seem still to have the wind-up clock. The electric clock, introduced as an improve-

The 1940 2½ litre Saloon featured this newly-introduced heater and separate control panel. This car, chassis 80090, was shipped new to Switzerland, thus the KPH speedo. Note, too, the period Philco radio and a rather large speaker.

ment, proved throughout its life in this and the subsequent Mark IV cars to be unreliable and subject to failure, a problem which persists to this day.

Other changes were made to the interior of the car, one of which was the introduction of unpleated upholstery on the six-cylinder cars, but as this required higher quality hides the upholstery reverted to the pleated form immediately after the war. They also had new door trims. The 1½ litre, including the SE version,

The unpleated upholstery in the back of this car – a 1940 2½ litre Saloon, chassis 80004 – was previously used by Jaguar in the 1935 S.S.I Airline. The door panels (far left) were trimmed to match.

Interior door panels of a standard 1940 1½ litre Saloon (chassis 70055), displaying a design that remained unchanged from previous models.

continued with pleated seats according to the factory brochures, and with an unchanged design of door trim.

Picnic tables were provided in the backs of the seats of the 1½ litre SE and six-cylinder saloons, and these seats were for the first time adjustable for height. The height adjustment for the seats was praised in the motoring press and

was written about in some detail in the reviews. The seat supports had a long adjusting screw, turned by a cranked handle on the front face of the seat squab, and this provided a height variation of some 3in (76mm), while the fore and aft movement of the seat permitted an adjustment of some 7in (178mm). Together with the adjustable steering column, this allowed any driver, large or small in build to find a thoroughly comfortable position. The standard model of the 1½ litre saloon and all the DHC versions retained the front seats that had only fore and aft adjustment, but no height adjustment, and no picnic tables.

The six-cylinder engines were largely unmodified, as was the radiator, though the cooling system was now fitted with the necessary hoses and pipes to carry hot water to the heater. The heater pipe was plumbed into the lower radiator hose and angled up to the bulkhead where it lined up with the heater unit inside the car. On

Height and reach adjustment was provided for front occupants of the 1940 2½ litre Saloon; here are the unpleated seats of chassis 80004.

Picnic tables in open and closed positions, as found in the seat backs of a 1940 2½ litre Saloon (chassis 80004).

Six-cylinder engines were largely unmodified. This 1940 2½ litre Saloon engine has a single fuel pump.

A 1940 2½ litre Saloon (chassis 80090) revealing the offside of its engine. The heater pipe can be seen running up at an angle between the exhaust manifold and the engine block.

the post-war cars, the water pump had its own back plate and was located higher up on the engine, so the heater pipe was then able to run horizontally to the bulkhead.

These cars were unchanged in price at launch, though the increasing cost of materials once the war had started soon affected them, as shown in the prices given in the sales brochure dated February 1940.

	Price at launch Aug 1939	Price in Feb 1940
1½ litre Saloon	£298	£325
2½ litre Saloon	£395	£435
3½ litre Saloon	£445	£490

All models were therefore some 10 per cent more expensive by February, which was a significant rise for Lyons to make, given his absolute determination to keep prices under tight control. To add insult to injury, Purchase Tax was introduced in June 1940, though by then new car sales were effectively Government controlled, requiring a licence from the Ministry of War Transport. The sales brochure for February 1940 does not show a price for either the 1½ litre SE or the DHC models as "the Coupé models and the 1½ litre Special Equipment model are no longer available". The price of the 1½ litre standard saloon in this brochure

however included the adjustable-height seats. The company at that stage was apparently completing whatever cars it had parts for and must have found itself over-stocked with the adjustable-height front seats for the 1½ litre SE model when the demand for the more expensive model collapsed. Therefore for two months in October and November 1939 it produced 55 of the standard 1½ litre cars fitted with the special front seats of the SE, with picnic tables.

When the company prepared the Car Record Book for the 1940 models, it divided the ledger between the three models and it is interesting to

The heater pipe take-off arrangement from the lower radiator hose of a 1940 2½ litre Saloon.

Chassis 70055 is a standard 1940 1½ litre Saloon, but fitted with adjustable front seats from the SE model.

note the volumes expected at that stage, which would probably have been in June 1939. With twenty cars to a page, for the 1½ litre 300 pages (6000 cars) were allocated, for the 2½ litre and 3½ litre 74 pages (1480 cars) each, or four of the 1½ litre cars to one each of the larger-engined cars. The war not only dramatically curtailed the production but also affected the proportion of each model, ending up with 688 1½ litre, 135 2½ litre, and 68 3½ litre cars made, a ratio of 10:2:1, instead of the 4:1:1 that had been anticipated, reflecting the near collapse of the overseas and home markets for the larger-engined cars.

These 1940 model cars were only produced in small numbers since the factory was rapidly changed over to the war effort. When car production was resumed in 1945 most of the changes that had been incorporated into the 1940 models were retained, with the notable exceptions of the unpleated upholstery on the six-cylinder cars and the quarter lights on the DHC cars.

By the time of the restart in 1945 other modifications had been made to the design for the post-war Mark IV model, and though the 1940 model was only produced briefly it must be classed as a separate type in its own right. There was a handbook issued for the 1940 model, but it was almost the same as for the 1938-39 cars, with some changes in the text but not in the illustrations, and was not therefore fully representative of the new model. *The Autocar* did manage to publish a road test of a 1940 2½ litre before fuel rationing made pleasure motoring impossible.

Owing to Pool petrol, this car had a low compression engine (discussed at the end of this section), and reached only around 80mph (129km/h), while acceleration was down as well.

The extras available for the period from 1938 to 1940 were similar to those quoted for the earlier cars, including Ace wheel discs in various finishes, a single Lucas FT58 fog lamp with mounting bar (for the 1½ litre model and the SS 100, as two fog lamps were now standard on six-cylinder saloons), a badge bar, a Philco long and medium wave radio, and fitted luggage for both Saloon and DHC models. A set of spring gaiters was now also offered.

Some owners of the all-steel cars

Most of the interesting first owners now preferred the 3½ litre model, and many were names we have already encountered as owners of the earlier 2½ litre cars, including the Prince of Baroda, the Earl of Northesk, Gordon Crosby, and Humfrey Symons. The most famous owner was however King Carol of Romania, the first time that a Jaguar was bought by Royalty; his son Prince Michael and his brother Prince Nicholas owned SS 100s. In the motor industry, Captain Black of Standard had a 3½, and two others were owned by his company, including a drophead. Leonard P Lord of the Austin Motor Company had a 3½ saloon and another was famously bought by Rolls-Royce who wanted to find out how Jaguar did it at a price which was a fraction of their Bentley's.

William Lyons himself had a 3½ drophead which he took on a holiday trip to France in 1938, and there were several other cars used by senior company staff. Of the gentlemen of the motoring press, Rodney Walkerley of *The Motor* and HS Linfield of *The Autocar* both had 3½ litre saloons. There was increasing Police interest in the Jaguars, and of the pre-war all-steel cars there were seven 1½ litre cars, seven 2½ litre cars, and three 3½ litre cars supplied to various forces. They included Glasgow, Hertfordshire, Leeds, Leicestershire, and the Metropolitan Police, the latter a 3½ apparently allocated to their driving school at Hendon.

The "Baby Jaguar" Sports Car

Lyons and Captain Black of the Standard Motor Company got together and made a small two-seater sports car based on the 1½ litre chassis and engine (some sources say the car was built on a Standard Flying Twelve chassis). This car was probably built by the experimental departments of the two companies, and the chassis and the engine both carried the same number EXP 501, denoting an experimental car. This was in 1939, but the car was unfinished at the outbreak of war. It was taken to Lyons' home, Wappenbury Hall, and kept there in the stables together with the factory SS 100, later registered LNW 100, for the duration. Some time after the war, "Lofty" England retrieved the car and put the finishing touches to it, after which it was given to Lyons' son John for everyday use, replacing his motorcycle. It was registered in December 1948 under HWK 10.

This car had possibly been intended as a production model, much like the SS 100 fixed-head coupé, but the war put a stop to this and the car ended up as a one-off, as after the war both companies were fully occupied in making as many normal cars for export as possible.

Another oddity is that in 1939, SS Cars apparently built a prototype small car, chassis number XD1, which was registered under EWK 700 in October 1939, but was not taxed after the end of 1940. All we know from the registration card is that it was probably a saloon and had a four-cylinder engine of 65mm bore, rated at 10.4hp. This is extraordinary as there was at this time *no* British car engine of this bore and hp rating. Most 10hp engines had a bore of 63.5mm. It *could* have been an over-bored version of the Standard Ten Engine (63.5mm by 100mm, 1267cc), or of the OHV version of this engine that Standard supplied to Morgan; 65mm by 100mm would give 1327cc. As late as 1943, Lyons was thinking about introducing a new range of small 10 and 12hp post-war cars, but in November 1944 the company issued an official statement that it was not going to mass-produce a small car after the war.

Low Octane Pool Petrol and Jaguar Engines

In the run-up to the war the Government introduced Pool petrol, with a much lower 72 octane rating against the 80 that had been the norm previously. Pool petrol would cause severe pinking on the relatively high compression SS Jaguar engines, so the factory needed to modify the cars to run on Pool. Some indication of how the company tackled this

The Baby Jaguar was a 1939 one-off resulted from the combined efforts of the Standard Motor Company and Jaguar, based on the 1½ litre chassis and engine. Development ceased due to the outbreak of war, but it was eventually finished and was given to Lyons's son John for everyday use.

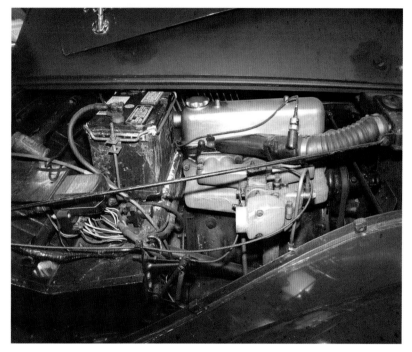

problem can found in the Instruction Books and Spares Catalogues.

The six-cylinder engines normally had compression ratios of 7.6:1 and 7.2:1 respectively and the 1939-40 Instruction Book carried the following statement relative to the use of Pool petrol:

"Whilst only Pool type petrol (72 octane) is available, the cars are sent out with the carburetter suitably tuned, and the ignition automatic advance curve has been suitably modified to suit this fuel. When a return is made to normal conditions, and 80 octane fuels are again available, an alternative carburetter setting and distributor curve will be made available through our Service Dept. at a nominal charge."

In addition to this the Spares Catalogue lists

SPECIFICATIONS OF 1938-1940 MODELS

	1½ litre	2½ litre	3½ litre
Dimensions			
Overall length	14ft 5in (4394mm); 1940: 15ft (4572mm)	15ft 6in (4724mm)	As 2½ litre
Overall width	5ft 5½in (1664mm)	5ft 6in (1676mm)	As 2½ litre
Overall height	5ft (1524mm)	5ft 1in (1549mm)	As 2½ litre
Wheelbase	9ft 4 1/2in (2858mm)	10ft (3048mm)	As 2½ litre
Track	Front 4ft 4in (1321mm), rear 4ft 7in (1397mm)	Front 4ft 6in (1372mm), rear 4ft 8in (1422mm)	As 2½ litre
Weight (saloon)	25 cwt (1271kg); 1940: 26cwt (1322kg)	31cwt 2qrs (1602kg); 1940: 32cwt (1627kg)	As 2½ litre
Engine			
Type	4 cylinder OHV	6 cylinder OHV	As 2½ litre
Capacity, RAC hp	1775.8cc, 13.23hp	2663.7cc, 19.84hp	3485.5cc, 25.01hp
Bore, stroke	73mm by 106mm	73mm by 106mm	82mm by 110mm
Bhp at rpm	65 at 4600	102 at 4600	125 at 4250
Crankshaft bearing diameters	Main journals 2.479in, big-end journals 1.894in	Main journals 2.439in, big-end journals 1.824in; from engine L 1051: main journals 2.479in, big-end journals 1.894in	Main journals 2.479in, big-end journals 2.086in
Con rods	Steel; bronze small-end bushes	As 1½ litre	As 2½ litre
Compression ratio	7.5:1	7.6:1	7.2:1
Tappet clearance	0.015in inlet, 0.018in exhaust	0.012in inlet, 0.015in exhaust	As 2½ litre
Carburettor	Single SU H4 vertical to K 1200, then horizontal on KA, KB engines	Twin horizontal SU H3	Twin horizontal SU H4
Fuel pump	AC mechanical	Single SU electric	Twin SU electric
Transmission			
Gearbox type	Double helical	As 1½ litre	As 2½ litre
Overall ratios	19.18, 11.80, 7.06, 4.86	16.20, 9.51, 6.18, 4.50	13.45, 7.90, 5.12, 4.25
Rear axle	ENV spiral bevel, ratio 4.86; 1940: Salisbury hypoid bevel	ENV spiral bevel, ratio 4.50	ENV spiral bevel, ratio 4.25

two other ways to deal with poor petrol. The first is the availability of a low-compression cylinder head that could be fitted to special order; it was the same casting as the standard head but was left 0.071in (1.8mm) deeper to create a marginally deeper combustion chamber, though there was no indication as to what the compression was lowered to with this head. There was also a steel compression plate (C1547) that could be fitted after the car had left the factory. This was assembled with two of the normal thin copper head gaskets, one on each side. The compression plate remained in the

Spares Catalogue for the Mark V cars as well, since Pool petrol was only phased out in 1953. It is likely that post-war, the special low-compression head was only fitted on request to cars destined for countries with exceptionally low-grade petrol, even worse than the 72 octane Pool petrol in the UK. Since the "low octane" distributor was fitted to the late pre-war cars and all post-war pushrod engines, then the majority of those still running may well have the low octane set-up.

The 1½ litre engines had a compression ratio of 7.5:1, similar to the six-cylinders, but the

	1½ litre	2½ litre	3½ litre
Electrical			
Headlamps	LBD166 Biflex; 1940 SE: P80 on SE model	P100R; 1940: P100L with fluted lens	As 2½ litre
Side lamps	Torpedo type 1130	Type 1185 integral in wing	As 2½ litre
Fog Lamps	FT58 on 1940 SE model only	FT58	As 2½ litre
Dynamo	C45 YV/3 V58; 1940: C45 YV/3 GC 24/0	C45 PV/3 L1/1	As 2½ litre
Starter	M418G GCO; 1940: M418G GC 24/0	M418 AL/1 V51/0	M45G GC20/0
Distributor	DKH4A GC24; 1940: DKYH4A GC29	DUH6A GC14	As 2½ litre
Control box	RJF 50; 1940: RJF 91	As 1½ litre	As 2½ litre
Trafficators	SF55J Type 28; 1940: SF55J Type 29	SF54G 1940: SF55J Type 23G	As 2½ litre
Chassis			
Springs, Suspension	Semi-elliptic leaf springs; beam front axle, live rear axle	As 1½ litre	As 2½ litre
Shock absorbers	Luvax vane type hydraulic; 1940: Luvax piston type	As 1½ litre	As 2½ litre
Steering box	Burman Douglas worm & nut	As 1½ litre	As 2½ litre
Brakes	12in x 1½in Girling rod, single leading shoe	14in x 1¾in Girling rod, single leading shoe, ribbed drums	As 2½ litre
Wheels	18in wire spoke	As 1½ litre	As 2½ litre
Tyres	5.25x18	5.50x18	As 2½ litre
Turning circle	38ft (11.6 metres)	As 1½ litre	As 2½ litre
Fuel tank	14 gals (64 litres), incl 2 gals (9 litres) reserve	As 1½ litre	As 2½ litre
Price	Sal £298 (Std), £318 (SE) DHC £318 (Std), £338 (SE)	Sal £395 DHC £415	Sal £445 DHC £465

company took a different approach in adapting them to Pool petrol. The Instruction Book carries the following note:

"All engines are normally tested on Ethyl Petrol, but in view of war conditions and only Pool Petrol being available, all cars are being sent out fitted with a cylinder head packing to lower the compression ratio, so that the engine will operate satisfactorily on the grade of fuel now available. When, however, the 80 octane rating fuel becomes available, the removal of the compression plate is recommended, so that the corresponding increase in performance obtainable with the better-class fuel may be gained."

In other words, only the compression plate is mentioned, there being no reference to any of the other changes made to the tuning of the sixes. Presumably all the four-cylinder engines had the compression plate fitted, but the Spare Parts Catalogue for them, unlike that for the six-cylinder engines, makes no mention of the plate as a separate item, though it might have been included in the "Joints (Gaskets) for Decarbonising Engine" that are not detailed but only listed under the part number Ass.307, for which no drawing exists today.

Chapter Four

The SS 100 Sports Car

With a larger engine, 1938's 3½ litre SS 100 was faster than its predecessor, and quickly became the preferred model. This car is chassis 39075.

In 1935 the company had built 24 short-chassis S.S.I 90 open two-seaters, based on the S.S.I chassis and powered by the 2664cc sidevalve engine, but this was only a short run near the end of the production of the S.S.I cars. The SS 90, as it was known, was allegedly capable of 90mph (145km/h) – it was never road-tested by the magazines – and was replaced in October 1935 (with production starting in April 1936) by the similar looking but overhead-valve SS Jaguar 100, which was tested to do 95mph (153km/h). For the first two seasons this car had the 2½ litre engine, but in late 1937 it was joined by a 3½ litre version that raised the bar to over 100mph (161km/h), and both models then continued in production until July 1939. It did not make a comeback after the war.

The 1936 and 1937 Models

The SS 100, as it was soon to be known, was powered by the 2664cc overhead-valve engine developed by Harry Weslake for the SS Company, and had a new specially designed chassis, which incorporated the main improve-

The SS Jaguar 100's chassis was similar to the shape of the S.S.I Saloon's but updated with rod-operated brakes.

The new SS Jaguar Tourer chassis (above) was widened and strengthened, and now altogether more substantial than the S.S.I Saloon chassis.

ments introduced for the SS Jaguar Saloon, though its overall shape remained similar to that of the SS 90 and it was the same length, with a wheelbase of 8ft 8in (2642mm). The SS 100 was something of a hybrid in terms of its chassis, with aspects of both the S.S.I and the SS Jaguar, though as can be seen more akin to the S.S.I in shape and construction. The central cruciform on the SS 100 was similar to that on the S.S.I but was located nearer to the rear suspension, since the wheelbase of the SS 100 was 1ft 3in (381mm) shorter than that of the S.S.I.

For the new SS 100 chassis, the outboard rear springs were retained, since the narrow two-seater body did not need the extra width that had been gained for the Saloon by moving the rear springs inboard of the chassis frame. The front springs were also kept outboard of the chassis, whereas on the 1936 Saloon and Tourer they were directly below the frame. The semi-elliptic leaf springs were damped by Luvax hydraulic shock absorbers all round, with additional Hartford friction dampers on the front. Some of the SS 90 cars had been fitted with André Telecontrol friction dampers on the front suspension which were adjustable from inside the car, and the SS 100 was offered with the optional Luvax "Finger-tip control" shock absorbers on all wheels, also adjustable by the driver from inside the car. The cost was £10 10s including fitting if they were specified at the time of ordering the car. It is not known if any of these adjustable dampers were ever actually fitted by the factory.

The SS 100 chassis did however incorporate the new Girling rod brakes all round, and the sliding trunnions for the rear mounts of the front springs. The wheels were the revised type as fitted to all SS Jaguars. The transmission was similar to the Jaguar Saloon and Tourer, with the four-speed Standard gearbox and remote gear lever.

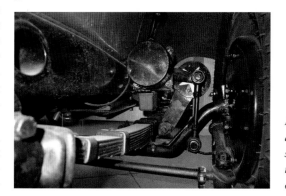

Luvax hydraulic vane and Hartford friction shock absorbers, as fitted to the front suspension of the SS 100.

This splendid 1939 3½ litre SS 100 (chassis 39112) was not just a pretty face – it was also one of the SS works team's entrants into the 1939 RAC Rally.

The dashboard of a 1938 3½ litre SS 100 (chassis 39075), complete with adjustable damper gauges.

Under the dashboard of a 1938 3½ litre SS 100 (this is chassis 39075) was the same wiper mechanism found in 1936 cars.

The design of the body was inherited from the SS 90 and it was ash-framed like the saloon, but unlike the saloon the panels, wings and bonnet were all made of aluminium. The use of aluminium and the compact dimensions of the open two-seater body reduced the weight of this model by 7cwt (356kg) to 22cwt (1119kg), a considerable saving and a significant contribution to the greater performance of the sports car

over the saloon. Thanks to the lower weight, the final drive ratio could be raised to 4:1, at least on the 1937 and later 2½ litre models; the 1936 cars appear to have had the 4.25 ratio of the Saloon and Tourer of that year.

The relatively soft aluminium wings were to some extent protected from damage from stones thrown up by the tyres by having a sheet of steel riveted to their underside, but as this tended to cause corrosion between the two different metals, any repairs to the wings were best made by replacing the steel with harder heavy-gauge aluminium plate. The heads of the two rows of rivets that secured the reinforcing sheets to the flared wings gave the SS 100 its characteristic appearance. The radiator had a wire-mesh stone guard rather than the vertical slats of the Saloon. Headlamps were the Lucas QK596 type as originally fitted to the Tourer, but some surviving cars have been fitted with P100 headlamps, which look somewhat large on an SS 100. The headlamps had wire-mesh stone guards matching the radiator, and were supported by the characteristic bracing bars, with a small medallion reading "100" in the centre of the horizontal main bar where the two lower diagonal bars joined up. Unlike the later Saloons, the SS 100 always had separate side lamps. Two external Alto horns were fitted below the headlamps, and later cars often had a single centrally-mounted fog lamp.

The instruments were the same as fitted on the 1936 Saloon, with clockwise rotation for both the rev counter and speedometer. On the later saloon the rev counter was changed to anti-clockwise rotation to eliminate the need for the right-angle reversing gear on its drive, but all the SS 100 cars continued to be made with the clockwise rotating instrument. The instruments had the same silver dials as on the early saloon but they were arranged differently, with the rev counter, speedometer, and oil pressure gauge directly in front of the driver, and the other three minor instruments – fuel gauge, ammeter, and water temperature gauge – located in front of the passenger. An oil temperature gauge could be fitted as an extra. Additionally, the SS 100 had a fuel reserve tap operated from the dash by a turn-knob in front of the passenger. There was a substantial grab handle directly in front of the passenger to aid getting in and out of the car, and for hanging on to when the car was being driven competitively, particularly on winding and bumpy roads.

A single Bakelite knob on the dashboard operated both the windscreen wipers together through a fairly complicated mechanism that parked them down and out of the way of the windscreen, so this could be folded forwards if desired. The use of this mechanism was continued on all SS 100 cars, though it was changed on the 1937 Saloons to enable each wiper to operate separately.

The steering wheel boss for these early models was the same as fitted to the Saloons of that period, though with only two levers since the SS 100 did not have trafficators, but it seems that some early cars still had a trafficator switch. When this switch was not fitted, its slot was blanked off with a Bakelite fillet.

The interior of the car had few luxuries and even had a simple chain or a fob instead of an interior door handle to operate the door lock. There were however external door handles. There were simple door trims with small map pockets, and two brackets for the side screens. The cabin was a snug fit for the driver and passenger, who sat low in the car with the seat cushion nearly at sill height.

The two seats were upholstered in unpleated leather and their backrests folded forward to give access to a small fully carpeted storage space in the tonneau for luggage, or maybe even a small child for a short journey. Behind this area was a vertical storage compartment for the side screens, with a cover fastened by two toggle clips. The car was supplied with a light-weight hood and a tonneau cover that was zipped down the middle to allow for the passenger side to remain covered; the hood had a very small rear window divided in two panels. The hood when folded fitted neatly around the top of the tonneau area and was provided with a hood envelope.

The windscreen could be folded flat forwards, by undoing a knurled knob with the SS hexagon on either side, and the cars were fitted with two aero screens mounted on the lower windscreen surround for use when the screen was folded down. Under the passenger seat there was a long lidded recess for the storage of tools, in particular the jack and its handle, as well as the starting handle, which was similar to but shorter than the one for the Saloon. The recess could also accommodate a limited number of other tools. There is no

A 1937 2½ litre SS 100 (chassis 18109) and its early dashboard, still featuring a trafficator switch on the manette, even though no trafficators were fitted to this model.

There were simple door trims with small map pockets, plus two brackets for the side screens. This is a 1938 3½ litre SS 100, chassis 39075.

The vertical storage compartment at the back of the SS 100's rear cabin was designed for storage of the screens.

Beneath the SS 100's passenger seat lived a neat tool storage compartment, here shown open to reveal the jack. Again, the car shown is a 1938 3½ litre SS 100, chassis 39075

Offside of a 2½ litre SS 100 engine bay, showing the small-diameter steering column fitted to 1936/37 cars. This car actually has the later exhaust manifold.

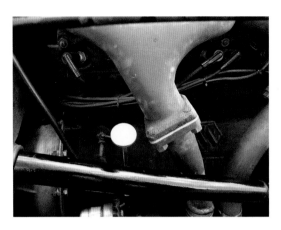

record of what tools were supplied by the factory when the cars were new.

The bonnet had louvres along the top as well as on the sides. The bonnet line was very low, barely clearing the top of the rocker cover, and the engine bay was also narrower than on the Saloon. This reduced space in the engine compartment brought with it certain constraints in the layout of the engine and ancillaries, thus the thermostat was fitted horizontally, so the engine was initially to the same specification as in the 1936 model 2½ litre Tourer.

However, the engines destined for use in the SS 100 cars, both the 2½ and the later 3½ litre, were fitted with different front and rear engine

mountings from those of the Saloons or Tourers, and were identified by an additional light stamping of "SS 100" on the block above where the engine number had been more heavily stamped. The SS 100 identification is easily and often hidden under layers of paint, however light. It does not appear that these engines went through any testing process, whether at Standard or at SS, to select the best units for the SS 100 cars. It should be noted that other Jaguar engines can be adapted to fit SS 100 cars, as some survivors are known to have post-war Mark IV or Mark V engines.

The engine was modified in August 1936, when the height of the block was increased by ¼in (6.4mm). There was no change to the 1937 model SS 100 as such, though production had been halted between October 1936 and January 1937. The cars completed up to October had chassis numbers 18001 to 18051 and engine numbers lower than 251164, so presumably all had the 1936-type engine, but from January 1937 the following 75 SS 100 cars, with chassis numbers 18052 to 18126, were made with same engines as the 1937 model Saloons.

The early SS 100 cars with the 18000 series chassis numbers had the long small-diameter steering column as used on all the Tourers and on the 1936 Saloon (although the column was

A recessed battery box was found in the centre of the SS 100's bulkhead; this is a 1938 3½ litre, chassis 39075.

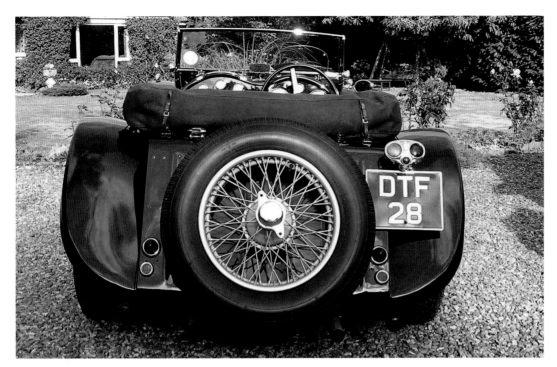

shorter on the Saloon). There was no space under the bonnet for the air filter and silencer assembly fitted on the Saloon, so the engine had no air filter at all. Many owners at that time would fit compact individual pancake filters to reduce induction noise and to provide some barrier to dust getting into the carburettors. With the bonnet line being lower than on the Saloon, there was no room for the battery to sit on top of the bulkhead, so it was housed in a recessed box in the centre of the bulkhead, which intruded into the cabin under the dashboard.

The SS 100 was not fitted with bumpers, front or rear, and the spare wheel was mounted on a sturdy tubular carrier sited centrally through the vertically mounted steel slab fuel tank. The fuel filler cap and the fuel level sensor were mounted on the top of the tank. Unlike the SS90, the rear of the tank and thus the spare wheel were at a forward angle. Normally one spare wheel would be carried, but if needed an extension was available to carry two spares. The factory only fitted one off-side rear owl-lamp that served as stop, tail, and reversing lamp, as well as illuminating the single number plate. As twin tail and stop lamps have been a legal requirement since the 1950s, latter-day owners usually like to have an owl-lamp and a rear number plate on each side, to make the appearance of the rear of the car symmetrical.

The 1938 and 1939 Models

By the middle of 1937, 126 of the 2½ litre SS 100 cars had been made to the original specification. Some modifications were then made, the chief one of which was the addition of a 3½ litre-engined car. This larger engine produced a faster car that quickly became the preferred model, following up the many successes that the SS 100 had already achieved in competition. The 2½ litre model was continued but was made at only half the volume of its bigger-engined stable mate.

The new 3½ litre model was introduced in October 1937. The final drive was raised to 3.8:1, and the gearbox had the same ratios as the 3½ litre Saloon. The engine, which is discussed in the chapter on the all-steel 1938 cars, from the outset had the stiffened crankshaft with bearings 0.040in (1mm) larger in diameter than those of the 2½ litre, and was fitted with thin-shell big-end bearing caps and steel con rods.

The 2½ litre engine also received the steel con rods with the thin-walled shells, but only in September 1938 after engine number L 1051, and these new engines were used only in the Saloon and DHC models. The SS 100 2½ litre was by that time near the end of its production run and the last ten cars made from November 1938 to September 1939 all had the earlier type engine with engine numbers lower than L 1051. These engines must have been made prior to

Among the 1938 engine modifications was a change in water pump design – it now mounted directly onto the engine block with no back plate. This 3½ litre SS 100 is chassis 39075.

A 1938 3½ litre SS 100 (chassis 39075), featuring the later steering wheel boss. Its design was essentially unchanged but the unused trafficator lever slot was blanked-off.

Offside view of a 1938 3½ litre SS 100 engine (chassis 39075). Note the later, larger-diameter steering column.

September 1938 and held in stock by SS Jaguar or by Standard, in readiness for any late orders for 2½ litre cars.

Otherwise, the engines in the 1938 and 1939 SS 100 cars were the same as those fitted in the 1938 model all-steel Saloons, with the same modifications as had been introduced on those cars. These included a change in the water pump design, eliminating the separate back plate and using the front face of the cylinder block as the back plate for the pump. The one-piece exhaust

manifold casting was replaced by two separate castings feeding the new dual exhaust system, each pipe having only one silencer, against two on each pipe on the Saloon.

These later cars were fitted with the larger diameter 2in (51mm) steering column, the same as on the Saloon, though of the longer type needed for the SS 100. The steering wheel boss was updated to the 1938 Saloon type, with its smaller horn-push, and the additional circular surround forming a shroud between the boss and the steering wheel itself.

Inside the cabin the driver had been given more foot space by creating a larger box for the foot pedals which intruded a little into the engine bay. The 3½ litre had a speedometer reading to 120mph, whereas the 2½ litre always had a 100mph speedometer.

The radiator badges now had the engine size shown instead of the name Jaguar on the elongated insert at the bottom of the winged badge, while the Jaguar name now appeared on the modified hexagonal insert at the top of the badge, together with the SS logo. As on the Saloon, the badge had cream enamelled inserts for the 2½ litre and black for the 3½ litre.

Interestingly, unlike the saloons, both the 2½ and 3½ litre SS 100 cars had the same size radiator and grille, since presumably it was considered that there was no need for additional cooling for the larger engine, and there would not have been enough space anyway to accommodate a wider radiator. This seems to have been the correct decision since the 3½ litre cars are no more prone to overheating than the 2½ litre models.

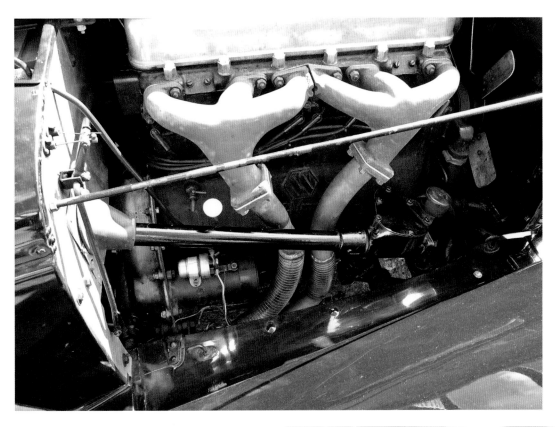

Compare the bulkheads of the 1936 2½ litre SS 100 (chassis 18016, left) and the 1938 2½ litre SS 100 (chassis 49033, below). Note the later car's casing beneath the steering column, which was added to give more space for the driver's feet.

Special or Extra Equipment

There are no records of what extra or special equipment was fitted to any new SS 100 cars by the factory. The Car Record Book only gives the colours of the exterior, interior, and sometimes of the hood. The extras quoted for the cars were Ace wheel discs, fog or pass lamps, chromium-plated badge bars, spring gaiters, and the Luvax "Finger-tip" shock absorbers mentioned above.

The most often asked question concerning factory-fitted special equipment, however, is not about any of these but about whether a car would have had chromed wheels from new. There are no references to chromed wheels for any of the SS 100 cars in the factory records but that does not mean that no car had them.

One car that did have chromed wheels was chassis number 18061. It was painted Maroon and had Maroon interior and hood, so was undoubtedly a special order. It was supplied by Loxhams Garages at Barrow-in-Furness in February 1937. The full story of the car was told to me by the son of the proprietor of that branch of Loxhams. The managing director of the large shipbuilding company Vickers Armstrong at Barrow-in-Furness, Sir Charles Worthington Craven, was a good friend of

The dark blue-coloured radiator badge (left) of the 1936 2½ litre SS 100 (chassis 18016). By 1938 the 2½ litre model's radiator badge was cream, and the 3½ litre SS 100's emblem was black, as shown (right).

William Lyons, and they had met at the 1936 Motor Show. Sir Charles was looking for a stylish car for his wife Constance and Lyons suggested that the SS 100 might be suitable, so Craven ordered one on the spot.

The car needed to be picked up from the factory and taken to Barrow, and that was where the son of the Loxhams distributor came in, as it was his job to deliver the car in a timely manner for such an important customer. He collected the car from Foleshill and drove it up to Barrow, where it was registered EO 6598 and taxed in Sir Charles' name on 18 February 1937, and then delivered to Lady Craven personally. The delivery driver had a quick conversation with her and questioned the advisability of having chromed wheels, since they would need much more attention to keep clean. Her response was that this did not concern her, as she would not be cleaning them herself. This supports his recollection of the car having had chromed wheels from new.

Lady Craven's ownership of the car was however short-lived, just three months I think, as she drove the car only a few miles and found it particularly unladylike for her to get out of the car when visiting the library. The upshot was that the car was returned to the factory and re-sold to a Mr WH Harrison. The factory warranty, normally only valid for the first owner, is recorded as having been transferred to the new owner, which was a major and unique concession on the part of Lyons and gives credence to the rest of the story.

The car survives, though it carries its subsequent registration number GOF 2 (a Birmingham issue of 1946). Interestingly the factory ledger does not make any mention of the real first owner, nor the date on which she took delivery. This is an eyewitness account of chassis number 18061, and establishes that the car had been delivered with chromed wheels, even though there is no record of it in the ledger. Any claim by an owner that his or her car had chromed wheels from new can only be confirmed from the car's own original documentation, and not by any records held in the Jaguar Heritage archive.

There were a few 2½ litre cars (but no 3½ litre models) that took a while before being sold by distributors, with the consequence that the their final despatch dates are considerably later than their manufacturing dates. The early history of some of them is known and this gives an idea of what happened to them and how they came to be designated as 1940 models in the ledger, despite having been made earlier.

49006 was made on 18 November 1937 and went to the distributor RC Bellamy in Grimsby. They used it as a demonstrator whilst trying to sell it. The famous pilot Alex Henshaw, who lived close by, used it for a weekend but did not buy it as he found it too unstable for his liking. He was a well-known celebrity, and was later somewhat put out to find that the distributor was advertising the car as having been owned by him. The car had to go back to the factory at some time for repair and refurbishment and was finally sold in September 1940, but the name of the first owner is not recorded.

49010 was made on 28 November 1937 and went to Henlys. It was returned unsold to the factory and then assigned to PJ Evans in Birmingham on 25 March 1938, but again was returned to the factory on 27 September 1938. It remained there until 4 August 1939, when it was again sent to Henlys but still remained unsold, and then probably went back in the factory until 1947 when it was sold to Ian Appleyard and registered for him under LNW 100 in Leeds in July 1947. This makes this car the last SS 100 registered but not the last one made. This car was fitted with a 3½ litre engine by the factory, and a post-war type radiator badge without the SS letters, and Ian Appleyard went on to win the 1948 International Alpine Rally outright in it.

49050 was made on 20 July 1938 and sent to Glovers in Yorkshire on 23 August 1938. It was not sold and was then passed to other distributors, Scottish Motor Traction of Carlisle, and PJ Evans, until finally returning to Glovers on 28 August 1940, and to the first unrecorded owner.

49056 was made in August 1938 and there is no record of what happened to it until it was shipped on 6 May 1940 to one Myles Standish, an American Vice-Consul in Marseille, just four days before the German invasion of France. Marseille ended up in the Vichy-governed "free" part of France and was not occupied by the Germans, but Mr Standish presumably beat a retreat when the USA entered the war in December 1941. Perhaps for that reason the car seems to have disappeared. Standish is incidentally honoured for issuing visas to Jews escaping to Portugal, and he helped Leon Feuchtwanger to escape from an internment camp.

The one-off 1938 3½ litre SS 100 FHC (chassis 39088) was finished in metallic Gunmetal Grey, and sold through Henlys in London during April 1939.

49061 was made in November 1938 and invoiced to Henlys in November 1940 but only shipped from the factory in March 1941; again the first owner's name is not recorded.

49064 was a chassis-only made in June 1939, presumably as a special order, but only reached its destination, the Jaguar distributors in Brussels, after the war in June 1947. It was then fitted with a one-off Vanden Plas body and was shown at the 1948 Brussels Motor Show (see chapter 7).

The Fixed Head Coupé

In 1938 the company produced a fixed head coupé version of the SS 100 which was shown at the Earls Court Motor Show. It had the 3½ litre engine but the body was quite unlike the normal SS 100.

It was a closed two-seater and the interior was more like the SS Jaguar Saloon, with a high level of trim, well carpeted, and a wood veneer dashboard with black-faced instruments similar to those fitted on the 1938 Saloon. There was even a lidded cubbyhole for the passenger. The

seats were bigger and deeper than in the SS 100, and the doors had internal handles and wind-down windows in place of the removable side-screens. The windscreen could be opened at the bottom like the Saloon and trafficators were also fitted.

The 1938 3½ litre SS 100 FHC's elegant rear view, revealing its twin fuel tank fillers.

Luxuriously appointed and plushly carpeted, the 1938 3½ litre SS 100 FHC's two-seater cabin contained a wood-veneered dashboard and Saloon-style instruments.

Externally the body was well rounded, with fully skirted helmet front wings, as opposed to the flowing wing line of the normal car, and spats over the rear wheels. The outline of the roof and rear quarters were somewhat similar to the Atalante coupé body fitted to the contemporary Bugatti type 57, and may in turn have inspired the post-war XK 120 fixed head coupé. There were no running boards or bumpers, and there was a traditional external boot, while the petrol tank was under the tail of the car and had twin filler caps. The bonnet top did not have any louvres.

In a short article on this car, *The Motor* for 18 October 1938 stated that "a demand has sprung up for a small closed car that would have the comfort of a Saloon model with the performance of the open sports car. These demands should be well met by the new Jaguar fixed-head two-seater coupé which was a last minute addition to the SS Stand No. 126 at Earls Court." It went on to state that "this car will be built in limited quantities for owners demanding exceptional performance with closed coachwork and will be priced at £595 with 3½ litre engine and at £545 with the 2½ litre engine."

The car was certainly very stylish and had attractive lines but maybe the additional £150 over the SS 100 price was too much for prospective owners as only the one 3½ litre car was ever

Reviewers reckoned the recessed battery box intruded a little too much into the cabin beneath the dash; shown here is 1938 SS 100, chassis 39075.

made. It can be assumed that there was insufficient interest at the show for it to be pursued any further. This model was never featured in any of the sales brochures of the time. The only car made was chassis 39088 registered EHP 111, it was finished in metallic Gunmetal Grey with silver-grey interior trim, and was sold through Henlys in London to one LT March in April 1939. Fortunately it still exists.

Reviews of the SS 100

The road tests of the cars naturally concentrated on their performance and handling. The visibility was considered good as both wings could easily been seen by the driver. The seats were reasonably comfortable with their coil springs and Dunlopillo overlay but the small cabin had a tendency to become hot from the engine. This occurred on both 2½ litre and 3½ litre cars. Unlike the Saloons the handbrake was of the fly-off type, always operating only on the rear wheels, and was effective and easy to use.

It was considered that there was a reasonable amount of luggage space behind the seats for the type of car. The recessed battery box intruded somewhat into the foot well, so depressing the clutch pedal required the use of the toe rather than the ball of the foot.

That the 3½ litre engined car had excellent acceleration was immediately obvious, with 50mph (80km/h) being reached in 7.4 seconds and 70mph (113km/h) in only 14.7 seconds. The rod-operated brakes were good and the engine very tractable, needing only third or fourth gears for most normal driving. The exhaust noise was scarcely noted at low speeds though it was harsh around 60mph (97km/h), but became quieter again as the speed was increased. The suspension was firm and there was no body roll when the car was driven hard, the combination of the front hydraulic and friction shock absorbers working well to keep the car stable. The car was very manoeuvrable, the light and positive high-geared steering needing only 2½ turns from lock to lock.

Overall the SS 100 was a genuinely fast, stable and exciting car to drive and it is no wonder that so many were successfully raced and rallied, and also that so many of them have survived, a number of them having had major repairs and rebuilds. It is one of the most desirable cars Jaguar has ever made and of the 309 cars made around 90 per cent are known still to exist.

Specifications of SS 100

	2½ litre	3½ litre
Dimensions		
Overall length	12ft 6in (3810mm)	As 2½ litre
Overall width	5ft 3in (1600mm)	As 2½ litre
Overall height	4ft 6in (1372mm)	As 2½ litre
Wheelbase	8ft 8in (2642mm)	As 2½ litre
Track	4ft 6in (1372mm)	As 2½ litre
Weight	22cwt (1119kg); 1938-39: 23cwt (1170kg)	As 1938-39 2½ litre
Engine		
Type	6 cylinder OHV	As 2½ litre
Capacity, RAC hp	2663.7cc, 19.84hp	3485.5cc, 25.01hp
Bore, stroke	73mm by 106mm	82mm by 110mm
Bhp at rpm	102 at 4600rpm	125 at 4250rpm
Crankshaft bearing diameters	Main journals 2.439in big-end journals 1.824in	Main journals 2.479in big-end journals 2.086in
Con rods	Dural, no small end bushes	Steel, bronze small-end bushes
Compression ratio	7.0 to 1; 1938-39: 7.6:1	7.2 to 1
Tappet clearance	Inlet and exhaust 0.006in to eng 251333, then 0.015in; 1938-39: 0.012in inlet, 0.015in exhaust	As 1938-39 2½ litre
Carburettor	Twin SU H3	Twin SU H4
Fuel pump	Twin SU electric	As 2½ litre
Transmission		
Gearbox type	Double helical	As 2½ litre
Overall ratios	1936: 15.30, 8.98, 5.83, 4.25; 1937 and later: 14.40, 8.45, 5.45, 4.00	12.04, 7.06, 4.58, 3.80
Rear axle	ENV spiral bevel, ratio 1936 4.25, 1937 and later 4.00	ENV spiral bevel, ratio 3.80
Electrical		
Headlamps	QK 596	As 2½ litre
Side lamps	Torpedo type 1130	As 2½ litre
Control box	RJF 50	As 2½ litre
Distributor	DUH 6A/0 GH14/1; 1938-39: DUH 6A GC 14	As 1938-39 2½ litre
Dynamo	C45 PV/3 L1/0; 1938-39: C45 PV/3 L1/1	As 1938-39 2½ litre
Starter	M418 AL V51/0	M45G GC20/0
Chassis		
Suspension	Semi-elliptic leaf springs; beam front axle, live rear axle	As 2½ litre
Shock absorbers	Luvax vane type hydraulic plus Hartford friction on front	As 2½ litre
Steering box	Burman Douglas worm & nut	As 2½ litre
Brakes	Girling rod, 13in x 1½in brake shoes, finned drums	As 2½ litre
Wheels	18in wire spoke	As 2½ litre
Tyres	5.25x18	As 2½ litre
Turning circle	36ft (11 metres)	As 2½ litre
Fuel tank	17 gals (77 litres)	As 2½ litre
Price	£395	£445

Chapter Five

After the War: The Mark IV Range

The front of a standard-model 1946 1½ litre (chassis 410275), wearing LBD166 Biflex headlamps.

Immediately after the end of the war there was a need for the company and the country to restart production of cars, particularly for the export market in order to earn hard currency. Two 1½ litre saloons were first off the line in September 1945. The first became a works car and the second was supplied through Henlys to Sheercraft Ltd, which no doubt got preferential treatment as a supplier to Jaguar. The 1½ litre cars were then made in volume but it was only in February 1946 that the 2½ and 3½ litre cars followed. Priority had been given to the production of the smaller car, as it was probably the easiest to start making in volume, particularly as the Standard Motor Company supplied the

engines and gearboxes. The SS 100 was no longer made, and the 1½ litre DHC was also dropped from the range. The six-cylinder DHC models would only make a brief appearance in 1948.

There was a real urgency to get cars made in volume and though there were a limited number of changes made from the 1940 model, not all were immediately incorporated in the first cars made. There were presumably stocks of pre-war parts at the factory and its suppliers, and these were used up first, which no doubt helped in getting a speedy start to production and in building up the volumes.

The most urgent change needed was to eliminate as many as possible of the SS logos that

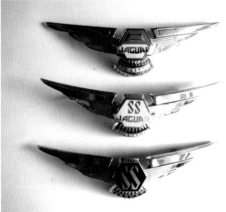

Radiator badges, from the bottom upwards: 1937 2½ litre in dark blue; 1938 2½ litre in cream; top: the badge used immediately post-war, featuring the same winged base casting and insert but with the SS logo omitted.

Left: *The Mark IV 2½ litre's cream "Jaguar" radiator badge*. Right: *Radiator grilles grew taller after World War II.*

appeared on the cars. Some were straightforward but others needed time and ingenuity to change. The pre-war radiator badge for instance displayed the SS lettering prominently, and new badges and winged castings would take time to make, so for the first cars the same winged casting was used, but the SS Jaguar enamelled insert with its characteristic shape was modified, retaining its shape but with the upper part left blank and with only the word Jaguar on it. This was soon replaced with a new design of the winged casting which included a flattened hexagonal lozenge-shaped insert with just Jaguar on it. The radiator shell frames were incidentally altered in design, with a thin bottom section so they could sit flat on the apron, from which the recess had been eliminated. The ID plate, the oil filler cap, the wheel wing nuts and the rear bumper badge could all be changed easily, but it was some time before all the castings for the cylinder blocks carried the Jaguar name rather than SS.

The post-war range was described in the magazines in 1945, by *The Autocar* on 21 September and *The Motor* on 26 September. Neither of these major articles was completely free of errors, thus *The Motor* was adamant that the six-cylinder cars now had Girling's new hydro-mechanical brakes with hydraulic front brakes, and *The Autocar* claimed to have enjoyed a run on a post-war 3½ litre car when it is unlikely that any car of this type existed as yet.

The 1½ litre cars

Externally the cars were largely unchanged from the 1940 models, but the rear number plate surround was replaced by a slightly modified post-war type, although only after the first 264

cars had been made; this change also applied to the six-cylinder cars.

The quarter-light channels were now chromed and the headlamps on the standard model were changed to the LBD 166 tripod version which was similar to the Biflex type but had three internal supports for the light shield. The headlights for the SE model remained the P80 type. The central motif on the front apron was shorter than that used on the six-cylinder cars and was unchanged throughout the production of the 1½ litre.

The SE model became by far the most popular model, 73 per cent of all the four-cylinder cars made having the SE trim. From a slow start with no SE models made in 1945, the numbers increased each year, ending up with 94

On the left is the post-war Mark IV grille, which sat on top of a flat apron. It replaced pre-war grille (shown on the right-hand-side) that sat in a recess, effectively hiding the deeper bottom frame member.

A front view of chassis 415384, a 1948 1½ litre SE model fitted with the P80 headlamps. The fog lights on this car are non-standard.

Chassis 412349, a 1947 1½ litre SE model, also fitted with non-standard front fog lights.

A 1946 1½ litre standard model (chassis 410275), showing the later number plate housing and the narrow back bumper with small scroll ends.

per cent of the production being SE cars in 1948.

The engine and the double helical gearbox were mostly unchanged to the end of production of the 1½ litre, and were supplied complete by Standard, who no doubt took the quickest route to volume production for their own cars, as well as for the engines and gearboxes supplied to Jaguar. This would have involved using whatever pre-war stock Standard might still have, and also using unmodified cylinder block moulds until sufficient numbers had been made, to allow time for the SS logo to be replaced by the word Jaguar, though not all the later engines had the Jaguar logo on the casting. Cylinder blocks with the SS logo were fitted to cars made up to February 1946, by which time 275 had been made. The same basic engine and gearbox were used on the post-war Triumph 1800 models, and the gearbox also on the Standard Twelve and Fourteen.

The main modification to the engine at the

The 1948 1½ litre SE's P80 headlights, unchanged forked central motif and Jaguar radiator badge.

start of post-war production was a new design of water-heated inlet manifold on to which the horizontal carburettor was bolted. The petrol/air mixture passed through this manifold to the cylinders, getting warmed on the way, which provided a welcome increase in power, claimed to be "nearly 10 per cent", and yet the post-war engine was still quoted as developing 65bhp, the same figure as pre-war. The new inlet manifold also served as the water outlet from engine to radiator. It required a modified exhaust mani-

LBD 166 tripod headlights of a1946 1½ litre standard model (chassis 410275), changed from the previous Biflex lamps.

The Mark IV was a handsome, well-proportioned car. This is a 1948 1½ litre SE model (chassis 415384), which became by far the most popular model.

Early and late post-war 1½ litre engines (right and below respectively). The February 1946 cylinder block still wore an SS emblem, but after this date it was swapped for a Jaguar logo cast onto the left-hand side of the block.

Offside view of a 1946 1½ litre engine, showing the ingoing fuel being warmed by passing it through the water manifold.

The 1946 1½ litre engine from the nearside, showing its oil filter casting bolted to the block. Its oil filter canister was shorter than the part found on six-cylinder cars.

fold which was just below it.

Also new were the water thermostat, air cleaner and silencer, and the oil cleaner and filter housing, which was similar to that fitted to the six-cylinder cars but with a shorter filter canister for the smaller engine. The water pump was unchanged and remained bolted directly to the front face of the engine block with no back plate. The four-blade engine fan was later supplemented with a six-blade option on cars that were destined for export to hot countries. The steel con rods on the four-cylinder engines were not changed and were used to the end of production. Export cars were available with a lower compression ratio of 6.8:1 rather than the standard 7.6:1, achieved by fitting the compression plate which had been used on some late pre-war cars.

The manual choke was retained since it was not possible to fit the automatic type used on the six-cylinder cars, and the distributor with the vernier micro-adjustment only appeared in July

1949 after 3252 cars had been made. The Lucas RJF 91 control box was fitted on these cars from the start but was changed to the Lucas RF95 type in July 1948, together with the addition of the Lucas type 6J junction box. The battery was moved from the central position on the bulkhead to the left side at the end of 1946, and in late 1948 the battery cradle was changed to one with side bars to secure the battery in position.

The single leading shoe brakes all round were retained, together with the Millenite cast-iron brake drums, the handbrake now operating

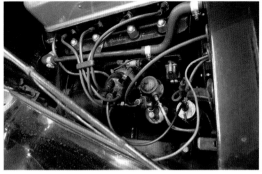

The engine bay of a 1948 1½ litre SE, complete with the factory-original heater feed pipes. .

A standard 1946 1½ litre's compact engine bay; this car has been modified to accept an aftermarket heater.

the rear wheels only. Luvax Girling P6 shock absorbers were fitted as standard but in 1948 Armstrong units were available as an alternative, as on the six-cylinder cars. In the transmission, the gearbox ratios were the same as on the pre-war cars, but the hypoid bevel differential had a ratio of 4.875:1.

Inside the car, the two interior lights in the rear cabin were now handed, and the dash panel was updated on the SE model to accommodate the heater controls and make provision for the optional radio. This layout was similar to the six-cylinder cars but the two controls for the heater and fan speed were reversed on the dash from those on the six-cylinder cars, since the hot water feed from the engine was on the opposite side for the four-cylinder engine. The sun visors were updated but the rest was much as the late pre-war cars, since the upholstery had remained pleated even on the 1940 SE model.

The 2½ and 3½ litre Saloons

Like the 1½ litre cars, the six-cylinder models were largely unchanged from the 1940 models. Since volume production of these cars only started in February 1946, there were fewer cars made with left-over pre-war parts and assemblies. Having said that, 132 and 147 respectively of the 2½ and 3½ litre cylinder blocks still carried the SS logo, even though the engines were now being made by Jaguar themselves. Of these, the engine numbers of the first 18 and 25 engines respectively still had the pre-war L and M prefixes, but all following engines, including

those with the rest of the SS logo blocks, had the post-war P and S prefixes. All engines with the SS blocks were fitted with steel con rods, but then the alloy con rods were introduced, and were fitted to all subsequent six-cylinder engines. The replacement of the steel rods with the lighter alloy rods with their integral oil-feed

A rear-seat passenger's view of a 1948 1½ litre SE model (chassis 415384). Note there were only trafficator and dip switches on the steering wheel boss.

Close-up of chassis 415384's dashboard (a 1948 1½ litre SE model). Note the heater and ventilation controls were reversed from six-cylinder models, since the hot water feed from the engine was on the other side.

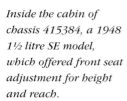

Inside the cabin of chassis 415384, a 1948 1½ litre SE model, which offered front seat adjustment for height and reach.

pipes between the main bearings and the gudgeon pins is today viewed by many as a poor technical decision, since the alloy rods are considered by some to be prone to failure, which though very rare is catastrophic if it does occur. However, in engines running hot the alloy con rods were prone to expand, resulting in lower oil pressure.

Some other changes were made to the engines. The water pump was changed to a more robust unit with its own back plate rather than having the front face of the block as the back plate, and the fan could therefore be mounted higher up on the engine, the better to cool the radiator. The oil pump too was upgraded and fitted with a deeper filter system to handle its higher output. The camshaft drive chain was changed to the duplex type. The rev

Front and rear door trims of a 1948 SE model; again, the car illustrated is chassis 415384.

counter drive gear for the six-cylinder engines consisted of two bronze castings, the adaptor that was bolted onto the block, and the right angle gearbox on to which the rev counter cable was secured. The rev counter gearbox was common to both but the adaptor for the 3½ litre had a two-bolt fixing and that for the 2½ litre had a triangular base secured with three bolts. At the end of 1947, the pair of castings was replaced by a single one on the 2½ litre engine and this single casting continued to be fitted to all the Mark V 2½ litre engines.

The engines were fitted with Fox austenitic steel exhaust valves, which had a long life and good resistance to failure under high tempera-

tures, and had "the additional virtue of being highly resistant to lead attack", according to *The Motor*, which also claimed that high percentages of lead had been added to the then-current Pool petrol. At the time it was commonly held that lead in petrol was the cause of burnt exhaust valves. On the 3½ litre engine only, a Metalastic torsional vibration damper was fitted on the front end of the crankshaft.

The six-cylinder engines were offered with normal and low compression to suit the available fuel, particularly in overseas markets. The compression was lowered by the fitting of a thick compression plate together with two normal Corrujoint gaskets, one on each face of the plate. The alternative compression ratios were, for the 2½ litre, 7.6 or 6.9:1, and for the 3½ litre, 7.2 or 6.6:1.

The first distributors fitted to the post-war six-cylinder engines were the same as those on the pre-war cars, with the advance and retard controlled by internal bob-weights, together with the advance and retard lever on the steering wheel boss if needed. These distributors were replaced in mid-1947 with units with micrometer vernier adjustment, useful for setting the timing in the first place, and the ignition

adjustment lever was then omitted from the boss. Later on, an additional vacuum control unit was introduced progressively, fitted first to the six-cylinder export saloons in September 1947 and then to the export DHC cars when they began to be made in 1948; the RHD 2½ litre cars were the last to have the new distributors, as late as January 1949. The vacuum control unit worked in conjunction with the internal bob-weights by instantly retarding the timing for fast acceleration if already travelling at a reasonable speed, when the bob-weights would have the

The majestic 1948 2½ litre Saloon. This car, chassis 511482, is equipped with the optional Ace wheel discs and P100L headlamps fitted with Difusa glasses.

A 1947 3½ litre Saloon (chassis 611244), still featuring the forked joining motif. Note the Ace wheel discs and the narrower chrome strips of the Mark IV.

ignition fully advanced. The sudden loss of the induction vacuum on opening the throttle would temporarily retard the ignition sufficiently to prevent pinking whilst the car gained speed. These vacuum distributors were similar to those fitted to all the Mark V cars.

At the end of 1946, the battery was moved from its position in the centre of the bulkhead to the left side and secured to its tray by two rods through holes in the lugs at each end of the special battery case. For the 1949 cars the fixing rods were replaced by two horizontal side clamp plates along the battery that no longer had the special lugs. It is probable that the control box was moved from the vertical face of the bulkhead under the fuel pumps, to lie almost flat along the top of the bulkhead away from the danger from possible fuel leaks from

Offside view of the 1948 2½ litre engine, complete with separate high-tension power pack for the optional factory-fitted Radiomobile 100 radio.

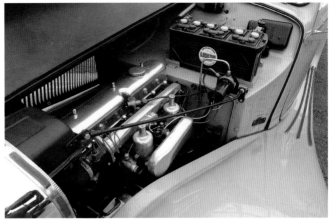

Under the bonnet of chassis 517039, a 1948 2½ litre DHC. The battery had been moved to the left-hand side on the bulkhead, with the new RF 95 control box and fuse box behind it.

A right-hand-drive 3½ litre, showing its close-fitting exhaust manifolds and steering box.

For the Mark IV, the water pump was more sensibly mounted with its own back plate.

the pump. This move in mid-1948 coincided with the change from the RJF91 control box with its integral fuse box to the RF95 control box with a separate Lucas type 6J junction box.

The gearbox on the six-cylinder cars was changed twice during the production run. At first the cars were fitted with the pre-war four-speed box, presumably still supplied by Standard, with double helical gears, but the internals differed from the pre-war boxes, as the bearings on the countershaft had been changed from bushes to needle bearings. This had proved to be a strong box and with synchromesh on the top three gears was relatively easy to use, though not giving a very fast gear change. The gearbox ratios quoted for the post-war cars were (approximately) first 3.37:1, second 1.94:1, third 1.35:1, and top 1:1, and

both the six-cylinder cars now used the same set of ratios.

The double helical box was retained until October 1947 when the single helical gearbox, called naturally enough the SH type, was introduced, in which the gears on the layshaft were

Later 1949 battery cradle with side bar clamping, which eliminated the need for a special battery case with fixing holes in the extended lugs at each end. The car shown is chassis 613452.

Chassis 611244, a 1947 3½ litre Saloon, welcoming passengers to its cabin – somewhat cheapened after the war, generally using pleated leather.

in a solid cluster, again running on needle bearings. This design of gearbox was made for Jaguar by the Moss Gear Company of Birmingham, and is universally known as the Moss box. The gearbox ratios on the single helical box were slightly changed to first 3.37:1, second 1.98:1, third 1.37:1, and top 1:1. The starting chassis numbers for the new gearbox were 510881 (2½ litre) and 612041 (3½ litre) so more than 2900 post-war six-cylinder cars were made with the double helical gearbox.

At the end of 1948, Jaguar brought in another version of the single helical box, the JH type made by themselves (but usually also referred to as a Moss box), in which the gears on the layshaft were separate units as in the pre-war box. These two boxes, the SH and JH, were in

use at the same time until the end of the production of the Mark IV. The company continued with this practice of using both boxes in parallel throughout Mark V production, as well as on the XK 120.

Several other small changes were made at various times during the production run but there are no hard and fast points at which they were introduced, so the chassis numbers given in the Spare Parts Catalogue for when the changes were made should be used mainly as an indication of the when the changes were implemented, rather than being a precise statement.

The other main mechanical changes were the introduction of the hypoid Salisbury rear axle, and of the Girling two leading shoe brakes. The change to the Salisbury axle resulted from its successful introduction on the 1940 1½ litre model, and also to its extensive use in wartime vehicles in which it proved to be rugged, reliable, and quiet. The use of this axle allowed the transmission tunnel to be lower and gave more space for the passengers' feet in the rear compartment. The hypoid bevel differential had a final drive ratio of 4.55:1 on the 2½ litre and 4.27:1 on the 3½ litre.

The Girling two leading shoe brakes on all wheels introduced immediately after the war gave the cars stronger braking, since with this arrangement both brake shoes for each wheel gave the maximum forward braking force, with the least amount of braking effort. The new system employed more robust cast-iron non-ribbed brake drums, and the operating mechanisms for the braking system were new. As on the 1½ litre, the handbrake now worked only on the rear wheels. The shock absorbers were quoted as the Luvax-Girling P7 horizontal piston type. These were fitted to the cars until the end of the production run, though from 1948 onwards the vertical piston Armstrong shock absorbers could be fitted as an alternative to the Luvax type on both front and rear suspension.

The one-piece moulded rubber pre-war gearbox and clutch-housing cover was replaced with a steel housing in November 1946, and the new cover was screwed to the floorboards on the inside of the car. The rest for the driver's left foot was lost as it had been an integral part of the moulded cover.

The interior of the cars had been cheapened after the war, with the plain leather upholstery replaced by the pleated type that did not require the use of the expensive and probably unobtainable blemish-free hides. It should be noted that many cars between June 1947 and January 1949 had Bedford cord cloth upholstery, probably because of a general leather shortage, affecting nearly 500 Mark IV cars altogether. Picnic tables were no longer fitted to the backs of the front seats, but the "air conditioning" unit was retained. The controls for the heater were now fully integrated in the main dashboard. The heater and fan unit was of a more compact design and was moved further forward under the scuttle, to allow space for the installation of the control unit for the optional radio under the dash. The radio needed a high-tension power pack and amplifier that was a self-contained unit mounted under the bonnet on the offside on the bulkhead. As mentioned above, the ignition lever disappeared from the steering wheel boss in mid-1947.

The P100L headlamps were now all fitted with frosted "Difusa" glasses with a round central clear area. Some other changes were made to the exterior of the cars over the Mark IV production period. A minor change was the design of the chromed motif that joined the two front wings; the pre-war joining piece fitted in conjunction with the recessed radiator shell was forked at the radiator end, and this part continued to be fitted on the post-war cars, even though the recess for the radiator in the apron had been eliminated. In mid-1948 however, a new joining piece was introduced with parallel sides and a raised central ridge.

There was a variation on a small number of radiator shells in which the radiator slats and the radiator itself were set noticeably further into the shell, requiring a different shell and radiator to be used. There is no mention of this variation in the Parts Catalogue, nor does there appear to be any reason for it. The photo is of the shell fitted to chassis number 611613 made in July 1947 and shows the radiator slats set considerably back from the nose of the shell. The distance from the end of the nose to the hole for the radiator cap is the same for both this and the normal versions.

Extras were probably more or less the same as had been offered in the immediate pre-war period. The radio was now by Radiomobile, and a tow bar assembly seems to have been a new addition.

Girling horizontal shock absorbers on the front axle (left). Armstrong vertical shock absorbers (right) were introduced for later cars, but Girling continued to be fitted as an alternative.

A 1947 dashboard with heater controls; at the time there was still an advance/retard lever on the steering wheel boss.

P100L headlamps with Difusa glasses and the 1948-type parallel joining motif for the wings. This car wears export overriders, since it was sent overseas when new.

Normal shape for the six-cylinder radiator shell, showing the position of the slats.

A rare radiator shell with set-in slats and a protruding radiator nose. This variant is not recorded in Jaguar parts lists.

The Post-War Six-Cylinder Drophead Coupés

These models were made for a brief period, mostly in 1948, but the four-cylinder drophead did not reappear after the war. The first DHC cars assembled at the end of 1947 were all LHD and though Jaguar made thirteen of the 3½ litre version, only two were shipped before the end of that year. All other DHC cars were made between January and September 1948, when production stopped in preparation for the introduction of the Mark V DHC.

The post-war DHC was very similar in looks to the pre-war model, and incorporated all the changes made first to the 1940 cars, and then to the post-war saloons. However, the quarter-lights that had briefly appeared on the 1940 DHC, were omitted on the post-war cars, removed either to reduce costs or because they proved impractical for use with the design of windscreen and hood fixing. The rear window remained too small to be of any use, its only virtues being that it was glass and not the plastic that soon discoloured, and that it was small

This 1948 DHC is a RHD 2½ litre, chassis number 517039

The post-war DHC was very similar in looks to the pre-war model. This is a RHD 3½ litre DHC chassis 617001.

Large numbers of right-hand-drive DHCs didn't emerge from the factory until stocks of left-hand-drive versions had been built for the American market. This is a 1948 3½ litre DHC, chassis 617003.

A right-hand-drive 1948 2½ litre DHC, chassis 517039. With the hood raised, its rear window remained too small to be of any use.

Here we see the hood in de Ville position, while the photograph to the left reveals its pleated seats.

The headlamps of this 1948 left-hand-drive 3½ litre DHC (chassis 637373) retained the P100L shell but with modified twin-filament bulbs for left-hand dipping.

From this angle, the left-hand-drive 3½ litre's engine bay looked distinctly crowded with the intrusion of the steering column; this is a 1948 car, chassis 637373.

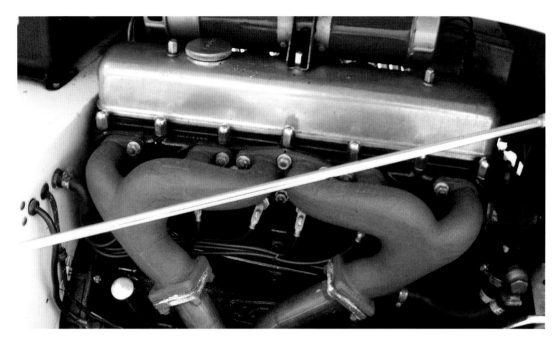

A left-hand-drive 1948 3½ litre's engine bay (chassis 637068), which looked remarkably empty with its steering column moved across to the opposite side.

enough to allow the hood to fold into the recess behind the rear seat. Some sort of additional external rear-view mirrors are by necessity often fitted to cars that are still in use today.

The 3½ litre engined LHD cars were the first to be made in volume and most of these went to the USA, but soon RHD cars for Australia started to appear in volume. In fact it would be six months before any more than a handful of the DHC cars became available in the home market. It may incidentally be noted that no home market price seems to have been quoted for the DHC models.

The Left-Hand Drive Cars

After the war the company needed to export a greater proportion of its cars, which meant producing the left-hand drive versions for markets that drove on the right. The first LHD car, a 1½ litre model, appeared in August 1947, and was soon followed by 2½ and 3½ litre versions. The LHD cars were needed in the potentially large markets of Brazil and the USA, and Belgium and Switzerland in Europe, although Switzerland also took RHD cars. Many export markets for saloons took all three engine sizes, except the USA, which only wanted the 3½ litre. When the DHC was introduced, the USA was also different from other export countries in wanting a higher ratio of DHC cars to saloons, with equal numbers of saloons and DHCs exported to the USA.

The Six-Cylinder LHD cars

The two six-cylinder engines were not designed with LHD in mind, so to convert them to LHD, Jaguar had to overcome a number of layout problems in the engine bay. In the RHD version the space on the left side of the engines was fully taken up by the dynamo, air filters and air manifold, the oil filter casting and its canister. The steering column on the RHD car, at around 2in (51mm) in diameter, was too large for the space available in the LHD version, so a thinner 1¼in (32mm) column was used, mated to a compact

There was no advance and retard lever on the steering wheel boss of the 1948 left-hand-drive 3½ litre, and no radio fitted either.

one-piece steering box in place of the bulky two-piece RHD box. Nevertheless, even with this slimmer steering column other modifications had to be made to the layout of the engine bay. On the RHD model an air manifold fed the two carburettors separately from two vertically mounted air filters that hung down on the left hand side of the engine, but to make room for the LHD steering column a new air manifold was used, rising upwards from the twin carburettors to a port in a new large single air filter mounted horizontally along the top of the engine.

The ignition coil also needed to be repositioned, and was now mounted on top of and in line with the steering column, and the oil filter and pressure relief housing unit were split into two castings connected by a pipe, to reduce its profile and allow it to be mounted closer to the cylinder block. These new arrangements produced a workable solution for the LHD model but made the engine and the ancillary equipment much less accessible on the left side, and left the right side looking somewhat empty of equipment. Interestingly, though the LHD steering column and box were smaller and more compact than those fitted to the RHD cars, there does not appear to be any evidence that the LHD unit was any less robust, so probably it was just a better design of steering box.

Apart from these modifications in the engine bay, a revised dashboard was fitted, and the pedals and controls were moved to the other side. Interestingly, the speedometer and the rev counter were left in the same positions as on the RHD cars. LHD cars had their own chassis number series (see chapter 9 on car identification). The six-cylinder engines on LHD cars were identified with an extra letter L after the normal prefix letter, so they became the PL (2½ litre) or SL (3½ litre) engines. There were no gearbox numbers recorded by the factory for LHD cars, which is curious since the majority of these cars were made after the gearbox numbers for the RHD cars began to be recorded in the ledger.

Overriders on the front and rear bumpers were fitted on all export cars regardless of whether they were LHD or RHD. The LHD cars were fitted as standard with twin double-filament bulbs with vertical dipping headlamps for some markets. On RHD cars, at least for the home market, the offside headlamp was switched off and the nearside dipped, since double-dip headlamps were not yet a legal requirement in the UK.

A very strange thing happened in 1948 when over 70 LHD export cars, mostly 3½ litre DHCs built during June and July of that year, were converted to RHD between August and November, and sold mainly in the home market. They were given new RHD chassis numbers and the tell-tale L in the engine number prefix was apparently removed. Jaguar must have considered that these cars were no longer saleable for export, and that home market demand warranted the no doubt expensive effort of converting them. About a dozen such cars are believed to exist and can be identified by having a blanking plate over the redundant hole for the steering column on the left-hand side of the bulkhead (see also chapter 7 on export cars).

The Four-Cylinder LHD Cars

The LHD version of the 1½ litre car was introduced in August 1947 and 95 per cent of the cars made were the SE model. For this car the conversion to LHD was less of a problem than for the six-cylinder models, but some changes were still needed, other than the obvious change of sides for the steering column and pedals, and a new dashboard.

In the engine compartment the steering column and box had to be relocated, but the RHD column being small in diameter could be accommodated, though again with a smaller one-piece steering box replacing the bulkier two-part unit of the RHD model. Also needed was the same split oil filter housing as used on the LHD six-cylinder cars but with the shorter filter canister. Unlike on the six-cylinder cars however, the air filter and cleaner did not need to be moved, as it already sat out of the way on the right-hand side at the top of the four-cylinder engine, though the coil was relocated to sit on the steering column and the dynamo adjustment bracket was modified to clear the column.

The headlamps on the LHD cars were both fitted with double filament bulbs for export and whilst the Lucas 80/2 unit for the SE model retained its same model number, the LBD 166 Tripod became MBD 166 when fitted with the double filament bulb.

Owners at home and abroad

The most famous owner of any of the early post-war Jaguars was undoubtedly the Hollywood film star Clark Gable who took delivery of

The 1½ litre engine bay was better suited for the left-hand-drive version, since the exhaust and inlet manifolds were on the right-hand side. This image shows a 1948 1½ litre SE model, chassis 430202.

a left-hand drive 3½ litre DHC from Roger Barlow of International Motors in Los Angeles, the first of several Jaguars that Gable was to own; unfortunately his name is not to be found in the Car Record Books. There were many titled owners, including the the Maharaja of Baroda, who had owned two Jaguars before the war, but now had a modest 1½ litre, as did another Indian Prince, Major General HH the Ameer of Bahawalpur, and it may be mentioned that this car is now owned by the Ameer's grandson. There were many titled owners in Europe, in particular in Belgium.

Of titled owners at home, there was the much-married Earl of Kimberley, the bobsleigh runner who was once described as a "rickety motorist", the Earl of Balfour, and also Lord Brabourne who married Patricia Mountbatten. Other intriguing names found in the records are George Formby, NS (Nubar Sarkis) Gulbenkian, Madame Onassis – presumably Tina, the first wife of Aristotle – and W (presumably William) Walmsley, Lyons' original business partner. Many of the early 1½ litre saloons were sold directly by Jaguar to their suppliers in the motor industry and it is not surprising that the names of Connolly, Dunlop, Girling, GKN, Lucas, Moss Gear, Sankey, S Smith, and Wilmot Breeden among others are recorded as first owners. Other company owners ranged from BEA (British European Airways), through impresarios Lew & Leslie Grade, to the *Manchester Guardian*.

There were at least 41 Mark IVs supplied as Police cars, of all three sizes, and an important new customer was the Lancashire County Constabulary which took no less than 24 cars; they had run many pre-war MGs, both sports cars and the big saloons, and continued as a good customer for MG sports cars into the 1960s. The Mark IV similarly found favour with their colleagues in Leicestershire, Manchester, and the West Riding of Yorkshire.

The Press on the Six-Cylinder Cars

These cars continued to attract favourable comments from the motoring press, which was as always very impressed by their grace, performance and comfort, as well as the value for money offered by Jaguar, even at post-war prices with Purchase Tax. In general the power output from the Jaguar engines was considered outstanding by the press and " whereas very few production type engines develop 2hp per square inch of piston area, the Jaguar range all

SPECIFICATIONS OF MARK IV MODELS

	1½ litre	2½ litre	3½ litre
Dimensions			
Overall length	15ft¾in (4591mm)	15ft 6in (4724mm)	As 2½ litre
Overall width	5ft 6in (1676mm)	As 1½ litre	As 2½ litre
Overall height	5ft (1524mm)	5ft 1in (1549mm)	As 2½ litre
Wheelbase	9ft 4½in (2858mm)	10ft (3048mm)	As 2½ litre
Track	Front 4ft 4in (1321mm), rear 4ft 7in (1397mm)	Front 4ft 6in (1372mm), rear 4ft 8in (1422mm)	As 2½ litre
Weight	26cwt (1322kg)	32cwt (1627kg)	As 2½ litre
Engine			
Type	4 cylinder OHV	6 cylinder OHV	As 2½ litre
Capacity, RAC hp	1775.8cc, 13.23hp	2663.7cc, 19.84hp	3485.5cc, 25.01hp
Bore, stroke	73mm by 106mm	73mm by 106mm	82mm by 110mm
Bhp at rpm	65 at 4600	102 at 4600	125 at 4250
Crankshaft bearing diameters	Main journals 2.479in, big-end journals 1.894in	As 1½ litre	Main journals 2.479in, big-end journals 2.086in
Con rods	Steel, small-end bronze bushes	Dural, no small-end bushes	As 2½ litre
Compression ratio	7.6:1 or 6.8 to 1	7.6:1 or 6.9:1	7.2:1 or 6.6:1
Tappet clearance	Inlet 0.015in Exhaust 0.018in	Inlet 0.012in Exhaust 0.015in	As 2½ litre
Carburettor	Single horizontal SU H4	Twin horizontal SU H3, with thermostatic automatic starting carburettor	Twin horizontal SU H4 with thermostatic automatic starting carburettor
Fuel pump	AC Sphinx mechanical	Single SU electric	Twin SU electric
Transmission			
Gearbox type	Standard double helical	Double helical, then Moss single helical	As 2½ litre
Overall ratios	19.23, 11.84, 7.08, 4.875	15.35, 8.80, 6.12, 4.55; SH: 15.35, 9.01, 6.22, 4.55	14.40, 8.25, 5.73, 4.27; SH: 14.40, 8.46, 5.84, 4.27
Rear axle and ratio	Salisbury hypoid bevel, ratio 4.875 to 1	Salisbury hypoid bevel, ratio 4.55 to 1	Salisbury hypoid bevel, ratio 4.27 to 1
Electrical			
Headlamps	LBD 166 with tripod; P80/2 (SE model)	P100L with Difusa lens	As 2½ litre
Side lamps	Torpedo type 1130	Type 1185 integral in wing	As 2½ litre
Fog Lamps	FT58 as extra for SE model	FT58	As 2½ litre
Dynamo	C45 YV/3 V58	C45 PV/3 L1/1	As 2½ litre
Dynamo LHD	C45 YV/3 GC24/0	C45 ZV G86	As 2½ litre
Starter	M418G GCO	M418 AL/1 L1-0	M45G Type GC20/0
Distributor	DKYH 4A GC29	DXH6A GC 30, then GC38, then DVXH6A GC40 with vacuum control	DZH6A GC38, then DXH6A GC 37, then DVXH6A GC31 with vacuum control
Control Box	RJF 91 then RF 95/2	As 1½ litre	As 2½ litre
Trafficators	SF55J type 23G	As 1½ litre	As 2½ litre
Chassis			
Springs, suspension	Semi-elliptic leaf springs; beam front axle, live rear axle	As 1½ litre	As 2½ litre

	1½ litre	2½ litre	3½ litre
Shock absorbers	Girling P6 horizontal then Armstrong vertical	Girling P7 horizontal then Armstrong vertical	As 2½ litre
Steering box	Burman Douglas worm & nut	As 1½ litre	As 2½ litre
Brakes	12in x 1⅛in Girling rod single leading shoe, plain drums	14in x 1¾in Girling rod two leading shoe, plain drums	As 2½ litre
Wheels	18in wire spoke	As 1½ litre	As 2½ litre
Tyres	5.25x18	5.50x18	As 2½ litre
Turning circle	38ft (11.6 metres)	As 1½ litre	As 2½ litre
Fuel tank	14 gals (64 litres), incl 2 gals (9 litres) reserve	As 1½ litre	As 2½ litre
Prices incl. PT			
Nov 1945	£684 (Std), £729 (SE)	£889	£991
Jun 1946	£787 (Std), £838 (SE)	£991	£1100
Mar 1947	£865 (Std), £921 (SE)	£1089	£1199
Feb 1948	£953 (Std), £1009 (SE)	£1189	£1263

substantially exceed this output and give 35bhp per litre". This high performance was attributed to the Weslake cross-flow cylinder head with downward inclined polished ports which gave it exceptional breathing at high rpm, complemented by the dual exhaust system which in itself contributed many extra horsepower.

Jaguar had prospered and grown in the years leading up to the war and "each year saw steady developments, not only in output, but also in worthwhile technical improvements and manufacturing resources". The company was considered "one of the major producers of British high performance cars and the release of the post-war range will afford satisfaction to many thousands of buyers".

The press was impressed by the trim of the cars and wrote that "the interior is most inviting, the front seats are large, comfortable and softly upholstered. The rear seat with its centre folding armrest is broad enough to give comfort for three people, the headroom is ample and the low floor level not only gives plenty of space for the legs but also makes entry or egress very easy".

The Autocar road tested the 3½ litre on 19 March 1948. The test car was the factory demonstrator GVC 677, chassis number 612175, and the reviewer wrote that "one does not have to make any special effort or use of very high speeds to find that distances are being covered in unusually short times. This is because on a normal main road the car will hold, almost irrespective of bend or gradient, a steady rate of

between 50 and 60mph without seeming to be exerting itself. At 40mph it appears scarcely to be moving". A 96-mile (154km) run was covered in exactly two hours, an average which 65 years later it would be difficult to equal on a UK non-motorway route! The article stated that a speed of 89mph (143km/h) measured by electrical speedometer was achieved within a mile of level motoring, and quoted a top speed of 91mph (146km/h). Fuel consumption, on Pool, was around 16-18mpg (approximately 17 litres per 100km).

The Motor did not road rest a Mark IV, but the sports editor RL Walkerley and the experienced old Monte Carlo hand Mike Couper gave the 3½ litre a good work-out in the winter of 1947 when, in the absence of a Monte Carlo Rally, they decided to run their own, and borrowed the Jaguar press car, FVC 879, chassis number 610669, from William Lyons. Before the war, Walkerley had been an enthusiastic owner of an SS Jaguar 3½ litre which he ran for 20,000 miles over a year in 1938-39. The post-war car proved just as satisfying, and got the intrepid pair safely through to Monte Carlo despite horrific weather and road conditions through most of France, although the travelling average was 25mph (40km/h) rather than the 32mph (51 km/h) which would have been necessary during a real rally, so they arrived two hours and fifteen minutes late at Monte Carlo, still receiving a warm welcome from the rally organiser M. Noghes. The car had never given the slightest trouble.

Chapter Six

A Jaguar at the Crossroads: The Mark V

By the middle of 1948 the Mark IV was showing its age, especially when compared with the increasing number of all-new post-war designs from other British manufacturers, in the specialist car class as well as among the mass-producers. Sales were still holding up reasonably well, at least in the home market, but a new Jaguar would normally have been available for delivery from August of that year, and many customers were no doubt getting impatient. The replacement car needed to be sufficiently modern to attract good overseas sales, particularly in the USA, but also had to capitalise on the Jaguar traditions for appearance, performance, and value for money. Furthermore, the car needed to appeal to the largest export market, Australia.

This replacement model, to be called the Mark V, while announced at the beginning of October 1948, was not however going to be made in any numbers before March 1949, so in the meantime the life of the Mark IV had to be extended to bridge the gap. Export sales of the Mark IV had effectively dried up in August 1948 as the overseas markets were hoping for a new model, and in consequence Mark IV production

Pressed steel wheels and wide cushioned tyres were standardised on the Mark V to provide a more comfortable ride. The photo shows chassis 624308, a 1950 3½ litre Saloon.

rates were slashed by half, which at least meant more cars for the home market, where waiting lists stretched for years into the future.

The Mark IV replacement was, for reasons explained in chapter 1, always going to be somewhat of a halfway house; this was a Jaguar at the crossroads between tradition and modernity. However, thanks to Lyons' feel for design the Mark V still emerged as a very stylish and more modern looking car, whilst retaining many of the Jaguar design trademarks including the radiator grille of the Mark IV. It was the last Jaguar model with the flowing combined front wings and running boards. The outline of the roof and rear end also showed a clear family resemblance to the earlier cars.

When the Mark V was launched in advance of the 1948 Earls Court Motor Show it did not disappoint the waiting customers. It was recognizably a Jaguar and, as reported by *The Autocar* in October 1948, it "had not departed from the nicety of the proportions that had made the pre-war Jaguars the prize winners at many *Concours d'Élégance*".

Mark V Chassis Design

Like many other British specialist cars of this period, the Mark V was that happy and appealing combination of a traditionally styled and very British-looking body fitted on a chassis

Front view of a 1950 3½ litre Saloon (chassis 624308), showing the faired-in Lucas PF770 headlamps and SFT700 fog lamps.

A 1949 3½ litre Saloon (chassis 627098), showing the rear wing cover fitted to all Mark V cars. Note the pointed front corner of the early quarterlight.

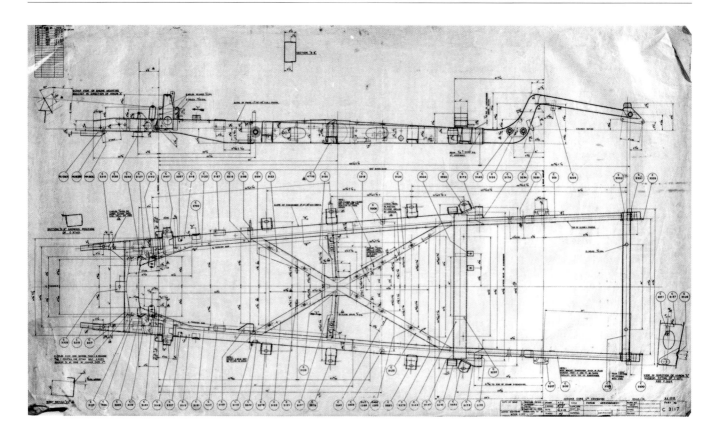

Factory drawing of the new Mark V chassis showing its much-changed design from the Mark IV, in particular the kicked-up rear end to provide longer travel for the rear suspension to match the new IFS.

of completely up-to-date specification. The chassis frame had the same 10ft (3048mm) wheelbase as before but was completely redesigned to improve its stiffness, to provide a suitable platform for independent front suspension. This had been under development in the factory since 1938 when a 3½ litre car had been converted by Heynes and Hassan with an experimental independent front suspension, but the Mark V was the first production Jaguar car to feature it.

The new frame had deep box-section side members to eliminate torsional deflection. At the front, the frame was strengthened by a strong box-section cross-member which provided a rigid mounting for the suspension. In the centre of the frame was a cruciform, supplemented by a cross-member, with a further cross-member at the front anchorage point for the rear springs. At its maximum, the side member box section was 6½in (165mm) deep and 3½in (89mm) wide and ran level the length of the car as far as the front of the rear springs, where it kicked up sharply by over 12in (305mm) and passed above the rear axle to provide longer travel for the rear suspension. This was a departure from the previous design in which the chassis was under-

slung. Behind the rear axle the chassis dropped gently downwards to the rear spring shackles almost at the extremity of the frame, which was more or less on a level with the main part of the side members, and there was a final cross-member at the rear.

Heynes had designed a remarkably slim but strong front suspension, with upper and lower wishbones each side joined at their outer ends by stub axles with hard-chromed ball-ends held in graphite bronze seats in the wishbones. This design for the stub axles had the added benefit of being self-adjusting to take up any wear. The main member of the lower wishbone had a deep I section that carried the weight of the car and it was to this arm that the splined front end of the torsion bar was connected. The forward member of the lower wishbone was a tubular strut running diagonally to an attachment point under the front cross-member, and which took up the braking loads. The upper wishbone was anchored to a bracket on the top of the frame. A Newton telescopic shock absorber was mounted at an angle from the lower wishbone to a bracket above the upper wishbone. There was a torsion anti-roll bar attached between the lower wishbones on each side of the car. The two 52in

(1321mm) long torsion bars ran longitudinally inboard of the frame to adjustable anchor points on the cross-member sited at the rear of the gearbox; this arrangement reduced the twisting forces on the chassis.

The new front suspension had longer travel than the beam axle of the Mark IV, and this needed to be reflected in the rear suspension, which therefore also had increased suspension movement. This was partly achieved by the new frame, and partly by increasing the length of the rear springs from 42in (1067mm) to 49in (1245mm) to soften the rear suspension. The rear springs were fitted as standard with leather gaiters, one for the front and one for the rear part of each spring. The gaiters were fitted with grease nipples to allow the springs to be lubricated but in practice heavy oil was more effective than grease. Horizontal Girling piston-type shock absorbers were fitted at the rear. The Armstrong vertical piston shock absorbers were no longer used.

Another innovation for Jaguar was the introduction finally of fully hydraulic Girling brakes all round. The braking surfaces were large, being 2¼in (57mm) wide and operating in 12in (305mm) diameter cast iron drums, and the front brakes had cooling air ducts in the back plates. Both the front and rear brakes on the early cars were of the twin leading shoe type. The front brake shoes were individually operated by their own securely fixed-pivot slave cylinders, and the rear brakes had single large external slave cylinders, mounted perpendicularly to the back plate, and operated the brake shoes by means of bell-cranks and pushrods as on the Mark IV. The handbrake cable was attached directly to cone-shaped plungers that operated the hydraulic slave cylinders mechanically. On later cars made from January 1950, the rear brakes were changed to single leading shoe, with one sliding pivot slave cylinder per wheel located inside the drum. Sitting on top of each slave cylinder was a drawbar and tappet assembly operated mechanically by the handbrake cable. This was a neat but not very efficient solution for the handbrake.

The steering was updated to the Burman Douglas worm and recirculating ball type in place of the worm and nut unit of the previous model. Also new for this model was the use of pressed steel wheels, which were heavily dished and had wide 5-inch rims to accommodate the smaller diameter but wider 6.70x16 Dunlop Super-comfort tyres. Jaguar was the first company to standardise these tyres, which gave a smoother and more comfortable ride. The wheels were fitted with chrome-plated hub caps partly over-painted in body colour and with the Jaguar name in a lozenge shape in the centre.

Engines and Transmission

The engines were largely unchanged from the Mark IV, but the two downpipes from the exhaust manifolds were now joined together to create a single exhaust system. The con rods in the early cars were alloy in both engines, but in September 1949 on the 3½ litre engine these were changed to steel. The 2½ litre engine continued to be fitted with the alloy rods to the end of its production. A new single large capacity SU electric fuel pump was fitted on both cars, relocated from the bulkhead to a position on the chassis close to and lower than the fuel tank. All cars now had the long cylindrical air filter mounted above the rocker cover.

The Borg and Beck single dry plate clutch was 9in (223mm) in diameter on the 2½ litre, and 10in (254mm) on the 3½ litre. The Moss single helical gearbox with synchromesh on second, third, and top, type SH or JH, was basically unchanged, with ratios first 3.37:1, second 1.98:1, third 1.37:1, and top 1:1, and was fitted with Jaguar's traditional short remote gear lever. For the first time a divided Hardy Spicer prop shaft was used. A short length of shaft from the gearbox had a universal joint just behind the cruciform connecting it to the longer rear shaft,

Cooling air scoops on the front brakes. There were plates supplied in the toolkit to close the vents if needed.

A right-hand-drive 3½ litre engine shown from the left. All Mark V engines had the air filter mounted along the top of the engine, and the fuel pump was out of sight near the petrol tank.

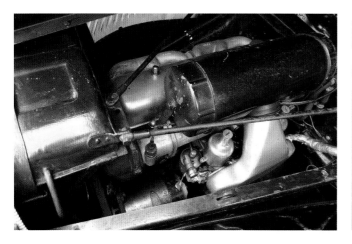

The rare 2½ litre right-hand-drive engine, here photographed from the left. The fuel lines have been insulated to keep them cool and reduce the risk of vapour lock in traffic in this poorly-ventilated engine compartment.

A right-hand-drive 3½ litre engine, here shown from the right. The battery was set into the bulkhead, and the RF95 control box and fuse panel rested to the right of the engine, probably for ease of making the expected high numbers of left-hand-drive cars.

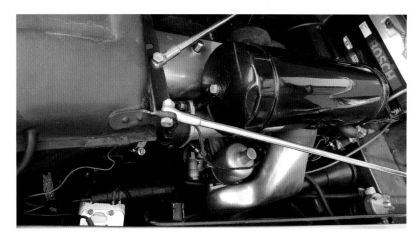

The crowded engine compartment of a left-hand-drive 3½ litre, which looked very similar to the 2½ litre.

and was supported at the divide by a rubber-insulated housing. As well as reducing vibration, this two-part shaft ran lower in the car to the Salisbury hypoid rear axle, and provided a nearly flat floor in the passenger compartment with no intrusive transmission tunnel. For the

1950 model the central bearing was spring-loaded to reduce vibration in the car. The final drive ratio was 4.55:1 on the 2½ litre and 4.30:1 on the 3½ litre.

Body Styling

The lines of the car had been lightened and modernised, without losing its traditional elegant and characteristic Jaguar look. An important change was the introduction of half-doors with thin chrome-plated channel frames around the side windows, which gave a noticeable increase in the glass area. A first in Jaguar styling was the well-rounded rear quarter-lights which slightly overhung the rear door shutline. They eliminated the closed-in look of the rear passenger compartment, and also matched the front quarter-lights. Altogether, the new side window shape gave the car a sleeker and more elegant appearance. On the early cars the front quarter-lights had pointed leading edges and were shut by the same captive bell-crank devices as were used on the rear ones, but in October 1949 the catches on the front lights were replaced by a lever type, and the front bottom corners of the windows were rounded off.

The windscreen was still of the flat single-pane type but was more raked than on the Mark IV. It no longer opened, which allowed for a slimmer header rail. This too improved the appearance of the side profile of the car. The bonnet sloped gently from the windscreen to the radiator, which had been moved forwards.

The rear compartment of a 1950 3½ litre Saloon (624308), displaying its unpleated upholstery and completely flat floor.

Chassis 622934 is a 1950 car, thus the quarterlights featured rounded front corners.

The Mark IV louvres had been removed from the side panels of the bonnet. Though this did give the car a more streamlined look, it reduced ventilation for the engine, and made it susceptible to overheating, to the point that nowadays a lot of owners have fitted auxiliary electric fans to keep the engine cool. The side panels were fixed in place, though they could be removed for maintenance purposes. The two top panels of the bonnet were hinged in the centre and opened sideways. They were fastened by plungers operated from the inside of the car by cranks under the dash. These were later changed to rods and levers with sufficiently long travel to prevent accidental opening.

The radiators and the grilles for the Mark V were now the same size for both engines, being the wider 3½ litre type, no doubt to save on tooling but also to try to compensate in part for the reduced cooling of the engine compartment. Only the wording and the colour of the radiator badges, black for the 3½ litre and cream for the 2½ litre, distinguished the two cars from each other externally. For the 1950 cars, a concealed crossbar was fixed behind the vertical slats, and this reduced the wind noise from the grille. The horns on the early cars were under the bonnet, with the offside unit mounted on a bracket on top of the steering box. Later cars were fitted with horns mounted externally under the chassis at the front. The externally mounted P100 headlamps of the Mark IV were replaced by faired-in smaller-

diameter Lucas PF770 headlamps, the first time a Jaguar had built-in headlamps, and two slimmed-down SFT700 fog lamps were lifted from bumper height and mounted just below the headlamps. The side lamps were still faired into the tops of the front wings.

The Mark V retained one traditional and much-cherished feature, a sliding sunroof, which was standard on all cars, and would

Front view of a 1950 2½ litre Saloon (chassis 520842) with the same-sized radiator grille as that of the 3½ litre car.

The heater unit on early cars was mounted on the bulkhead in the engine bay; this image shows chassis 620263, a 1949 Saloon.

Draught sealing fillet fitted on later cars, found on the inside of the bottom of the front door.

remain so on the Mark VII and subsequent models until 1961. The early models had no ventilation vents in the scuttle but this proved to give inadequate ventilation in the cabin, so adjustable scuttle vents were introduced in November 1949, sited between the bonnet and the front doors. At this time too the Clayton Dewandre heater and demister unit was moved from its position on top of the bulkhead under the bonnet to a location inside the cabin under the dash. Filtered fresh air from the front of the car could be drawn in for ventilation.

Both front and rear doors were now hinged on the centre pillar, with concealed hinges, and were fitted with fixed push-button door handles on the waistline chrome trim moulding. This made the rear doors safer in case of accidental opening whilst in motion, but the front doors remained "suicide doors". Thanks to the angle of

the front shutline and the sweep of the front wing, the doors assumed a rather extreme shape. A courtesy light was now provided which operated when a front door was opened, with the switch housed on the sill of the doorframe. The sealing on the front doors of the early saloons proved to be ineffective and in June 1950 an additional cast aluminium sealing fillet was fastened to the bottom of both front doors. This seal was also available as a retrofit kit for the earlier cars.

The front wings still swept into running boards which continued to the rear wings, but this was the last Jaguar to have running boards. A single frame containing a one-piece rubber mat now replaced the separate tread strips and beading on each running board. The sleek lines of the car were further helped by hiding the fuel filler cap away in its own lidded lockable enclosure on the rear wing. The lower profile of the car was accentuated by the smaller wheels. The rear wheels were covered by full spats which further modernised the look of the car, and, like the side window shape, began a new and long-running Jaguar styling tradition. The spats initially fitted to the Mark V were awkward to remove, so the securing system was changed for the 1950 model. The spat was then fastened at the top by a budget lock and the bottom slid into two hinged sockets.

With all these measures to streamline the look of the car, it was odd that it was fitted with heavy double-bar bumpers both front and rear. They were undoubtedly welcomed in the US market, but they were rather massive and perhaps the least successful part of the overall design. The rear bumper was in two parts, separated by the central number plate mounting panel, which hinged down to give access to the spare wheel and the wheel brace which was clipped to the inside of the cover. The number plate itself was no longer protected behind glass, and this was the last Jaguar to have the bottom-hinged boot lid that could be used to carry additional luggage if needed. An automatic boot light was now fitted, and the earlier cars had a recessed lip to the boot lid, but this was eliminated in 1950. The tool tray was considerably altered with the addition of three open-ended spanners, now for the first time of AF sizes, and a kit for bleeding the hydraulic brakes, whilst the jack, handle and wheel brace were moved to the spare wheel compartment.

Interior

The dashboard was redesigned with export markets in mind, since it could be easily configured for either RHD or LHD, although the layout was similar to the Mark IV. All the instruments were mounted symmetrically in a centre console, identical on RHD and LHD cars, which was angled and mounted further forward than the panel either side. The front of the centre console could be easily hinged down to give access to the backs of the instruments and to all the wiring. On each side of the centre console were two separate smaller panels, the one on the driver's side with a small lidded cubbyhole outboard of the steering column, and the other with a larger lockable glove box for the passenger. The dash and other interior woodwork were in walnut veneer.

At the bottom centre there was a pullout ashtray drawer that was replaced by the optional radio if fitted, though on later models two ashtrays were mounted on the garnish rail at the top of the dashboard. Four blue (also referred to as "ultra violet") lights mounted on the front of the dash illuminated the instruments from above, but in October 1949 the number of lights was reduced to two. New instruments were fitted to the dashboard, the speedometer closest to the driver, the rev counter – still running anti-clockwise, still with a built-in clock – opposite, and the three smaller gauges in a line between them. The dials were black with an unusual stylised typeface for the white numbers and letters, believed to have been shared only with the Jowett Jupiter.

The four-spoke 18in (457mm) steering wheel had telescopic adjustment for reach on the column and a new-style boss with a pointed-dome horn push which had the profile of a jaguar head moulded into it. There was only one lever switch on the boss, for the direction indicators, since the dip switch was now floor mounted.

The Mark V had an umbrella pull-type handbrake mounted between the steering column and the door which followed the current fashion for this type of brake. It got over the difficulty of fitting a floor-mounted handbrake, as the front bearing mount for the prop shaft was now where the handbrake would have been located. The handbrake was never very efficient, nor much liked; *The Autocar* described it as "convenient" but to *The Motor* it was "awkward". When the Mark VII came out with its floor-mounted central

The instrument panel was designed for easy access to the instruments. This is a later version, with just two dash lights and its heater unit relocated to the car interior, beneath the dashboard.

A shot showing the dashboard layout of a left-hand-drive 1950 3½ litre DHC (chassis 647097). The instruments were in the same positions as the right-hand-drive version, and the dashboard required minimal effort to swap them around.

The dashboard layout of a right-hand-drive 1950 3½ litre, chassis 624308. The new manette with a conical centre and Jaguar motif housed only the indicator switch, since the headlamp dip switch was now floor-mounted. The handbrake lever was down by the door.

Expensive unpleated seats greeted occupants of the 1950 3½ litre Saloon, chassis 624308. Note the umbrella handbrake handle just inside the doorway

The front seats were individual, each adjustable for height and reach, and the rear bench seat had a retractable centre armrest and side armrests. On 1950 cars, the backs of the front seats were made less upright to make them more comfortable for the occupants. The interior of the car was opened out for the rear passengers by the almost complete elimination of the intrusive transmission tunnel, achieved by the use of the two-piece prop-shaft combined with the hypoid rear axle.

With the Mark V Jaguar returned to using the more expensive unpleated upholstery, which gave the car the air of luxury that overseas buyers were expecting from a Jaguar, and which had been used on the S.S.I Airline in 1934 and then on the short-lived 1940 model SS Jaguar. It is also possible that customers had complained that dirt collected in the pleats, but the plain upholstery required the use of expensive flawless hides, so the company reverted to pleated seats on the Mark VII in 1950. Some Mark Vs had contrast-colour piping for the seats and door trim panels.

Each door was fitted with an internal safety lock. On the early cars this was a small chromed lever, but this was replaced in March 1950 by a circular chromed casting with a raised finger grip across it to turn it. This was used later on the Mark VII. The front door trims incorporated capacious zipped pockets and there were smaller pockets on the rear doors. The early cars had the rear ashtrays set into the backs of the front seats but these were moved in May 1950 to inserts in the garnish rails of the rear doors, and at the same time the front ashtrays were relo-

handbrake, this was offered by Jaguar as a retrofit conversion kit for the Mark V. It is not known how this would have been fitted, or whether any such conversions were ever carried out.

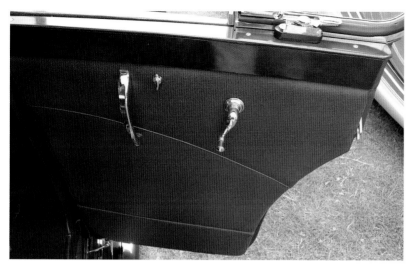

The 1950 3½ litre Saloon (chassis 622934) featured very simple rear door trims. In the centre was a small lever to turn the standard safety locks.

The front door trim of a 1949 3½ litre Saloon, featuring a zipped pocket. The car shown is 621364.

cated into the facia rail.

Extras quoted included a badge bar, a selection of different HMV Radiomobile radios, a fitted luggage set, a tow bar assembly, a plastic Windcheat radiator shield, and finally the Jaguar mascot for the radiator cap.

The Drophead Coupé (DHC) model

This model was announced together with the saloon in 1948 but only went into production about a year later, with both engine sizes. It proved very popular in overseas markets, particularly in the USA. It is not surprising, given the fast luxury car market for which it was designed, that the biggest demand by far was for the larger-engined cars. Over the production period only 29 of the 2½ litre DHC were made as against 971 of the 3½ litre.

The design of the Mark V DHC was similar in many ways to its predecessor but with the sleeker more elegant profile of the new saloon. The hood had the same three-position configuration as before; fully opened, fully closed, or in the half open de ville position, when the landau bars supported it. The landau bars were, as a styling feature, considerably wider than those on the Mark IV. The front windscreen was more raked and had a deep header rail, which allowed the front edge of the hood to butt up to the back of the header for fixing, unlike the Mark IV where the hood sat on top of the windscreen. This improved both the aerodynamics and the weatherproofing of the car. The rear window was by necessity still very small so that the hood could be folded into the recess behind the rear seat; even so, as on the Mark IV, only part of the hood fitted into this recess, and the folded hood still protruded well above the waistline of the car.

The DHC was fitted with front quarterlights, a feature that had first appeared briefly on the 1940 SS Jaguar DHC models. The quarter-light assembly had a substantial fixed chromed frame. This eliminated the feature of the Mark IV whereby both the front and rear door window channels could be folded flat when the window was fully wound down, but the rear window channel could still be folded down out of the way when the hood was open. Like the saloon, the first quarter-lights had the pointed front corners, soon to be replaced by the rounded type whose frame became a convenient place to mount a much needed rear-view mirror, in the triangular area in the front part of the frame.

Two-tone Cars

A number of Mark V cars, both saloons and dropheads, are now painted in two-tone colour schemes and there are some contemporary photos taken in the USA of such cars. The style and design of the car seems particularly suited to being painted in two colours, and the American market obviously liked this treatment, but Jaguar themselves only ever produced two such cars. In May 1951 a 3½ litre Saloon was painted

The Mark V DHC was styled with a sleeker, more elegant profile than the new saloon. The hood now butted up to the windscreen frame rather than sit on top of it, and the landau bars were made wider in profile as a design feature. Chassis 647097 is a left-hand-drive 1950 3½ litre DHC.

by the factory in Red and White with a Red interior, and was sold through Ritchies of Glasgow. Unfortunately the first owner is not named in the Car Record Book and it is not known if the car has survived, but its registration was JGE 96. The other two-tone car was a 1950 DHC exported to New York, in Suede Green with Black wings, Suede Green trim and a Black hood.

Since all other cars left the factory in a single colour, those wealthy US customers who wanted two-tone cars must have commissioned them from the local distributors, Hoffman in New York and Hornburg in Los Angeles, who would have had the cars re-painted on arrival in the USA. In this way the factory could mass-produce single-colour cars, and the distributors could then customise the paintwork, which kept this costly process away from the factory.

Road Tests of the 3½ litre Saloon

The road test carried out by *The Autocar* described the running and handling of the 3½ litre car on test as "silky and a distinct step-up in the inherent quality of feel of a model which already was on the shortlist of outstanding British specialist cars. For its remarkable combination of virtues it might well be expected in these days to cost several hundred pounds more than it does, and that is a very big tribute to pay a car. It is a car for long journeys that can put 50 miles and more into an hour, yet it is thoroughly tractable for the short pottering or shopping expeditions."

The comfort and stability of the ride was attributable to the independent front suspension and the softer rear suspension together with the big-section Dunlop tyres on the wide rims. The Burman re-circulating ball steering was light at all speeds, accurate throughout the range and gave confidence because it did not call for concentration to keep the car on the straight and narrow, whilst on corners the car followed an accurate course with the minimum of attention. Fairly heavy cars impose a significant task on the braking system but the Girling fully hydraulic system worked well with only light pressure, though the handbrake needed to be pulled hard to hold the car on a slope.

The performance of the 3½ litre was reported

The Mark V DHC retained a small rear window to allow the hood to fold down fairly flat. Again, this is a 1950 3½ litre DHC, chassis 647097.

The uncluttered interior of chassis 647097, a 1950 left-hand-drive DHC.

Test, date	SS Jaguar *The Motor* 31 May 1938	Jaguar Mark IV *The Autocar* 19 March 1948	Jaguar Mark V *The Autocar* 8 July 1949	Jaguar Mark V *The Motor* 5 April 1950
Top speed	91.8mph (147.7 km/h)	91mph (146.5 km/h)	91mph (146.5 km/h)	90.7mph mean, 91.8mph best (146-147.7 km/h)
0-50mph (80km/h)	9 sec	11.9 sec	13.5 sec	9.9 sec
0-60mph (97km/h)	n/q	16.8 sec	18.9 sec	14.7 sec
0-70mph (113km/h)	n/q	25.6 sec	28 sec	20.4 sec
10-30mph on third/top	6.0/7.4 sec	7.1/9.8 sec	6.2/8.4 sec	5.5/8.0 sec
30-50mph on third/top	7.7/8.5 sec	7.7/10.3 sec	7.5/9.4 sec	6.4/8.9 sec
Standing 1/4 mile	19.4 sec	n/q	n/q	20.2 sec
Fuel consumption	18-20mpg	16-18mpg	15-18mpg	18.2mpg

as very satisfactory and the power was delivered smoothly, accelerating the car with supreme ease. The seats were considered comfortable and the driving position very satisfactory, while visibility for the driver was good, though under some circumstances the rear view mirror mounted on top of the dash rail caused a blind spot to the left. The quality of the unpleated hide of the upholstery came in for particular praise, as did the flat floor in the rear for the passengers.

It is interesting to compare the performance of the Mark V with its predecessors, all fitted with the same size 3½ litre engine.

This suggests that there was very little difference in performance between the three different generations, allowing for the fact the two post-war road tests in *The Autocar* were carried out on inferior Pool petrol, which *The Motor* in 1950 avoided by taking their Mark V into Europe. The Mark V 2½ litre was not tested by the magazines, but it may be supposed that this too would have had a performance similar to the pre-war model, with a top speed around 85mph (137km/h).

The Mark V had successfully met its design brief for a car that was unmistakably a Jaguar, and had all the attributes of comfort, speed, style and stability which had come to be expected from the cars made by the company. It was the last of the pushrod-engined Jaguar saloons. The Mark VII model that followed was powered by the twin-cam XK engine with 160bhp, and would set a new benchmark for saloon performance with a top speed of 100mph (161km/h). It was to take Jaguar to increasing fame as a saloon car producer, as well as being a maker of prodigiously successful sports and racing cars.

Mark V owners

Again there were many titled owners, including the Dukes of Sutherland and Portland. The Earl of Kimberley had two Mark Vs, supplied very quickly one after the other, in December 1949 and April 1950, so one wonders whether he crashed the first one. The Prince of Baroda remained faithful to Jaguars, the Ameer of Bahawalpur replaced his Mark IV 1½ litre with a Mark V 3½ litre, and the Raja Muda (or Crown Prince) of Perak in Malaya also had a 3½ litre. In the world of show business, film director Joseph Losey had a drophead, and like Gable he patronised International Motors, as did one R Mitchum, who may be Robert Mitchum. Actor David Niven and New Zealand crime writer Ngaio Marsh both took advantage of the PED scheme (see chapter 7) when they bought their Mark Vs.

Among Mark V owners were also the Viscount Curzon, son of Earl Howe, and Sir Hartley Shawcross, the attorney general in the Attlee government, who had been chief British prosecutor at the Nuremberg trials. The Ministry of Supply bought a Mark V. Among company owners was Goodwood Road Racing, meaning probably the Duke of Richmond and Gordon. Another company to use Mark Vs was Leyland Motors, which had two of them. There were again many Mark Vs sold as Police cars, for some reason especially in Scotland, where they were bought by the Police in Dumfries and Galloway, Edinburgh, Glasgow, Greenock, and Motherwell and Wishaw; perhaps they recognised value for money when they saw it, but on Jaguar's doorstep the Warwickshire Police also used Mark Vs. Two Mark V dropheads exported to Denmark were bought by the national Danish traffic Police, which had used pre-war Buick convertibles. One of the Danish Police Mark Vs may be found today in the collection of Jaguars in Ole Sommer's museum.

The XK-engined Mark V Cars

The XK 120 sports car was introduced in October 1948, and Jaguar at that time probably wanted to get some experience of how its XK engine might perform in a large saloon car. In February 1949 one of the first Mark V cars made, chassis number 620004, which became a works car, was fitted with a Mark IV engine, number S 3392, made in July 1948. The car was registered in Coventry under HRW 488 and was destined to become the test-bed for at least two XK engines.

The first XK 120 engine fitted in it was W 1003-7, though the date of the engine change is not recorded. The car and engine were subjected to extensive tests by the Experimental Department and then this same car became chassis number 623173 in March 1950, when it was fitted with another XK 120 engine, number W 1110-8, and went through more tests.

The car was sold in January 1954 to JE Bird Autos Ltd by which time it had reverted to its original chassis number 620004. There is no record of why this was done or when, nor is there any explanation for the final entry in the Coventry City registration records which show that the car was at that time fitted with a third XK 120 engine, number W 1187-7. The car still exists today but there is no record of the number of its current engine, which is presumably still a twin-cam XK unit.

Another Mark V, chassis number 623053, was fitted with an XK 120 engine, number W 1130-7, by the factory, and this was the only Mark V car built from new with an XK engine. It was made in March 1950 and was a company car for William Lyons' personal use. It was Coventry registered under JVC 441 in the company's name. In August 1951 it was sold to a George Hack, an engineer with the Bristol Aircraft Company, who was reputedly a motorcycling friend of Lyons, which might explain how he managed to acquire such a unique car.

There is no record of this car having been used as a test-bed, and it is unlikely that at that time it would have been needed for testing, since the prototypes of the new Mark VII would have been available. This car has survived to this day, still with its original engine. The XK engine

The unique ID plate for Lyons' personal XK-engined Mark V, chassis 623053.

Lyons' XK-engined Mark V, with its chassis number (623053) in two places on the chassis.

did not just "drop" into the Mark V engine bay, and since significant modifications were required it is not surprising that only two cars were modified by the factory to take this engine; however, other cars have since been converted privately by their latter-day owners.

To fit the longer XK engine into the Mark V's engine bay, the factory let this recess into the bulkhead of chassis 623053.

SPECIFICATIONS OF MARK V MODELS

	2½ litre	3½ litre
Dimensions		
Overall length	15ft 7½in (4763mm)	As 2½ litre
Overall width	5ft 9½in (1765mm)	As 2½ litre
Overall height	5ft 2½in (1588mm)	As 2½ litre
Wheelbase	10ft (3048mm)	As 2½ litre
Track	Front 4ft 8½in (1435mm), rear 4ft 9½in (1461mm)	As 2½ litre
Weight	33cwt (1678kg)	As 2½ litre
Engine		
Type	6 cylinder OHV	As 2½ litre
Capacity, RAC hp	2663.7cc, 19.84 hp	3485.5cc, 25.01 hp
Bore, stroke	73mm by 106mm	82mm by 110mm
Bhp at rpm	102 at 4600	125 at 4250
Crankshaft diameters	Main journals 2.479in, big-end journals 1.894in	Main journals 2.479in, big-end journals 2.086in
Con rods	Dural, no small-end bushes	Dural, no small-end no bushes, then from eng T 6791 and Z 1501 steel with small-end bushes
Compression ratio	7.3:1	7.2 :1; 6.75:1 with compression plate
Tappet clearance	Inlet 0.012in, exhaust 0.015in	As 2½ litre
Carburettor	Twin horizontal SU H3 with thermostatic automatic starting carburettor	Twin horizontal SU H4 with thermostatic automatic starting carburettor
Fuel pump	Single SU electric located near fuel tank, type PP31/LCS	As 2½ litre
Transmission		
Gearbox type	Moss single helical	As 2½ litre
Overall ratios	15.35, 9.01, 6.12, 4.55	14.50, 8.52, 5.87, 4.30
Rear axle and ratio	Salisbury hypoid bevel, ratio 4.55:1	Salisbury hypoid bevel, ratio 4.30:1
Electrical		
Headlamps	Lucas PF 770	As 2½ litre
Side lamps	Type 1185 integral in wing	As 2½ litre
Fog lamps	SFT700	As 2½ litre
Dynamo	C45/PV4 86	As 2½ litre
Starter	M418G L4	M45G type GC20/0
Distributor	DVXH6A GC40 with vacuum advance	DVXH6A GC42 with vacuum advance
Control box	RF 95/2	As 2½ litre
Trafficators	SF34/N	As 2½ litre

The XK engine needed 4in (102mm) more than was available in the Mark V engine bay so the radiator was moved forwards by 2½in (64mm), and a recess of 1½in (38mm) was carved into the centre section of the bulkhead, to accommodate the wide head of the twin cam engine. As the radiator was moved forwards, the front apron was noticeably shorter as a result, and the car required a longer bonnet. Though built by the factory to fit the longer XK 120 engine, the modifications that were made to the basic Mark V seem to have been done in a knife-and-fork manner, probably by the Experimental Department. The recess in the bulkhead consisted of a piece cut away in the centre of the standard bulkhead and in its place was put a

	2½ litre	3½ litre
Chassis		
Springs, suspension	Front: Independent with torsion bars; rear: semi-elliptic leaf springs, live axle	As 2½ litre
Shock absorbers	Newton telescopic (front), Girling horizontal piston (rear)	As 2½ litre
Steering box	Burman Douglas worm & re-circulating ball	As 2½ litre
Brakes	12in hydraulic 2LS fixed pivot all round; later sliding pivot 1LS on rear only	As 2½ litre
Wheels	16in pressed steel five-stud fixing	As 2½ litre
Tyres	6.70x16	As 2½ litre
Turning circle	35ft (10.7 metres)	As 2½ litre
Fuel tank	15 gals (68 litres)	As 2½ litre
Prices incl PT (sal and DHC same)		
Oct 48	£1190	£1263
Aug 49	£1246	£1262
Apr 51	£1519	£1538

sheet of hand-formed aluminium, making the arrangement look somewhat unprofessional, but no doubt Lyons wanted to keep the costs for this special personal car as low as possible.

Possibly a simpler solution would have been to take the full 4in (102mm) off the bulkhead, but this would have reduced legroom for front seat occupants. It would also have moved the centre of gravity of the engine further back in the car to the detriment of its handling, which would certainly have been unacceptable to Lyons, who as an accomplished driver would have noticed it.

The Experimental Department sent a memo to Lyons on 29 March 1949, giving the test results of HRW 488; the car accelerated to 60mph in 16 sec, to 70mph in 23.3 sec, the standing quarter-mile came up in 20 sec, and the top speed was measured as 90mph (145 km/h) although it was stated that "This figure falls slightly short of the ultimate speed as the car had not quite reached its maximum when entering the measured distance". The XK engine was of 3442cc against the 3485cc of the OHV engine, but gave 160bhp rather than 125bhp, and it is interesting to compare the factory's findings for this type of engine with the figures for the standard Mark V with the OHV engine as reported in *The Autocar* and *The Motor* at the time (see above). There is no clear-cut answer,

and in practice there was probably very little difference between them, with the XK engine in the state of tune that was fitted in the Mark V. Clearly the poor aerodynamics of the Mark V also played their part; the Mark VII to come would have a much more efficient body design, enabling it to reach 100mph (161km/h).

This short joining motif on the apron of chassis 623053 came as a result of the radiator being sited further forward to accept the XK engine.

Chapter Seven

Exports, Assembly Abroad, and Special Bodied Cars

The Export Challenge

One of Lyons' most notable achievements was his post-war success in exports, starting as early as October 1945 and then going from strength to strength; indeed, his knighthood in 1956 was awarded for services to export. Only by looking at the export volumes in the pre-war years and comparing them with the post-war surge can the magnitude of this be appreciated.

During the time the S.S.I and S.S.II cars were made, from 1932 to 1935, Lyons had a large number of individual customers around the globe but only a few significant distributors, in particular in Holland, New Zealand, Argentina, Spain and India. In 1935 some 255 cars were exported to a total of 72 distributors, and though this accounted for 13 per cent of production, most destinations received only one or two cars. Inevitably there was little or no after-sales

support for owners, so presumably the prestige of owning such cars abroad compensated for the difficulty in obtaining spare parts and getting the cars competently repaired.

Exports in 1936 and 1937 at around 5 to 6 per cent of production were lower still, and the pattern of distribution was similar in both years, with around 45 overseas outlets. Again there were no really volume distributors, the largest markets being Switzerland, Holland, and Belgium in Europe, and Australia, Malaya and India in the Empire. More unusual destinations during these two years included Argentina, and even the USA.

This was still the case when the all-steel cars came on stream in 1938, and for the rest of the pre-war period 463 cars, or an average of 5.5 per cent of production, were exported. There were now 39 outlets, with Switzerland still the

TABLE 8.1 – SUMMARY OF PRE-WAR EXPORTS BY MODEL AND YEAR

	1935-36	1936-37	1937-38	1938-39	1939-40	Total	Total production for model	Total Percentage exported by model
1½ litre	18	49	30	83	43	223	7335	3.0%
2½ litre	93	171	72	84	26	446	5407	8.2%
3½ litre			43	44	7	94	1309	7.2%
SS 100	4	13	22	9		48	309	15.5%
Total exports	115	233	167	220	76	811		
Total production	2241	3628	2162	5437	892	14,360	14,360	
Percentage exported	5.1%	6.4%	7.7%	4.0%	8.5%	5.6%		All years: 5.65%

Worldwide desirability was a key to the company's export success. This 1938 photo shows the fifth-produced 3½ litre Saloon (chassis 30005), owned by King Carol of Romania, together with the first-off-the-line 3½ litre SS 100 (chassis 39001), sent for his son's sixteenth birthday.

front runner followed by Australia and the Far East, Malaya and India. Significantly the 1½ litre, which was the best-seller at home, was not very popular in export markets, where the six-cylinder models were more in demand, and the SS 100 was relatively the most successful model for export, although the actual numbers were naturally modest.

In an era where the British Empire was acknowledged to be the best outlet for British cars, it is perhaps surprising that of the 811 export sales, no less than 402 were to Europe, followed by 171 to Asia including many Empire markets, 45 to the Americas, 11 to various African markets, while Tozer, Kemsley and Milbourn which supplied Australia, New Zealand, and South Africa, took 164 cars, and the last 18 went to various destinations which have not all been located.

No other market took more than ten cars between 1935 and 1940 (see also appendix for more detail).

After the war, Lyons had to increase exports substantially and quickly, so he concentrated on developing some key markets, which became Australia, Belgium, Switzerland, USA, Brazil, India and Pakistan until independence in 1947, and South Africa, particularly with regard to the provision of spare parts, service, and support for the cars. This concerted effort was very successful and with it Jaguar was able to

TABLE 8.2 – BEST PRE-WAR EXPORT MARKETS BY RANKING, ALL MODELS AND YEARS	
Country or distributor	Number
Switzerland	192
Tozer, Kemsley and Milbourn	164
Malaya	64
India	62
Belgium	36
Holland	30
Ireland	28
Argentina	20
Czechoslovakia	19
Portugal	19
Germany	16
Hong Kong	14
USA	14
Romania	12
Austria	11
Total of above	701

increase its exports of the Mark IV cars to 3832 over the period this range was made, which was a very impressive 32 per cent of production of 11,969 cars.

To supply some large overseas markets, Jaguar introduced left-hand drive (LHD) cars in 1947. This was particularly important to address the potentially very large market in the USA, and

Rare photo of the two blanking plates, one round and one rectangular, screwed to the bulkhead to cover holes left behind when the car (chassis 511660) was converted from left- to right-hand drive by the factory after it had remained unsold.

Introductory letter for customers for the Mark IV sent out by Jaguar Car Distributors, Brussels in 1948, giving the prices of the cars at the time. It showed the effect on them of local assembly of 3½ litre cars, making them almost the same price as imported, fully-assembled 2½ litre models.

it really paid off when the Mark V came on line in 1949. The introduction of LHD cars and the drive to increase exports made it desirable for Jaguar to predict accurately how many LHD cars could be sold. This was illustrated by the fact that 12 2½ litre cars and 61 3½ litre LHD cars remained unsold, so these were converted in the factory to RHD. The cost of conversion can not have been trivial but was kept to a minimum where possible; in particular by blanking off the two holes now unused on the left-hand side of the bulkhead, when the steering column and the throttle arm were relocated to the right-hand side. In this rare photo of a converted car the voltage control box has been moved to the right-hand side, though it is unlikely that this was done by the factory, as it would originally have been fitted on the left-hand side on both LHD and RHD cars.

In Australia there were several distributors of Jaguar cars when the Mark IVs started to arrive. Standard Cars in Australia had sold some Jaguars, but this abruptly ended when Standard in the UK bought Triumph with the intention of competing with Jaguar. Andersons Agencies were operating in Brisbane, MS Brooking in Perth, and Dominion Motors in Adelaide, but all these sold small numbers of Jaguars and none could deliver on Lyons' determination to sell hundreds rather than tens of cars in this market. One other company, Brylaw of Melbourne, managed by the energetic and able Jack Bryson, was willing to accept the challenge and was quickly appointed as distributor of Jaguars for Victoria, New South Wales, and Tasmania, despite having hitherto imported mainly motorcycles and Morgans. For a time, Brylaw became by far the largest overseas Jaguar distributor in the world, with 693 cars to their credit by the end of Mark IV production, out of a total of 927 exported to Australia. As Bryson, they remained the premier Jaguar importer in Australia until the British Leyland days in the 1970s.

Australia was followed by Belgium with 558 cars, Switzerland with 447, the emerging US market with only 308 cars at this stage, Brazil with 183 cars, British India with 169 cars, and South Africa with 159 cars. The USA only imported the 3½ litre model, as American drivers were accustomed to powerful big-engined cars. Brazil switched to LHD cars once they became available, though Switzerland continued to take a mixture of LHD and RHD cars.

The scene was therefore set for the much-needed increase in the proportion of Jaguars for export when the long-awaited Mark V started to come off the production line. The delay in the start of Mark V production meant that exports had virtually dried up from November 1948 to March 1949, since none of the overseas customers wanted the old Mark IV cars any more, and the new eagerly awaited Mark V had yet to make an appearance in dealer showrooms.

Once Mark V sales got going, Jaguar went from being predominantly a home market

Madame Joska Bourgeois, owner of the Brussels distributor, Jaguar Car Distributors.

Showroom of Emil Frey, the largest Swiss Jaguar distributor, displaying a Mark VII, two Mark Vs and an XK120.

A Mark V in its as-shipped state arriving in Australia and destined for the distributor Brylaw.

Brylaw's lubrication plate, added to its Mark V cars sold in Australia.

supplier with a good record in exports, to being a major exporter which also supplied some cars to the home market. In fact, of the Mark V range 58.5 per cent of production was exported, 6145 cars as against 4354 home sales out of the 10,499 cars made. This rise in exports was phenomenal and stood Jaguar in good stead for later models.

First to receive the Mark V was again the Australian market. Brylaw made good on its promise to Lyons and imported 1711 Mark V cars out of a total of 2292 sent to the country as a whole. To put this in perspective, Australia took 37 per cent of all Mark V cars exported, and Brylaw alone accounted for 28 per cent. It is therefore no wonder that so many of these elegant cars survive there, and are obviously much cherished. After the accompanying photograph of Mark V cars at a wedding in Australia had been taken, yet another Mark V arrived. This turnout would put any other country to shame; Brylaw can be proud of the Jaguar legacy it gave birth to.

The introduction of Purchase Tax had dramatically increased the retail prices of cars sold to UK residents. The Government wanted to encourage sales of cars to overseas buyers and introduced the Home Delivery Export Scheme (HDES), which allowed cars to be bought tax-free in the UK, on the understanding that the car was to be exported within one year, or it would become liable for the Purchase Tax. The car was issued with a pink log book to identify its tax-free status. This scheme appealed

particularly to visitors to the UK, mostly from Australia and New Zealand, UK personnel working in the Commonwealth and visiting the UK on leave, and later US service personnel on a tour of duty in the UK.

Cars sold under this scheme, often referred to as Personal Export Delivery (PED) cars, were registered by the factory in Coventry, so they can be identified in the Coventry City Registration Records, and they made a significant contribution to the export business, with a total of 582 of the 6145 export sales. After a year abroad, the original owner could repatriate the car without incurring Purchase Tax, and after another year in the UK it could be sold on tax-free to a third party.

Lyons had been successful as usual in keeping the costs of manufacture of the cars under control, but he was unable to prevent the steep increase in prices of the cars after the war, which was due to inflation and the introduction of Purchase Tax. The upshot was that whereas the pre-war 2½ litre cars could be sold for £395, when post-war prices were announced in November 1945 this had risen to £889 including the Purchase Tax of £194, and there were corresponding increases for the basic 1½ litre to £685 and for the 3½ litre cars to £991. Since inflation and Purchase Tax affected all makes of cars, Jaguar cars still offered exceptional value for money for luxury sports saloons. This hefty burden on the domestic selling price of the cars made the export of the cars even more attractive.

Assembly Abroad

Before the war, Lyons had sent a few kits of parts to be assembled in Eire by Frank Cavey & Sons in Dublin, but post-war he was keen, and indeed he very much needed, to increase drastically the number of cars exported, so that the company could get a bigger quota of steel for the factory to run efficiently. Although Jaguars were reasonably priced, not all countries were financially in a position to import them, and some countries set a maximum value on cars that could be imported, which was the case in Belgium. Other countries

An impressive number of Mark V cars lined up for a wedding in Australia. Australia was the largest market for the Mark V, with 2292 cars sent there in all.

Personal export of a Mark V being flown across the Channel by Silver City. HVC 297 was chassis 620014, ordered through Brinkman in Singapore and registered in Coventry in March 1949.

charged a lower import duty on incomplete cars, whether in chassis form, or as Completely Knocked Down (CKD) kits, and were anxious to create local employment in assembly plants, or to encourage supply of locally-made components. These countries included Australia, South Africa, and New Zealand.

Accordingly, Jaguar instigated a complementary business of supplying CKD kits to some overseas companies for local assembly in various countries. These kits made a useful contribution which increased the volume of export sales. In our period there were three overseas assembly operations, starting in a small way with Eire, then after the war considerably increased in volume with the addition of Belgium and New Zealand as overseas assemblers. In later years, Jaguars came to be assembled in South Africa, and in a few other unusual markets such as Mexico. And as this book was being written, the first locally-assembled Jaguar XFs were put together in India… with China apparently to follow.

Frank Cavey in Eire

The Irish Republic was never going to be a large market for cars especially at the luxury end, yet nevertheless Frank Cavey wanted to be involved in selling SS Jaguar cars, and also in the assembly of CKD kits. His Dublin facility was the first to assemble SS Jaguar cars shipped in CKD form. In total 206 cars, complete and in CKD form, were sold by Cavey, starting with the odd one in May 1937 and building up to a total of 127 Mark IV cars before declining to 58 Mark V

An Irish-assembled CKD by Frank Cavey in Dublin, in Irish Green, this 1½ litre Mark IV is chassis 414803.

cars. Of the 206 cars, 138 were fully assembled by Jaguar, and 68 were sent out in CKD form.

Little has been recorded by the Jaguar factory or by any of the assemblers about the exact state in which the kits of parts were sent. Before the war just twelve kits had been sent to Eire between July 1937 and February 1939, and this was then restarted in August 1948 with the shipment of twelve CKD kits for the Mark IV, progressing to 44 Mark V kits sent in the period from October 1949 to February 1951. These kits were shipped in lots of four cars' worth of parts and sub-assemblies at about three-monthly intervals. These were very low volumes for these complex cars to be made in and it is surprising therefore just how much of the manufacturing and assembly work was actually undertaken by Cavey. In July 1938 an article in the *Irish Times* gave a good description of just was involved in the production of the first all-steel bodied SS Jaguar cars. The article states:

"The first 1939 SS motor car to be assembled in Ireland will be ready for delivery tomorrow. When I visited the premises of Messrs. F Cavey and Sons at 54 Camden St, Dublin, yesterday, the proprietor showed me the machine with some pride. It is a 2½ litre Jaguar saloon, finished in a restful grey shade with red leather upholstery. It has the sleek, graceful lines which the S.S. more than any car of its price possesses, and the frontal appearance is made more than ordinarily attractive by the out-size headlamps with which the car is fitted.

"Mr Cavey has been assembling S.S. cars for about a year now. His premises are not large, but he has arranged them admirably for the work which he is doing. The welding of the body parts and the fitting of them to the chassis is done in a loft, and the car is then swung down to the ground floor, where the final stages of assembly, upholstering, painting, etc., are completed. In a small establishment like this, each car receives the maximum possible attention, each item of its assembly being undertaken with care and constant supervision.

"Only a small output is attempted. The next car will not be ready for three or four weeks. Mr Cavey considers it better that he should turn out half a dozen machines, in each of which he can take a personal interest and satisfaction, than that he should attempt to produce on a big scale as yet."

This article is illuminating as it describes the

level of assembly undertaken, though it is some-what misleading in claiming that Cavey had been assembling SS cars for about a year at that time, since only three cars (two 1½ and one 2½ litre models) had previously been sent in CKD form in July 1937 and these had been the coach-built cars, which were a very different proposition from building the all-steel bodied 1938 cars. Nevertheless, for Cavey to undertake this major assembly task, with the high costs in setting up the facility and of training the work-force, gives a strong indication that even at that stage he intended to produce a regular supply of Irish-built cars for the local market in the future. By the time the war intervened a year later, Cavey had however only received a total of nine all-steel bodied CKD cars (five 1½ and four 2½ litre models).

Production restarted of the similar Mark IV model in June 1948, with twelve kits (four 1½ and eight 2½ litre models) shipped between July and September 1948. There was then another significant change in production facilities and skills needed to make the 44 Mark V cars (24 2½ litre and 20 3½ litre models) from September 1949 to February 1951. Cavey also took 115 Mark IV and 14 Mark V cars in built-up form.

Jaguar Car Distributors in Belgium

In 1946, Belgium became one of the main export markets for Jaguars, as it had substantial wealth from its colonies, in particular the Belgian Congo, and so was one of few Euro-pean countries able to pay for imported cars with hard currency, convertible against US Dollars. In that year Jaguar Car Distributors imported 105 cars, of which 73 were 1½ litre models, and all were of course still RHD. This rose to 266 in 1947, again mainly the 1½ litre RHD model, but in that year the Belgian Government imposed restrictions on the value of cars that could be imported, in order to keep some control on the outflow of foreign currency. They set a limit of £600 for any imported car, which did not affect the 1½ litre as it came below this figure, but hit the 3½ litre which was beginning to achieve some popularity. In its category, Jaguar was in a privileged position as a supplier of luxury cars, since its basic costs were so much lower than those of its competitors, but nevertheless to keep within the limit and be able to export the larger-engined cars Jaguar had to make arrangements to assemble CKD kits

Final colour defined on the back of the dashboard of an Irish 1½ litre Mark IV CKD, chassis 414803.

of the 3½ litre cars in a factory in Belgium.

Madame Joska Bourgeois, together with Australian-born Nick Haines, arranged with William Lyons to have cars assembled locally by the Belgian Vanden Plas Company, which was not related to the UK company of the same name. A team of twelve Jaguar personnel went out to help set up and to supervise the opera-tion, which obviously went well since the first CKD kits sent to Belgium on 22 December 1947 were delivered as completed cars to the customers in mid-February 1948. Again there are no records of what work was carried out by Vanden Plas, but it is likely that much work on the cars was done in the UK, since the bodies left Coventry already painted, and the upholstery was probably fully made up and supplied, since the paint and trim colours appear to have been determined before the kit left the Jaguar factory.

From the Jaguar records it can be seen that despatches of 3½ litre cars to Belgium started in December 1947 and went on until August the following year, with all aspects of the cars recorded in Coventry. Each car was entered in the Jaguar ledger with its chassis number, and an engine number pre-allocated from one of the engines that were shipped to Belgium. The body numbers for CKD cars were unique, PP on saloons and DH on dropheads, where Jaguar used prefixes of respectively B, later D, and C on its fully assembled saloons and dropheads.

The CKD scheme had the desired effect in keeping the price of the 3½ litre car competitive and attractive to Belgian customers. The Belgian prices of the time, converted to Sterling, show the following comparison with the UK prices, including Purchase Tax.

TABLE 8.3 – BELGIAN AND UK PRICES, CA. 1948

Engine size	Belgian price £	UK price £
1½ litre std	£866	£953
1½ litre SE	£895	£1009
2½ litre	£1030	£1189
3½ litre sal	£1048	£1263
3½ litre DHC	£1109	n/a

The smaller-engined cars were exported fully assembled from the UK, and although cheaper than in the UK by 9, 11, and 13 per cent respectively, the 3½ litre benefited noticeably from having been assembled in Belgium, as the Saloon was 17 per cent cheaper. Not only did it avoid the heavy surcharge by the Belgian Government for the more expensive cars, but it was also cheaper to finish at the Vanden Plas factory. From the above price list it is obvious why only eight of the 2½ litre cars were ever sold in Belgium, when its price was so similar to that of the 3½ litre.

Only 3½ litre cars were assembled in Belgium and the operation was a considerable success, ending in July 1948 by which time 139 cars had been assembled of which 49 were dropheads; all had left-hand drive. Belgium in fact took a total of 558 Mark IV cars, including 338 1½ litres, 8 2½ litres, and 73 built-up 3½ litres in addition to the 139 CKD cars. Of note too is the fact that the Jaguar ledger contains the names of the majority of the first owners of cars assembled in Belgium, as well as correcting the number of the engine actually fitted to a car that in all the cases was different from the one that had been nominally allocated by Jaguar at the time of shipment of the kits. Since Jaguar could only record names of first owners when they returned their warranty registration forms, it is fair to assume that the Belgian-assembled cars were covered by the same warranty as was offered by Jaguar for its own fully assembled cars, and this would only have been acceptable to Jaguar if it had its own supervisors and inspectors in the Vanden Plas factory in order to be sure that the cars were made to an acceptable quality standard.

Assembly in New Zealand

New Zealand had been a regular and enthusiastic importer of SS cars since the early 1930s through the export agent Tozer, Kemsley and Milbourn (TKM). TKM was the agent for South Africa as well as Asia and the Far East, Australia, and New Zealand, but the number that actually went to New Zealand is not precisely known. While TKM handled 164 cars in total from 1935 to 1940, only 21 have their final destinations recorded in the factory ledgers, and of these only eight are shown as having gone to New Zealand, but the actual figure could well have been much higher.

After the war New Zealand imported 79 Mark IV cars fully assembled, evenly distributed between the three engine sizes, but was to face onerous import tariffs that made cars markedly more expensive to import. Unlike Belgium which imposed restrictions on the more expensive cars, in New Zealand all cars were affected. In 1949 Shorters, of 55 Shortland Street, Auckland, followed in the footsteps of the Belgian assembly facility, and received the help of a team of Jaguar personnel. They had also embarked on local assembly of Citroën and Singer cars, for which they were the distributors in North Island. They took a total of 30 Mark V cars in kit form. Archibalds of Christchurch and Independent Motor Sales of Wellington, the main distributors in South Island, also undertook local assembly, but the numbers were much lower, at ten and five cars respectively.

Again the details of what exactly was shipped in the CKD kits is not known since the state of disassembly is not recorded in the Jaguar records, but in 2010, Mark Shorter, grandson of company founder Eric Shorter, remembered certain aspects of the assembly of the Mark V, which he recounted as follows:

"The cars arrived in purpose-built boxes with all the necessary bits in the main box and a separate box for the engine and gearbox; these were shipped in bulk with four or five to a box. The mudguards etc. were disassembled before shipment and taped to avoid damage. The assembly and painting was done in their [Shorters] workshop that was staffed by excellent craftsmen with the best plant and equipment. [He was uncertain about colours but mentioned White, Silver, Metallic Light Blue, Royal Blue, and Black.] The body parts were kept together as a kit and some were interchangeable. The ID plates came stamped from the [Jaguar] factory and were matched up with the correct engine at assembly time. The upholstery and door panels etc. were all done at Shorters by their expert tradesmen in a well equipped trim shop using New Zealand leather supplied by Sutherlands. Tan was the most popular along with Red. The seat frames were supplied in the kit. The main idea was to use as much local content as possible so other items like tyres, batteries and exhausts were supplied locally."

The cars assembled in New Zealand also had PP prefix body numbers though the actual cars made up from the chassis, engines and body numbers given by the factory were unsurprisingly not in the same sets as recorded in the factory ledger, since there would have been no necessity for feedback from New Zealand as they were responsible for the warranty for the cars they had assembled. The Jaguar ledgers do occasionally give details of first owners for the cars made in New Zealand or Eire, so it is a reasonable assumption that these cars were also covered by the normal warranty.

A total of 45 Mark V cars were assembled in New Zealand, ten of which were 2½ litre models which all went to Shorters, and 35 3½ litre models, of which Shorters assembled twenty. Shorters were very successful in their business and went on to sell and assemble many later Jaguar models, taking 692 complete and CKD cars from 1950 to 1959. However, the close co-operation on the CKD cars of Jaguar with the Belgian distributor was I think unique, probably because of the high volumes and the relative proximity of the factories in the UK and in Belgium.

Mark V ID plate with the PP prefix body number for cars assembled from CKD kits in New Zealand.

PP prefix body number tag plate on a New Zealand-assembled Mark V CKD.

Finally it should be mentioned that MS Brooking of Perth in Australia took seventeen Mark IV cars, eleven 2½ litre and six 3½ litre cars, which may have been in CKD or a similar form, as they are recorded by Jaguar as being supplied in primer rather than painted, but otherwise there is no clue in the records to confirm that they were definitely sent out in kit form.

Special Bodied Cars

Lyons supplied a small number of chassis over the years, possibly in recognition of the help he had received from established car manufacturers who had supplied him with rolling chassis when he had started making his own cars in the 1920s. These chassis were consigned to the usual distrib-

TABLE 8.4 – CHASSIS-ONLY DELIVERIES BY MODEL AND COUNTRY

Model	Number	UK	Switzerland	Belgium	Romania	Greece	unknown
SS Jaguar 1½	2	2					
SS Jaguar 2½	22	5	17				
SS Jaguar 3½	11	4	7				
SS Jaguar 100	6	2	2	1	1		
Mark IV 2½	2		2				
Mark IV 3½	12		10	2			
Mark V 2½	2					2	
Mark V 3½	3	1				1	1
In total	60	14	38	3	1	3	1

See appendix for a detailed list of all chassis numbers.

The 1937 Salmons-bodied 2½ litre DHC, chassis 251946. This car was probably forerunner to the design of the SS Jaguar DHC that came out in 1938. Note the P100R headlamps.

utors, and most of them were exported, so there is no factory record to show which coachbuilders bodied them. The numbers and destinations of rolling chassis for the period from 1936 to 1950 are detailed in the table on page 143.

Some coachbuilders produced bodies that were very similar externally and internally to Jaguar products, using the same radiator grille, some body parts (wings and bonnet), headlamps, and dash. These additional parts were no doubt ordered from Jaguar, and delivered together with the chassis.

At the other end of the scale were cars such as the two made by the Belgian Vanden Plas company for Mme Bourgeois who owned Jaguar Car Distributors in Brussels. One was based on an SS 100 and the other on a Mark IV chassis. They were both very different from the standard Jaguars, with only their radiators giving a hint as to their origin. Only a few of the special-bodied cars are known to have survived, many appear to have disappeared completely, and others have been given replicas of standard factory bodywork. The survivors are now very desirable and many are being lovingly restored.

J Gurney Nutting

This UK company made the body for the very first SS Jaguar chassis supplied to a coachbuilder. The chassis was number 11797, ordered by the Swiss distributor Emil Frey and shipped from the SS Jaguar factory in October 1936. The only body built by J Gurling Nutting on an SS Jaguar chassis, it was a Sports Saloon similar in appearance to the Bentleys the firm were bodying at the time. Gurney Nutting were

Rear view of the 1937 Salmons DHC. The spare wheel was mounted on the boot lid, rather than the side-mount of contemporary SS Jaguars. The rear window was already very small to facilitate folding the hood.

normally engaged in making bodies for Rolls-Royce and Bentley, and had notably built the body for Malcolm Campbell's 1931 Bluebird world speed record car.

Salmons (also known as "Tickford")

In December 1936 one 2½ litre chassis, number 12290, was sent to the Salmons company of Newport Pagnell in the UK, who built a three-position drophead coupé body on it. This was the first chassis to be bodied by a UK coachbuilder and the car which resulted undoubtedly influenced the design of the SS Jaguar drophead introduced some fifteen months later. In fact, at

The 1937 Salmons DHC door trim, complete with adjustable-height armrest.

Interior of the 1937 Salmons DHC, featuring SS Jaguar-style pleated upholstery with added pockets for the rear passengers.

Freestone and Webb's 1938 "razor edge" concours-winning Saloon (chassis 30180). This was the only body put onto an SS Jaguar chassis by the company, which normally made bodies for Rolls-Royce and Bentley cars.

roughly the same time as the Salmons drophead was made, SS Jaguar produced its own drop-head prototype on chassis number 12306. The Salmons car survives to this day but the first factory prototype does not, so no meaningful comparison can be made between the two. Salmons went on to become the supplier of drophead bodies to MG and Rover for the rest of the 1930s, and after the war the company was bought by David Brown, who turned their premises into the Aston Martin factory.

Freestone and Webb

This company was based in Willesden, North London, and specialised in making their trade-mark "razor edge" styled bodies for Rolls-Royce and Bentley in low volumes of around 15 per annum. They are generally credited with the invention of the razor edge style in about 1935. It was one of the last design innovations of a British coachbuilder. The company made just one body for a 3½ litre Jaguar chassis in 1938, on chassis number 30180, which was delivered by the factory on 5 April 1938 and completed in time for the car to be entered in the Ramsgate Concours in July, where it was awarded first prize for Mrs Guy Olliver in the category of "Smartest car entered and driven by a lady".

Mulliners (of Birmingham)

Captain John Black, the chairman and managing director of the Standard Motor Company, had a great deal to do with the SS Company in its

formative years, and he himself owned many SS and SS Jaguar cars. In 1939, he commissioned Louis Antweiler of Mulliners in Birmingham to build a razor-edge touring limousine, with an electric division, on an SS Jaguar 3½ litre chassis, as a present for Mrs Black. It was finished in black, with black leather to the front seat and fawn West of England cloth to the rear, and was very well equipped indeed. The couple were so pleased with this car that a duplicate was soon built for Captain Black himself; the two cars were respectively chassis 30948 and 31002, registered ERW 470, and EWK 480. A suggestion that plans were being laid for marketing further replicas came to nothing with the outbreak of war. Post-war, Mulliners developed a further razor-edge design for Black in the shape of the Triumph 1800 saloon. They ended up as major suppliers of bodies to Standard-Triumph and were finally taken over by them.

Maltby

This company based in Folkestone built bodies on chassis including Austin, Bentley, Lagonda and Rolls-Royce. In 1938-39 they built some "Redfern" drophead coupés on SS Jaguar saloon chassis, and one was exhibited at the 1938 Motor Show; they called this style a "Coupe de Ville". The car resembled the standard drophead but had a distinctive bulge in the soft-top line, and a rather heavier tail-end treatment. As a special-bodied car it needed to provide some advantages over Jaguar's own car and Maltby addressed the task of lowering and raising the hood, never easy in those days for dropheads, especially for such a bulky and well-padded hood as was fitted to Jaguars. Maltby came up with an electro-hydraulic mechanism that made "the hood easy to operate" according to a review in *The Autocar* in 1939. The downside of this innovation was that it gave the car a rather heavy profile when the hood was in the partially open de ville position, and the price was quoted as £575 in 3½ litre form, or £110 more than the standard drophead. It is believed that the car featured in the magazine was 3½ litre chassis 30998 but Maltby also bodied at least two 2½ litre chassis and probably two 1½ litre chassis, possibly more. The two smaller cars were quoted at £510 and £413 respectively, where the standard dropheads cost £415 and £318.

Avon

Sammy Newsome, who successfully campaigned SS Jaguar cars in rallies and hill climbs, ran one of SS Jaguar's most important and active distributors, SH Newsome of Coventry. In 1938 he wanted Lyons to make a de-luxe drophead version of the SS 100 with better weather protection, but either Lyons was not willing to extend the range of the models he was making, or wanted to give preference to his own fixed-head coupé. Newsome then arranged with a local company, Avon of Warwick, to make two demonstration cars on SS 100 3½ litre chassis supplied by the factory. The first car on chassis 39109 was registered EHP 7 and the second on chassis 39115 was EVC 587. These cars had similar bodies but EHP had a fold-

down windscreen with aero screens and EVC had a fixed screen. Both cars had doors with wind-down windows and covered rear wheels.

Though Newsome had planned for Avon to make more of these cars, as stated in his letter of June 1939 to prospective buyers, the project came to a halt with the outbreak of the war with only these first two made. Both cars survive but one has sadly been fitted with a replica of the standard SS 100 open two-seater body.

Maltby's 1938 2½ litre DHC with its hood in de Ville position, showing the deep profile of its electro-hydraulic hood mechanism and the resulting shallow side windows. The mechanical assistance for operating the hood was no doubt welcome, but not very attractive in looks.

Left above: *The first of two 1938 Avon-bodied SS 100 cars, chassis 39109 and registered EHP 7, was equipped with a fold-down windscreen.*
Left below: *The second 1938 Avon-bodied SS 100, chassis 39115 and registered EVC 587, featured a fixed windscreen.*

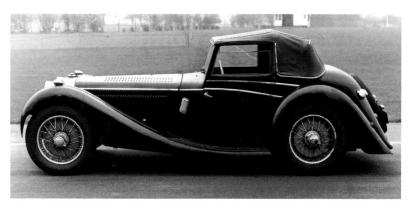

EVC 587, chassis 39115, a 1938 Avon SS 100 with fixed windscreen.

Bugatti-inspired styling of the 1938 3½ litre FHC Graber, chassis 30182.

Magill

This obscure company of Sheffield has some times been credited with bodying a 1½ litre as a drophead coupé, registered in Coventry under EDU 238; in fact this car was a factory-bodied drophead, chassis 56358, although it was apparently sold through the Sheffield distributor Hatfields – but the first owner of record lived in Hertfordshire. It took part in the 1939 RAC Rally.

Turning now to those chassis which were exported and bodied by foreign coachbuilders, I shall start with Switzerland. The Swiss import duty was calculated by weight, so it was cheaper to import a chassis than a complete car, and the country had a flourishing coachbuilding industry specialising in drophead coupé or

cabriolet bodywork; a few companies survived into the 1960s. These bodies were most likely commissioned by the Swiss distributors, Emil Frey in Zürich, and Garage Claparede in Geneva. It must be added that many of the Swiss cabriolet bodies of the 1930s tend towards the same rather Germanic look, and can be difficult to distinguish and identify unless they have a coachbuilder's plate attached. For information on the Swiss coachbuilders, I am grateful to Urs Ramseier of the Swiss Car Register and Dr Christian Jenny of the Swiss Jaguar Drivers' Club.

Bernath

Willi Bernath of La Chaux-de-Fonds built an estimated 25 bodies between 1945 and 1947 on a wide variety of chassis, probably mostly second-hand pre-war cars which he re-bodied. His designs showed both American and Italian influences. He re-bodied a 1937 SS Jaguar 2½ litre Saloon chassis 13141 in a rather florid modern style, with a full-width front including a horizontal grille behind which the headlamps were hidden. This car had originally gone to Garage Claparede in May 1937. The Bernath-bodied car still survives in Switzerland. One source suggests the Bernath-bodied car was SS 100 chassis 39092 but that was in fact bodied by Worblaufen, see below.

Graber

This was the best-known and most famous of the Swiss coachbuilders. In 1925 Herman Graber took over his father's company, which had made horse-drawn carriages, and built his first car bodies two years later. Graber specialised in high-quality luxury coachwork on US and European chassis such as Packard, Cadillac, Duesenberg,

Inside the 1938 Graber FHC, chassis 30182, was a one-piece front seat squab, albeit with split backrests to allow entry into the rear compartment.

Side view of the 1938 Graber FHC (chassis 30182), looking as if the SS Jaguar FHC SS 100 followed its lead.

The longer boot of the 1938 Graber FHC came as the result of the car being made on a Saloon chassis rather than the SS 100's.

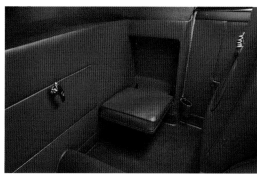

The 1938 Graber FHC's dashboard featured SS Jaguar instruments and a three-blade windscreen wiper driven by a motor mounted on the lower rail of the fixed windscreen.

This unusual side-facing occasional seat was found in the back of Graber's 1938 FHC.

Bugatti, Hispano-Suiza and Mercedes-Benz. After World War Two many bodies were designed and built on British chassis such as Alvis, which led to a Graber design becoming the standard Alvis 3 litre body. A number of bodies were built on Jaguar chassis before the war, including a 1937 2½ litre DHC, and a DHC and a FHC both built on 1938 3½ litre chassis.

Langenthal

This company based near Bern made bodies on Delahaye and Mercedes-Benz chassis, among others. In 1947-48 the company produced a splendid drophead coupé on a Mark IV 3½ litre chassis, with full-width bodywork and smooth lines, the front end with a narrow grille, four built-in lamps, and double bumpers looking very Alfa Romeo-like. The car was displayed on the official Jaguar stand at the Geneva Motor Show in 1948, together with an alternative more traditional design (but interestingly fitted with spats over the rear wheels) by Worblaufen, and a factory DHC. They are thought to have built at least two other bodies on Jaguar chassis.

Reinbolt & Christé

This Basel-based company had a longer history than most and had made a motor car body as early as 1900. They had made several drophead bodies for the big MGs in the 1930s, and after the war made similar bodywork on the Riley 2½ litre. Their Jaguar Mark IV, seen at the 1948 Geneva Show, was more modern, with a full-width front and built-in lamps, while the grille looked a bit like the Mark VII which was yet to come. The front wings ran through the doors, and the rear wings were fitted with spats over the wheel arches. This is thought to be their only Jaguar body.

Sécheron

An obscure small coachbuilder of Geneva, the successor to Gangloff whose off-shoot at Colmar in Alsace is better known thanks to their association with Bugatti, after the war Sécheron bodied one Jaguar of which photos exist, but the car can not be positively identified.

Tüscher

The Tüscher company, founded in 1909, was based in Zürich and was principally concerned with making motor coaches, trams and trolley buses. They did however make a number of car bodies on various chassis in the period up to 1940, after which they reverted to producing their original lines. The company built the lion's share of the pre-war Swiss drophead coupé bodies on SS Jaguar chassis, with at least thirteen cars to its credit, including twelve 1937 2½ litres and one 1939 3½ litre, all of which had been shipped to Emil Frey. Tüscher are also thought possibly to have built a drophead body on an SS 100 chassis, although if so, this must have been a standard car which they re-bodied.

Worblaufen

This coachbuilder is also known as Ramseier after the family who owned and ran the company at Worblaufen near Bern. They produced their bodies on Mercedes-Benz, Alfa Romeo, Delahaye, Hispano-Suiza, Peugeot and at least nine Jaguar chassis. To the order of Garage Claparede, they built a drophead body on a 2½ litre chassis which was on the SS Jaguar stand of the 1937 Geneva Motor Show. They then worked for Emil Frey and built dropheads on two 3½ litre chassis, and just before the war, similar bodies on SS 100 chassis 39092 and 39113 which had been sent to Frey in respectively December 1938 and April 1939, but it is not known if either of these were ever exhibited at a Motor Show, whether pre- or post-war. It appears that 39092 was eventually re-bodied in near-standard form.

After the war, they bodied at least four of the chassis sent to Switzerland, two each to Garage Claparede and to Emil Frey, and one of their cars was on the 1948 Geneva Motor Show Jaguar stand. Their 1947 body on a 2½ litre Mark IV chassis for Emil Frey, featured here, was a stylish drophead built about a year before the factory restarted the production of its own post-war drophead. The car was unmistakably a Jaguar, with the standard radiator grille, headlamps, dashboard and steering wheel. The interior was of Worblaufen's own design, with differently styled seats and an armrest between the two front seats. The folded hood sat high up behind the rear seats, since there was no recess for it similar to that found on Jaguar dropheads. This was a styling compromise to allow for an elegant swept-down line of the rear end of the car, and it could only be achieved by putting the spare wheel inside the boot under a dividing shelf with the luggage space above it. This necessitated keeping the full height of the boot

A post-war 1948 Worblaufen-bodied 2½ litre DHC (chassis 510455) with its hood closed. The rear quarterlights gave improved visibility for back-seat passengers.

The 1948 Worblaufen 2½ litre DHC's rear quarterlights could be partially opened.

for luggage, without an intruding recess for the hood. The petrol filler cap was also placed inside the boot, so as not to spoil the line of the car. The overall effect was very pleasing and very much worth the effort of designing and producing such a body.

A few chassis went to other European countries, but details are not always available, and apart from those mentioned below it must be noted that there is no information on the bodywork eventually fitted to the three Mark V chassis exported to Greece.

Rear view of the 1948 Worblaufen 2½ litre DHC. The hood sat noticeably high when open, since there was no recess for it behind the rear seats.

The 1948 Worblaufen 2½ litre DHC housed a simple interior with a useful centre armrest between the front seats.

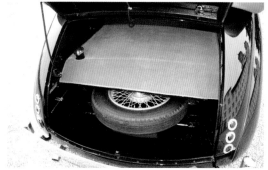

Inside the boot of the 1948 Worblaufen 2½ litre DHC. The spare wheel and fuel filler were put inside the luggage compartment to enhance the line of the car. The recess for the hood was sacrificed as a result.

Worblaufen's 1948 2½ litre DHC (chassis 510455) featured an unusual arrangement for the heater/ventilation intake ducting and a special tool storage compartment on the bulkhead in the engine bay.

Leonida (Romania)

This company was in Bucharest, and had close contacts to the Romanian Royal family. Two complete cars were supplied to the Royal family, an early all-steel 1938 model 3½ litre saloon for King Carol II in November 1937, and the very first 3½ litre SS 100 for his son Prince Michael in October 1937. However, in May 1938 a complete SS 100 chassis was sent out to the Romanian distributor Anglo Cars, and was bought by King Carol's mother for her other son, Prince Nicholas. The mechanic for the Royal cars working at the coachwork company Leonida designed and made the body, and the complete

*Leonida-bodied 1938
SS 100 made for
Romanian King
Carol's brother,
Prince Nicholas.*

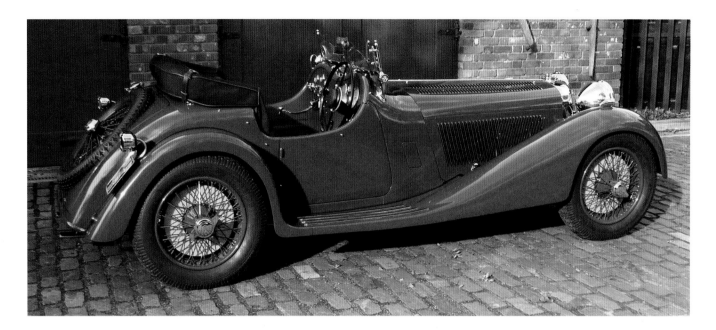

Above: *Side profile of the 1938 Leonida SS 100. The bonnet appears to be standard but the wings were special and the car had a completely different rear end treatment, including a boot.*

Right: *Inside the boot of the 1938 Leonida SS 100 – it was an unusual feature for an SS 100.*

car was delivered to Prince Nicholas. This was the only special-bodied Jaguar car made by the Leonida company, and was very different from the normal SS 100.

Vanden Plas (Belgium)

This company was actively engaged with Jaguar as they assembled the CKD kits for the 3½ litre Mark IV saloons after the war (see above). Madame Joska Bourgeois of the Belgian Jaguar Car Distributors in Brussels bought a saloon chassis and an SS 100 chassis on which she had two stunning special bodies built which were shown at the 1948 Brussels Motor Show, and both have survived to this day. The saloon chassis was made into a stylish drophead, and the SS 100 into a luxurious open two-seater car; both cars had rather a lot of chrome-plated decoration, in the manner of the French

company Figoni & Falaschi. Another Vanden Plas drophead body is thought to have started out as a Mark IV saloon. A third Mark IV chassis was a chassis-only display at the 1948 Brussels Show, and was then bodied by Vanden Plas, again as a drophead, with a modified wingline, and was possibly intended for the following year's Brussels show.

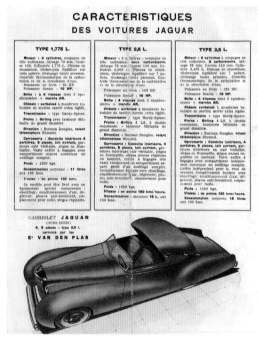

Belgian Vanden Plas brochure of 1948, showing the Mark IV Cabriolet.

The stunning 1948 Vanden Plas-bodied 2½ litre SS 100, chassis 49064, was a luxurious open two-seater in the style of French company Figoni & Falaschi.

Several other standard cars were re-bodied or modified post-production. Particularly well known is the Pycroft Special, with a streamlined body fitted to an SS 100 chassis after World War Two; while it survives, it was apparently much later fitted with a standard body. Another SS 100 was partially re-bodied by the famous French coachbuilder Saoutchik, a third SS 100 was re-bodied in a more modern style in Czechoslovakia after the war, by Uhlik or Pulda, and a fourth was given streamlined all-enclosing coupé bodywork by Les Leston in the UK. Yet another SS 100 was rebodied by Bidee in Belgium to look just like the same designer's Alvis TA14 sport, with head-lamps behind a pear-shaped radiator grille. There was even a Mark V drophead in the UK which ended up with a home-made half-timbered estate car body.

The Vanden Plas DHC (chassis 611423) and SS 100 Cabriolet (chassis 49064) on the 1948 Brussels Motor Show parade.

The 1948 Vanden Plas 3½ litre DHC, chassis 611423 was designed with a long, sleek appearance and extended boot.

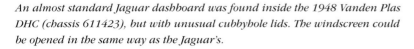

An almost standard Jaguar dashboard was found inside the 1948 Vanden Plas DHC (chassis 611423), but with unusual cubbyhole lids. The windscreen could be opened in the same way as the Jaguar's.

The 1948 Vanden Plas DHC's very wide doors gave easy access to its rear seats. Again, this is chassis 611423

Chapter Eight

The SS Jaguars in Competition

Lyons was keen to encourage owners to take part in the various motor sport events of the day, and while not consistently sponsoring an official works team, he did support many entrants in road rallies by giving them access to the company's service department.

In 1932 five S.S.I cars had taken part in the RAC Rally with moderate success, and 1933 saw the first entries of S.S. cars in the Monte Carlo Rally, in which Prideaux Budge in an S.S.I Coupe came 58th after crashing during the rally. In that same year a works-supported team of three S.S.I Tourers was entered for the International Alpine Trial, and though two cars failed to finish, the remaining car did manage eighth in class, bracketed by two other S.S.I cars which were sixth and 11th in class. In the 1934 Alpine event, a team of three S.S.I Tourers finished complete, for a third place in class behind the Talbot and Adler teams which tied for first.

The S.S.I cars appeared in increasing numbers in rallies in 1934 and 1935, with improving results, which supported Lyons in his aim to develop a more competitive image for his cars. The S.S.I and S.S.II cars were also frequently successful in the *Concours d'Élégance* contests around the country, since the cars were distinctive and attractive, and much admired by all.

Before the war there were many events in which one could drive or display one's car, and many SS Jaguar owners were enthusiastic participants. The events ranged from international rallies such as the Monte Carlo and the Alpine held in Europe, through the essentially national RAC, Scottish, and Welsh Rallies in the UK, to many small local events often held by car clubs,

either for single makes of cars, or based on a particular area.

The big European events were renowned as being the toughest tests for both men and machines, the Monte Carlo as it was held in the middle of winter when weather and road conditions across most of Europe were usually atrocious, the Alpine as it was held on poorly surfaced, narrow, and twisting mountain roads, while in both events it was demanded that competitors achieve a minimum average speed.

The larger UK rallies were held over three or

J Willing receiving the trophy for Grand Prix d'Honneur and Concours de Confort in the 1938 Monte Carlo Rally.

four days and involved about 1000 miles (1600km) of fairly gentle motoring on public roads, until arrival in one seaside resort or another, followed by speed and driving control tests on special sections, and ending with the coachwork *Concours* competitions. Lyons liked these rallies since they gave considerable exposure of the cars to the general public, and showed to advantage their elegant looks coupled with their impressive performance. These events were also widely reported in the national motoring press, again to the advantage of the company.

The Monte Carlo Rally

This Rally was first run in 1911 and again in 1912, after which there was a break until 1924. The first S.S. car took part in 1933. The models covered in this book were all at some time entered in the Rally in increasing numbers and with increasing success, but none ever won the Rally outright, the best finish being by Irishman C Vard and co-driver A Young who in 1951 drove their 3½ litre Mark V Saloon to third place overall.

Despite not actually winning the Rally, these Jaguar cars were both competitive and elegant

Irishman Cecil Vard and his Mark V came third overall in the 1951 Monte Carlo Rally, the highest place ever achieved by a pushrod-engined Jaguar.

and attracted very able drivers and owners, thus laying the basis for the successes that the Mark VII and subsequent cars achieved in the 1950s.

In 1936 there was only one SS Jaguar entrant, driven by the Hon Brian Lewis, who finished ingloriously 70th out of 72 overall, but did pick up second place in the *Concours de Confort* with his 2½ litre SS Jaguar Saloon. From 1937 there was an increasing contingent of Jaguars each year, reaching six cars in 1939. When the 3½ litre became available, this quickly became the preferred model and JOH Willing used one of these cars in the 1938 Rally to win the main award in the *Concours de Confort*, a fine achievement for a normal production car costing only £445. He had also finished 42nd overall in the Rally itself. In 1939 the team of Harrop, Mangoletsi and Currie achieved the highest placing to date, with tenth overall in another 3½ litre Saloon, all the more meritorious as they had chosen to start from Athens and thus had to negotiate the Balkans, rated in those days as the most difficult route.

After the war, the Rally did not restart until 1949. The proposed 1948 Rally was called off due to the French Government's refusal to

supply the petrol. A paragraph on the problem in the *The Autocar* in December 1947 stated: "every year at this time the indefatigable M. Noghès lays his plans for reviving this classic event and every year as the time of the start approaches the Rally is cancelled and we have to possess our souls in patience, buoyed up by the hope that by next year things will have improved sufficiently to permit us to set off through snow and ice, riding in a strange device." Such hope and patience were finally rewarded in 1949 when the first post-war rally was held, and for this there were two Jaguars entered, with J Rockman's 3½ litre Mark IV Saloon coming 75th overall while the Posnard/Felix Jaguar did not finish.

From 1950 onwards participation by Jaguars in the Monte Carlo Rally increased year on year and results improved markedly. The 1950 Rally saw the first entry of the Mark V and this was to prove to be the most successful of the pushrod-engined cars in this event, though not in 1950 when even the highest placed entrant, Rockman, only managed 122nd overall.

In 1951 things continued to improve for Jaguar and this turned out to be the best year for the Mark V cars. In all there were eight entrants driving Mark V cars and a number of awards were picked up by them. Undoubtedly the best achievement however was by Vard and Young, who came in third overall in a 3½ litre Mark V, and also won the Barclay's Bank Silver Challenge Cup for the highest placed British car, and the Royal Scottish Automobile Club Cup for the best performance for a starter from Glasgow. Of the eight starters, seven finished, and after Vard's third place the next best placing were Waring and Wadham who came ninth, again a very creditable performance. This pair was awarded the Late Public Schools Challenge Trophy for the best placed ex-Public School pupil and came second in the *Concours de Confort* in the over 1500cc class.

This was the peak year for the pushrod cars in this Rally, since the XK-engined Mark VII which appeared in 1952 quickly became the car of choice for the Monte (the XK 120 could not take part as the organisers at this time did not allow open two-seater sports cars). In that year there were fifteen Jaguars entered, of which only two were Mark Vs, neither of which was well placed in the results.

By 1953 the event was totally dominated by

the Mark VII, with fifteen out of the seventeen Jaguar cars entered, but Cecil Vard, still in his Mark V, managed to come fifth overall and with it a share in the *Equipe* Team Challenge Cup awarded for the best-placed three cars of one make, the other two being the Mark VII cars of Appleyard who came second, and Bennett who was eighth overall.

In 1954 there was but one Mark V out of the twelve Jaguars entered, and in 1956 came Jaguar's first and only win in the Monte Carlo Rally, with the Mark VIIM of Ronnie Adams and Frank Biggar. The Jaguar company had by then concentrated its efforts on the Le Mans 24-hour race, gaining significant and very prestigious victories in the 1950s with the C- and D-type sports cars.

The International Alpine Trial and Rally

The International Alpine Trial, first held in August 1928, was a popular and successful event organised jointly by the automobile clubs of several countries, with a route often going through France, Switzerland, Italy, Austria, and Germany, sometimes even Yugoslavia. Some S.S. cars took part in 1933 and 1934, but there was no rally held in 1935. When the Alpine Trial was held again in 1936, there was only one SS Jaguar entry, which was a borrowed SS 100 driven by Tommy and Elsie Wisdom, chassis 18008 registered BWK 77 (of which more later). This single car however did extremely well, finishing second in the 2000–3000cc class, and gaining

Ian Appleyard took first place in the over-3000cc class in his SS 100 on the 1948 International Alpine Rally.

The Danish Mark V entry of Herrmann and Schnackenborg finished eleventh in Class One on the 1952 Tulip Rally.

one of 17 Glacier Cups which were awarded for individual performances as opposed to team performance. It earned a very complimentary write-up in *The Autocar*, which reported that "Wisdom's Jaguar SS 100, too, has shown that it is one of the fastest sports cars on the market today, at any rate where widely different conditions are encountered".

This was the eighth and last in the pre-war series of International Alpine Trials. With the annexation of Austria to Germany in 1938, the last two-pre-war events were simply national German events, but meanwhile the *Automobile Club de Marseille et Provence* in France had taken up the challenge of hosting its version of the Alpine Rally, which it had done in a modest way since 1932 as the *Rallye des Alpes Françaises*, and this was to become the famous International Alpine Rally in post-war years. An SS Jaguar is recorded as having taken part in the last French pre-war event in 1939. The first post-war rally was held in 1946, and it attracted a few British entries. In 1947 there was a stronger British presence, including the first Sunbeam-Talbots to be entered in a major European rally, but also Ian Appleyard, the 23-year old son of the Jaguar distributor in Leeds, who entered a secondhand nine-year-old SS 100 3½ litre (chassis 39029, registered EXT 207) with co-driver Peter Musgrave. They were unfortunate to be held up when a bald tyre burst, but still managed to finish third in the over 3000cc class, and eighth overall.

There was only one more year, 1948, in which the pushrod Jaguar cars took part. This

time Appleyard was again the only Jaguar entrant, now in chassis 49010, registered LNW 100, built as a 2½ litre 1938 model but unsold and later upgraded with a 3½ litre engine (see chapter 4), with Dr Richard Weatherhead as co-driver. He comprehensively swept the board, being first in the general classification for the over three litre class, and also picking up his first *Coupe des Alpes*, the *Coupe de la Ville de Marseille*, and the *Coupe du Syndicat* for the best-timed climb of the Col d'Izoard, which was a tremendous achievement. Ian Appleyard did go on to win the Alpine outright for the first time and to collect more Alpine cups, including a rare gold cup for three cups in a row, but that was in his even more famous XK 120, NUB 120.

The Tulip Rally

After the war, in 1949, the Dutch set up The Netherlands Tulip Rally which was similar in format to the Monte Carlo and rapidly attracted a good number of entrants. There were a number of starting points in various countries in Europe, including London, and around 2000 miles (3200km) of driving around Europe before finishing in the Netherlands at Noordwijk, near the Zandvoort race track where the concluding speed trials were held. There was some concern expressed at that time by the organisers that "we are in great difficulties regarding foreign currency for the Dutch competitors, so that we do not yet know how many of them will be in a position to compete". There were however 163 in all of which 19 were from Britain, two of whom were driving Jaguars, with Ian Appleyard and Stuart in the SS 100, and F Edwards probably in a Mark IV. Appleyard and Stuart were second overall, having lost first place to Ken Wharton's Ford Anglia for stopping just short of the line in the final test, but were at least first in class 1.

In 1950 the Rally was run in appalling weather conditions and a good number of the 302 starters retired or failed to make the checkpoints in time. There were five Jaguars entered, four of which were probably Mark Vs, and three of these managed to finish, the best placed being the Dutch pair of Hora Siccama and Bloem, who came 20th in their class, followed by Barslay at 22nd in class.

By 1951 the XK 120 and the Mark VII, both with the twin-cam XK engine, had largely taken over from the pushrod Mark V in competitive events. The success of the Tulip Rally continued with an entry of 303 cars. In all there were four-teen Jaguars with eight of them identified as XK 120s, two as Mark V, one as an SS, probably an SS 100, and three listed only as Jaguar with no indication of the model. Appleyard won this event, but this time in his XK 120. One of the unidentified cars, driven by Barslay and Cookson, is stated as being a Mark V in a report on the rally in *The Autocar*, leaving the remaining two as being probably Mark Vs as well, so I have included these in the list in the appendix for completeness. Apart from the winner, the most successful Jaguar was Ainsworth and Beckett at 15th overall and ninth in Class 1. The Danish Mark V entry of Hermann and Schnackenborg was 30th in Class 1. Both entered again in 1952, when Ainsworth did not finish, but the Danish team finished 98th overall and 11th in class. These were probably the last Mark V entries in the Tulip rally.

The RAC Rally

The RAC Rally was the premier UK event before the war and was arguably the most popular rally with SS Jaguar owners. Pre-war from 1936 there were each year at least fourteen SS Jaguar entries, and on two occasions there were works or at least works-supported teams participating. It was a particularly popular event with SS 100 drivers, who did consistently well in the RAC. Each year the Rally finished at a different seaside resort, which no doubt spread the burden of organising, but also added to the interest for the participants and spectators alike.

In the 1936 Torquay Rally there were four-teen S.S. and SS Jaguar entries, one of which was the first SS 100 made, a 2½ litre car driven by Lewis, who had continued his close connec-tion with the company. The rest of the cars were a mixture of the previous year's S.S.I cars and the new SS Jaguars.

For the 1937 Hastings Rally there were fifteen entries, of which five were now SS 100 cars. Three of these cars made up the works team, driven by Wisdom, Lewis, and Rankin/Jacobs, and they did very well, finishing second, 25th, and fourth respectively to gain the Manufacturers' Team Prize. The individual winner of the Rally was however Harrop in his non-works SS 100, who also took the Buxton Starting Control Prize.

Success continued at the 1938 Blackpool Rally, in which out of 22 SS Jaguar entered thir-

B Hickman in his 2½ litre SS Jaguar Saloon during the 1936 RAC Rally.

teen were SS 100 cars. By now the 3½ litre engine was available in the SS 100 and five of the entries had the larger engine. Once again Harrop came out overall winner, this time in a 3½ litre SS 100, with Newsome and Bradley in similar cars coming fourth and fifth respectively.

There was one more Rally before the war in 1939, to Brighton, in which 23 SS Jaguars took part, of which ten were SS 100 cars, only two of these having the 2½ litre engine. There was a works team in this rally and all three cars had been made at the same time, having chassis numbers 39110, 39111 and 39112, and also

Jacob, Rankin, Lewis and Wisdom being congratulated by Lyons (second from right) for winning first place in the Manufacturers' Team Prize on the 1937 RAC Rally.

Misses Watson and Streather drove SS 100s in the 1939 RAC Rally. Miss Watson finished 11th out of 35 in that class, while Miss Streather retired.

J Harrop driving to victory in Group Five for open cars over 15hp in his 3½ litre SS 100 on the 1938 RAC Rally.

The Works Team of Harrop, Newsome and Wisdom and their 3½ litre SS 100s on the 1939 RAC Rally.

sequential Coventry registration marks EHP 201, 202 and 203. This time Harrop had been enlisted into the works team together with Newsome and Wisdom, and they had some success by finishing sixth, second and 22nd respectively, though the Manufacturers' Team prize was won by the Frazer-Nash BMW team, no doubt to the great chagrin of Lyons as the BMW 328 model was the arch-rival for the SS 100. There were other awards, with second place for the SS Club Team of Gordon in ninth place, Gibson in fourth, and Mann in seventh, and for two other SS Jaguar cars which came second in their classes in the Coachwork Competition. In this rally, Mrs Greta Lyons joined Mrs Wisdom in a 3½ litre saloon, chassis 30935 registered EDU 615.

After this rally no more were held until after the war in 1951, and by then the Mark V was the preferred car, though it was soon to be overtaken by the Mark VII with the XK engine, and the XK 120 itself. There were ten Mark Vs out of fourteen pushrod engined entries as well as thirty-six XK-engined cars in 1951, but there were no particular successes for any of the Jaguars, whether with OHV or with twin-cam engines. This was effectively the last year in which the pushrod-engined cars took part in the RAC Rally.

The Scottish Rally

The Royal Scottish Automobile Club ran its Scottish Rally around the end of May each year, attracting some 180 entries in 1936. The Rallies

T Bridgewater's 3½ litre DHC took first place in his coachwork class at the 1939 RAC Rally.

A signed photo of Norman Jackman driving his 1937 2½ litre SS Jaguar Saloon on the 1937 Scottish Rally.

SPLENDID SPORT.
SS ING IN
"SCOTTISH" SUCCESSFULLY
May 18th 1937   SINCERELY YOURS   Norman Jackman

The 1937 Scottish Rally. This was one of the three SS Car Club teams entered, here with B Matthews, G Matthews, E Jacobs, R Hunnan and W Vaughan

were first run in 1932, so 1936 was the fifth time it had been held. There were ten entrants that year driving a mixture of S.S.I, S.S.II and SS Jaguar cars, including two SS 90s and one SS Jaguar 100. The newer overhead-valve SS Jaguar cars were the most competitive of these cars and took three of the first six places, the best finisher being C Bembridge who came in third in his 2½ litre SS Jaguar Saloon. In all nine of the cars were placed, with only one non-finisher.

The 1937 Rally was named the Coronation Rally in honour of King George VI's accession to the throne. It attracted 180 entries in total including 23 SS Jaguars, notable for the high number of SS 100 cars and also for the high proportion of lady drivers, who made up six of the entries. There were thirteen 2½ litre SS 100 cars, five of which finished in the top ten in the class for open cars over 2200cc. Miss Jessie Sleigh, who came third in that class, put up the best performance for the SS 100, winning her the Ladies' Cup for the Rally. The seven 2½ litre Saloons also did well with HF Dixon finishing third and Norman Jackman eighth in the closed car class. There were four SS Car Club Teams, made up of mostly SS 100 cars with three cars per team, no doubt chasing the cup for the winning Team in the Rally, whilst also competing as individuals for the other honours. The placings for the Car Club teams have not been recorded but the winner is known to have been the Yorkshire Sports Car Club.

The 1938 Rally was called the Empire Exhibition Rally after the Empire Exhibition, which was held at the Bellahouston Park in Glasgow from May to December of that year. The overall number of entries had swelled to 208, and the SS Jaguar entries were maintained at a high level with 22 cars. There were 13 SS 100 cars, ten of which were the new 3½ litre cars showing their improved performance against the 2½ litre model, which was still being made though in smaller numbers than before. There were four cars with the recently introduced 1½ litre OHV engine, three Saloons and one DHC, together with four of the 2½ litre Saloons and one of the new 3½ litre DHC cars. The SS 100 cars were generally well placed, with three cars in the top ten of the open class, Bernard Matthews was the best placed at second in his 2½ litre SS100, beating the larger number of 3½ litre entries. Those competing in the closed car categories did less well, with only William Crawford in a 1½ litre saloon finishing in the first ten, in his case sixth out of 43 in the class. Four of the cars were non-starters.

In 1939 the threat of war affected the total number of entrants, which was down to 138, a drop of around 30 per cent; the SS Jaguar entrants fell by half to 11 in total. Those entered were SS 100s except for a single 2½ litre saloon driven by John McCubbin. Despite or maybe because of the reduced number of entrants, the top three SS 100 cars finished second, fourth, and sixth out of 20 in the class, with a 2½ litre version, this time driven by J Montgomery, again beating the larger-engined SS 100 cars. This eighth Scottish Rally was to be the last before the war, and also the last that the pushrod Jaguar cars would compete in, ending four years of considerable enjoyment and achievements for the drivers of the SS Jaguars.

The Welsh Rally

This Rally was run by the South Wales Automobile Club, starting with 1000 miles (1600km) on Welsh roads, each year ending up in Cardiff, where there was a special test section and the Concours on the last day.

In 1936 there was a total of 90 entrants, of which seven were SS Jaguars, but only 76 actually started and six cars failed to finish. The Welsh roads were tortuous and narrow, making it a testing experience with little time for sleep and meals. Despite this the SS Jaguar cars were well placed, with Hand and Jacob coming first and second in the class for closed cars over 16hp, and Sandland who came first in the class for closed cars under 16hp, and also first in the coachwork competition in the £251 to £350 four-door closed car category.

The 1000-mile section of the Rally had involved night driving, but this was modified for the 1937 event by reducing this to 500 miles over two days. This made the Rally more attractive for the competitors and the spectators and consequently the number of entrants overall rose to 118, thirteen of which were SS Jaguars. There was a works team of SS 100 cars driven by E Rankin, E Jacob and G Matthews, and there were entries of a further four SS 100s and six Saloons. The 2½ litre SS100 driven by Jacob was outstanding in the competition and won the Premier Award, in effect the outright winner, and it also won the Eliminating Prize for the best performance in the closing tests of the rally. Jacob was also a member of both the SS Jaguar Manufacturer's Team and the SS Car Club Team, which came first in their respective categories. *The Autocar* described Jacob's performance in the eliminating tests in the following words: "Jacob on the SS 100 electrified the crowd as he skidded into the bays with locked wheels and screaming tyres, reversed out with the front wheels sliding and shot off to the next box with rear wheels spinning, to make fastest time of the day, 1 min 3.5 sec". This was a very impressive performance which can be best gauged by comparison with Rankin's and Matthews' fast times of around 1 min 12 sec each. To complement these driving awards, Hetherington in another SS 100 won the coachwork competition in the £351 to £500 open car class.

1938 saw yet another increase in the number of entrants to 151. The contingent of SS Jaguar cars had risen to seventeen, eleven of which

The 1937 Welsh Rally's winning works team of Jacobs, Rankin and G Matthews, here with Mrs Hetherington's car for the photo shoot. The team also won the Team Club prize for the SS Car Club.

were SS 100s, five being the new 3½ litre, introduced that year. The Rally retained the same format as in the previous year and was held in unusually dry weather. This made the eliminating tests the deciding factor for the Rally and there was no Premier Award that year, each class instead having its own declared winner. In the open class over 15hp the two SS 100 cars of Mrs Hetherington and Miss Streather came first and second, and Mrs Hetherington also picked up the Supporters Prize. Bryden in his 1½ litre DHC won the under 15hp drophead coupé Coachwork prize.

The 1939 Rally was held at the end of July and the Government was by then issuing warnings about petrol rationing to private motorists, who would receive ration books in the event of war. The impending war reduced the entries but there were still 118 cars, of which nine were SS 100s and three were closed cars. Three SS Jaguars were non-starters and one DHC retired with a snapped half-shaft. It poured with rain all through the rally but this did not dampen the spirits of the competitors, who reportedly remained cheerful throughout.

With only 12 SS Jaguars competing the results were pretty modest compared with previous years. Norton in his 3½ litre SS 100 won the over 15hp open car class and Miss Watson, also in an SS 100, won the Ladies' Prize for open cars. There were two Starting Point Prizes for Miss Watson and A Gordon, who also won the Welsh Rally Supporters Prize. There were no successes

for the SS Jaguars in the coachwork competitions. The 1939 Welsh Rally was the last one in the series as the event was not re-introduced after the war.

SS Car Club Rallies

Apart from the international and national events, there was a plethora of local rallies and trials held at weekends. There were also car club events, either for a single make or put on by local area clubs taking all makes, and for the SS Jaguar owners in particular there was the very active company-sponsored SS Car Club.

The SS Car Club was founded in 1936, and after the treasurer had absconded with the funds at the first rally held in Blackpool, leaving an unhappy Lyons to foot the hotel bill, it was essentially run by Ernest Rankin of the SS Company. Each year a number of rallies, trials, races and speed events were held, and for example in a fifteen-month period from July 1937 the following events had been run or at least planned:

July 1937	Kentish Trial – 17 entries	
Sept 1937	Scottish Trial – held to attract Scottish owners but out of 21 entrants only three came from Scotland	
Nov 1937	Bournemouth Trial – 16 entries	
Feb 1938	Works Visit and Speed Trials - held on company premises with 32 entries	

April 1938   Buxton Trial – 21 entries
May 1938   Donington Race Meeting –
             36 entries
June 1938   Scarborough Rally – 60 entries
Sept 1938   Southern Rally at Ramsgate –
             planned but not run due to lack
             of support

This was a very full season and most events were well supported and no doubt helped a good deal in promoting the sales of the company's cars. All the events ended with a dinner dance, and hotel accommodation was available for those who needed it. At the dinners there were the customary award ceremonies at which prizes and hallmarked silver trophies were presented.

Races and Hill Climbs

In these other categories of motor sport the Saloon and DHC models did not figure, but the SS 100 occasionally did, although Lyons was mindful of the fact that it was a road-going sports car and not a racing car, so he always preferred to see the cars entered in rallies, and is even said to have personally persuaded a would-be entrant of an SS 100 in the 1938 Tourist Trophy race to withdraw. The handling characteristics of the SS 100 were dictated by its chassis design, old-fashioned by the standards of the late 1930s, especially when compared with the rival BMW 328; the SS 100 gained a reputation for being skittish at high speed. Of the race tracks in Britain before the war, the SS 100 was happiest on the new road circuit at Donington Park, and had its moments at Brooklands, but did not shine on the short and twisty Crystal Palace circuit.

Another notable category of competitive events was the hill climb, which consisted of a timed run up a winding track, and these were especially suitable for the SS 100 with its high power-to-weight ratios and excellent acceleration. In this category, Shelsley Walsh was the most important venue, in use since 1905, but there were other venues such as Prescott, which hosted its first hill climb in 1938.

Of the many SS 100 cars used in competition, the most famous was 18008 registered BWK 77, also known from its chassis number as "old number 8", which Wisdom had used in the Alpine Trial of 1936. It is often described as the factory development car, and undoubtedly

Walter Hassan was much involved in the development of the engine, although the records suggest it was owned by the Coventry Jaguar distributor SH "Sammy" Newsome. Newsome and Wisdom both used the car, with Newsome usually doing the hill climbs and Wisdom the track racing. Newsome was fastest in class at Shelsley at several meetings and in June 1939 climbed in less than 43 sec. Wisdom took the car to Brooklands on a number of occasions and won the Long Handicap race at the BARC meeting in October 1937 at an average speed of nearly 112mph (180km/h), with a fastest lap of 118mph (190km/h). BWK 77 was much developed over its active career; in 1937 it was fitted with a prototype 3½ litre engine and with a compression ratio of 12.5:1 (or even higher) was said to develop 160bhp on methanol-based racing fuel, while even more power was extracted in post-war years. For racing and hill climbs, it usually ran stripped, minus wings and lamps. At a final pre-war outing at Brooklands, Wisdom lapped at 125mph (201km/h) in practice, but, alas, the crankshaft broke before the race itself. Newsome went back to Shelsley Walsh in 1946 but could not better his pre-war time; that was only improved on in the 1970s in the hands of a later owner of the car, David Barber. Elsie Wisdom won the Ladies' Class in the 1947 Bouley Bay hill climb in Jersey with the car, but it then passed into different ownership and for some time disappeared from sight, until re-discovered and restored in the late 1960s.

Finally, I should mention the SS Car Club event at Donington Park in May 1938 where a "trade race" was held, with William Lyons, William Heynes, and Sammy Newsome in three identical SS 100 cars; Lyons' car was the company press car and demonstrator, DHP 734, a 3½ litre model, chassis 39053. His performance was typical of him as an ambitious and determined go-getter: he twice started too early and had to be pulled back to the starting line, and when finally the race got under way he took the lead and held it to the end, with Newsome second and Heynes third. Lyons also put in the fastest lap of the day, quicker than any of the other SS 100s, some of which were race-prepared. As has often been stated, it must be some sort of a record for a driver to only enter one motor race, win it, and then never race again!

For lists of entrants and placings for each rally see Appendix 4.

Chapter Nine

Car Identification and Tool Kits

Identification Numbers

From the very early days of the motor industry, car manufacturers identified their individual cars with unique numbers allocated mostly to the chassis, and usually also to the engines. This was at first done for the maker's own convenience, and most manufacturers seemingly took some pride in being able to attach a prominent brass plate with their name or logo and the relevant number or numbers. In Britain vehicle registration was introduced with the Motor Car Act of 1903, but there was as yet no statutory requirement for registration authorities to record chassis and engine numbers. This was only introduced with the 1920 act, when these numbers had to be recorded both on the newly-introduced Log Book issued to the owner, and by the authorities.

When the Swallow Coachbuilding Company began to make S.S. cars in 1931, they recorded the chassis and engine numbers, and usually also the body numbers; they were after all coachbuilders. However, all S.S. cars came from the Standard Motor Company in chassis form, therefore the chassis and engine numbers were allocated by Standard, and the ID or commission plate with the chassis number was often attached to the engine. In 1935, SS Cars Limited began to build its own chassis, and from now on introduced its own design of commission plate, usually attached to the bulkhead behind the engine, clearly stamped with chassis, engine and body numbers. SS Jaguar cars were now issued with five-figure chassis numbers of the company's own devising, although the engine numbers continued to follow the system estab-

lished by the Standard Company. The following is a run-down of what ID marks and numbers there actually were, where they were located, and what form they took.

1936 and 1937 Models

Chassis number: There were no numbers actually stamped on the chassis on either of the two Saloon models made during this period. The Tourer and the SS 100 did however have their chassis numbers stamped in fairly faint numbers near the sliding trunnion housing on the offside vertical face of the chassis. On the SS 100 the number was stamped at the rear of the housing and on the Tourer just forward of it. Since it was only lightly stamped, the chassis number was easily hidden by over-painting or even lost altogether during the process of cleaning off rust, so the numbers are often invisible or missing nowadays.

SS 100 chassis number stamped on the offside chassis.

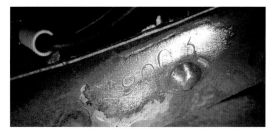

Chassis number stamped faintly on the chassis of a 1936 Tourer.

A 1936 2½ litre engine with the number stamped on the offside block.

Commission and body number plates of a 1936 1½ litre Saloon, etched with basic details about the car.

Engine number: The 1936 engines had an identifying number stamped directly onto the offside of the block, at the top rear of the engine by the bulkhead.

The SS 100 had an additional stamping of "SS 100" in larger letters alongside the engine number, possibly to identify these engines at the Standard factory as being destined for fitting into SS 100 cars. The only likely difference however between the SS 100 engines and those for the other cars was that they would have been fitted with the special front and rear engine mountings required for the SS 100 before leaving the Standard factory. It is unlikely that the engines designated for the SS 100 cars had been specially tested and selected by Standard.

On the slightly different 1937 cylinder block, the engine number was stamped on a raised boss in the same location as the engine number on the 1936 engine.

Commission plates: The first type of a more informative brass commission plate was introduced for the 1936 model cars. The plates were etched with the basic details of the engine and the dimensions of the cars. The chassis, engine and body numbers for the particular car were stamped on the plate, which was then riveted to the vertical face of the bulkhead on the offside. The plates were made of soft brass and the etched raised letters were small, so nowadays on many of the original plates the lettering has become indistinct due to frequent cleaning and polishing by proud owners.

Commission and body number plates seen on a 1937 2½ litre Saloon.

Engine number stamped on the cylinder block of a 1936 SS 100.

The 1937 engine number was now stamped on a raised boss on the engine, but in the same location as 1936 models.

The commission plate of a 1937 1½ litre Saloon, showing the 9ft 0in wheelbase and 4ft 0in track.

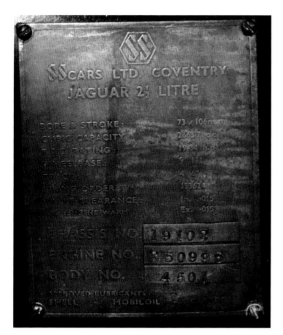

Tourer commissioning plate from 1937. The same basic blank plates were used throughout the 2½ litre range.

The same basic blank plates were used for the 2½ litre Saloon, Tourer, and the shorter wheelbase SS 100, so the wheelbase given on the plate for the SS 100 was incorrect since it was in fact 8ft 8in against 9ft 11in of the other two models on which the plate was used. The track at 4ft 6in was however the same for all three models. The 1½ litre cars had their own plates, with the 9ft 0in wheelbase and 4ft 0in track.

For the body number, the company continued the practice of riveting a small rectangular aluminium plate with large raised reverse-embossed numbers. This was moved from the nearside where it had been on the earlier S.S.I and S.S.II models, to a position on the offside of the bulkhead, above the new commission plate.

1938, 1939, and 1940 Models

Chassis number: The Saloon and Drophead cars continued without the chassis number stamped on the frame, though the Instruction Book states that the chassis number was "given under the bonnet at offside of engine". This however refers to the commission plate, which was in this position on the car. Occasionally, when a car has been stripped for restoration or repair, the chassis number is found stamped or written on some of the wooden parts of the body, but as these were hidden from sight when assembled, they were probably put on as an assembly aid by the factory. As the Tourer was no longer being made, the only model to have the chassis number stamped on the chassis was the SS 100, in the same position as before.

Engine number: The engines continued to have the raised boss cast on the block on the offside just by the bulkhead, on which the engine numbers were stamped. As before, the SS 100 engines carried the additional identification of SS 100, stamped above the engine number boss.

The engine numbers were now given letter prefixes, K, L, and M depending on the engine size, with KA and KB on later 1½ litre cars. They also had a suffix letter E stamped on the block, but the E only appears sporadically in the factory ledgers, even though present on the cylinder block and on the commission plate. The E was therefore probably not an important part of the engine number as far as Jaguar was concerned, but was a legacy from Standard who identified engines with the E suffix, since Standard from the late 1930s onwards typically used the same letter prefixes for chassis ("commission") numbers and engine numbers on any model.

Commission plates: For the 1938 model cars these were essentially the same as used on the earlier models, but some of the information etched on the blank plate had been updated for the new all-steel bodied cars, and also for the larger OHV engine of the 1½ litre car.

The plates for two six-cylinder cars had the individual details of the two engine sizes. They had an increased wheelbase, 1in longer at 10ft 0in exactly, and the track widened by 2in to 4ft

A 1939 engine number on a raised boss cast onto the offside of the cylinder block.

A 1940 Saloon commission plate, showing the new winged logo.

8in. Since the plates for these cars were common to all six-cylinder models, they produced an even wider disparity for the SS 100 cars between the dimensions as quoted on the plate and as found on the cars, since SS 100 chassis dimensions remained unchanged, so both wheelbase and track dimensions were now incorrect on the plate.

The 1½ litre cars had also grown a little in size with the wheelbase increased from 9ft 0in to 9ft 4.5in which was shown on the plate, and the track which had been 4ft 0in was now 4ft 4in at the front and 4ft 7in at the rear. The commission plate however only gave the single dimension of 4ft 7in for the rear track.

About May 1939 the format of the plate was changed, as the simple hexagon with the SS letters at the top of the plate was replaced by a winged badge with a central hexagon containing the SS letters, mimicking the badge on the radiator. No doubt the company introduced this change progressively, so it is unlikely that the introduction date was the same for the three models.

The body number plate was the same in style as before, but now with an S prefix on both the all-steel Saloon and the new Drophead, though the commission plate did not show the prefix. The factory ledger only gives the S prefix for the first two cars made, and then just the number with no prefix for the rest of the cars. When the

number series reached 8500 in October 1938, an A prefix was introduced for the Saloons in the ledger, but again only for the first 40 cars and the prefix was then omitted for subsequent cars; the A prefix body numbers seem to range from 1 to 1500, and then from 3501 to 4400, and were used at least to March 1939. It then appears that Saloon body numbers between March and July 1939 had a D prefix, with numbers between 8501 and 9350. The Dropheads continued with their original body number series through the 1940 model year. For the 1940 Saloon models with their revised bodies, a B prefix was introduced for the body numbers which started all over again from 1, and the B prefix was also used on the post-war Mark IV saloons. The body number prefix letters appeared on the commission plate. The body number plate was repositioned to just above the commission plate.

The tables 10.2, 10.2 and 10.3 opposite and overleaf give a breakdown of the numbers used. The years referred to in these tables are model years, i.e. "1937" is broadly speaking the period from August 1936 to July 1937, and so on.

Mark IV

Chassis number: It was only on the post-war cars that the chassis number was first regularly stamped on the chassis. The Instruction Book repeats the information from the pre-war book that the chassis number was "given under the bonnet at offside of engine". In fact the chassis number not only appeared on the commission plate as before, but was now also stamped on the vertical face of the nearside dumb-iron, though since the surface there was not very smooth, the stampings were very light and faint. It was however a step forward for the company in establishing some sort of permanent and visible chassis numbering on the chassis itself, rather than it just appearing on the removable commission plate. The post-war Jaguars had six-figure chassis numbers, at first commencing with 4, 5, or 6, for the 1½ litre, 2½ litre, and 3½ litre models respectively.

Engine number: The location and style of the stamping for the engine number was the same as used for the pre-war cars, but now with KB, P, and S prefixes for the three engine sizes; on the special six-cylinder engines adapted for left-hand drive cars, it became PL and SL. With Jaguar now making the larger engines, there was no need for the E suffix to the engine

TABLE 10.1 – PRE-WAR CHASSIS NUMBERS

	Chs no.s from	In	Chs no.s to	In
1½ litre sv sal 1936	20001	Feb 1936	20700	Jul 1936
1½ litre sv sal 1937	20701	Aug 1936	22194	Jul 1937
1½ litre sv sal "1938"	22195	Oct 1937	22250	Nov 1937
1½ litre sal 1938	50001	Oct 1937/Jan 1938	50600	Jul 1938
1½ litre sal 1939	50601	Aug 1938	53754	Jun 1939
1½ litre DHC 1938	56001	Mar 1938	56031 (plus two higher numbers)	Jul 1938
1½ litre DHC 1939	56032	Jul 1938	56643	Jun 1939
1½ litre sal and DHC 1940	70001	Jul 1939	70688	Jul 1940
2½ litre sal 1936	10001	Oct 1935	11449	Jul 1936
2½ litre sal 1937	11450	Aug 1936	13445	Jul 1937
2½ litre tourer 1936	10003; then 19002 on	May 1936	19060	Jul 1936
2½ litre tourer 1937	19061	Aug 1936	19105	Jul 1937
2½ litre sal 1938	40001	Nov-Dec 1937	40669	Jul 1938
2½ litre sal 1939	40670	Aug 1938	41450	Jun 1939
2½ litre DHC 1938	46001	1 car in Oct 1937; then from Apr 1938	46061 except 10 no.s	Jun 1938
2½ litre DHC 1939	46062 and 10 lower no.s	Jun 1938	46273	Jun 1939
2½ litre sal and DHC 1940	80001	Jul 1939	80135	Jul 1940
3½ litre sal 1938	30001	Oct 1937	30545	Jul 1938
3½ litre sal 1939	30546	Aug 1938	31003	Jun 1939
3½ litre DHC 1938	36001	Mar 1938	36078 except 8 no.s	Jun 1938
3½ litre DHC 1939	36079 and 8 lower no.s	Jun 1938	36238	Jun 1939
3½ litre sal and DHC 1940	90001	Jul 1939	90068	Sep 1939
SS 100 2½ litre 1936-37	18001	Oct 1935/Apr 1936	18126	Aug 1937
SS 100 3½ litre 1938-39	39001	Oct 1937	39118	Jul 1939
SS 100 2½ litre 1938-40	49001	Oct 1937	49065	Sep 1939

TABLE 10.2 – PRE-WAR ENGINE NUMBERS

	Eng no.s from	In	Eng no.s to	In
1½ litre side-valve 1936	27058	Feb 1936	approx. 35000 *	Jun 1936
1½ litre side-valve 1937	approx. 55000	Jun 1936	60682 *	Nov 1937
1½ litre OHV 1938	K 3	Oct 1937/Jan 1938	K 1200	Sep 1938
1½ litre OHV 1939	KA 1	Sep 1938	KA 3500	Aug 1939
1½ litre OHV 1940	KB 1	Aug 1939	KB 401	Jul 1940
2½ litre 1936-37	249501	Oct 1935	253183	Jul 1937
2½ litre 1938-40	L 1	Oct 1937	L 1996	Jul 1940
3½ litre 1938-40	M 1	Oct 1937	M 1466	Sep 1939

* The spread in these engine number series must be because the same engines were used in Standard Twelve cars, however from around 59350 virtually all numbers seem to be issued to SS Jaguars.

SS 100 engines had engine numbers in the normal series for 2½ and 3½ litre engines.

TABLE 10.3 – PRE-WAR BODY NUMBERS

	Body no.s from	In	Body no.s to	In
1½ saloon 1936	0002	Feb 1936	0701	Jul 1936
1½ saloon 1937	0702	Aug 1936	0999	Nov 1936
1½ saloon 1937-38	3000	Nov 1936	4250	Nov 1937
2½ saloon 1936	9001	Oct 1935	9999	Apr 1936
2½ saloon 1936-37	1000	Apr 1936	2999	Apr 1937
2½ saloon 1937	5000	Apr 1937	5438	Jun 1937
2½ tourers 1936-37	4401	May 1936	4504	Jul 1937
SS 100 all years	4724	Oct 1935	5039	Sep 1939
All saloons 1938	5501	Nov 1937	7350	Jul 1938
All saloons 1939	7301	Aug 1938	8500	Oct 1938
All saloons 1939	A 0001	Oct 1938	A 1500	Jan 1939
All saloons 1939	A 3501	Jan 1939	A 4400	Mar 1939
All saloons 1939	D 8501	Mar 1939	D 9350	Jul 1939
All saloons 1940	B 1	Jul 1939	approx. B 800	Jul 1940
DHC 1937-39	1501	Oct 1937	2000	Sep 1938
DHC 1939-40	2251	Sep 1938	2950	Aug 1939

A Mark IV chassis number, now stamped on the vertical face of the nearside dumb-iron.

Post-war commission plate with new Jaguar logo – similar to previous versions, and still found on the same place on the bulkhead.

numbers of these and it was dropped, but it was retained on the Standard-made four-cylinder engine, appearing on the engine block and on the commission plate.

Commission plates: The plates were similar in design and content to the pre-war ones and were fixed to the same place on the bulkhead. The plate itself now had a changed header, with the SS Cars Ltd, Coventry lettering replaced with the name Jaguar in a lozenge-shaped surround, which was the logo adopted by Jaguar for many future cars, and could be seen on hub caps and radiator badges.

As well as the commission plate, the cars now had a separate additional long narrow rectangular brass plate riveted below it, on which the gearbox number was stamped. The gearbox number however only appeared in the ledgers towards the end of the production of the Mark IV, so it is of little practical use for today's owners. Also introduced for these cars was a brass plate the same size as the commission plate and fitted next to it, showing the recommended lubricants for the engine, gearbox, rear axle and steering.

The body number was embossed on a narrow rectangular aluminium plate riveted to the bulkhead on the nearside. The Saloon prefix was changed from B to D when the numbers reached 9999, and the Drophead had a C prefix.

There are relatively few Mark IV cars which have the gearbox numbers recorded in the ledgers, but most six-cylinder cars appear to have had SH gearboxes, with the JH type gearbox coming in at the end of production, in December 1948 to February 1949. The 1½ litre cars with their Standard-made gearboxes may have had gearbox numbers prefixed with KB, as were their engine numbers.

TABLE 10.4 – MARK IV CHASSIS NUMBERS

	Chs no.s from	In	Chs no.s to	In
1½ litre sal RHD	410001	Sep 1945	415450	Feb 1949
1½ litre sal LHD	430001	Aug 1947	430311	Dec 1948 (only 2 cars made after Aug 1948)
2½ litre sal RHD	510001	Jan 1946	511682	Feb 1949
2½ litre DHC RHD	517001	Mar 1948	517073	Nov 1948 (only 3 cars made after Aug 1948)
2½ litre sal LHD	530001	Sep 1947	530075	Nov 1948
2½ litre DHC LHD	537001	Mar 1948	537031	Jul 1948
3½ litre sal RHD	610001	Jan 1946	613606	Feb 1949
3½ litre DHC RHD	617001	Feb 1948	617184	Sep 1948
3½ litre sal LHD	630001	Sep 1947	630254	Dec 1948 (only 1 car made after Aug 1948)
3½ litre DHC LHD	637001	Dec 1947	637376	Jul 1948

TABLE 10.5 – MARK IV ENGINE NUMBERS

	Eng no.s from	In	Eng no.s to	In
1½ litre	KB 1001 E	Sep 1945	KB 7202 E	Feb 1949
2½ litre	P 18	Feb 1946	P 1899	Feb 1949
3½ litre	S 26	Mar 1946	S 4455	Feb 1949

TABLE 10.6 – MARK IV BODY NUMBERS

	Body no.s from	In	Body no.s to	In
Saloons	B 1001	Sep 1945	B 9999	Jun 1948
Saloons	D 0001	Jun 1948	D 2313	Feb 1949
Saloons, CKD	PP 1001	Dec 1947	PP 1058	Aug 1948
Drophead Coupes	C 1001	Dec 1947	C 1551	Aug 1948
Drophead Coupes, CKD	DH 1001	May 1948	DH 1049	Jul 1948

The first 17 2½ litre cars had engines with prefix L, and the first 25 3½ litre cars had engine with prefix M, which may have been pre-war engines held in stock. Left-hand drive cars had engine prefixes PL and SL, with numbers in the same number series as engines for right-hand drive cars.

Some saloon CKD body numbers with prefix PP are duplicated, some have EPP prefixes in the ledgers, and some cars were assembled with different bodies from those recorded by Jaguar.

Mark V

Chassis number: The Operating and Maintenance Handbook for the Mark V states that the chassis number was "stamped on chassis frame side member at left hand front jack socket and three feet (0.9 metres) to rear of this point". This suggests that the chassis number was stamped in two positions, but in practice not many of the cars had the number in both locations. The early cars had the number stamped on the front left-hand chassis side member, and some then had this and an additional stamping on the top face of the bracket welded to the chassis midway along the engine. On the later cars, only this welded bracket was stamped. There are no hard and fast dates that I have been able to find for the changes. The bracket on which the chassis number was stamped was for mounting the brake master cylinder of LHD cars, and had the advantage that for the first time the chassis

A Mark V chassis number stamped on the left-hand-side chassis front extension.

The Mark V's chassis number was also stamped on a bracket welded to the left-hand-side chassis member.

An early Mark V with old-style commission plate and separate lubrication plate.

A later Mark V single larger brass plate, displaying ID and lubrication details.

litre, and T and later Z for the 3½ litre engines.

Commission plates: The plates on the early Mark V cars were of etched brass in the same style as on the Mark IV, and showed the various dimensions of the engine, wheelbase, and track. The plate was complemented by a similar looking recommended lubricant plate alongside, and a long narrow etched brass plate below carrying the gearbox number.

At some time towards the end of 1949, the style of the commission and lubricant plates were changed. They were merged into a single nickel-plated brass plate about 108mm by 165mm (4¼in by 6½ in) with the recommended lubricants listed below the stamped numbers of chassis, engine, body, and gearbox, while the inlet and exhaust valve clearances were added at the bottom.

Some cars sold by Brylaw in Australia had commission plates which had been modified by them. The top part of the Jaguar plate was retained but the lower part with the recommended lubricants was cut off and replaced with Brylaw's own separate plate specifically stating "Danger: Girling Hydraulic Brakes" and "The only product approved for the system is Wakefield Girling Brake Fluid" and also "Do not under any circumstances depart from this approval". Presumably this reflected the fact that hydraulic brakes had only recently been fitted to Jaguar cars, and it was important to get the message across to owners and garages alike to

Brylaw's own lubrication plate, found on some Australian imports.

number stamping on a Jaguar car was actually reasonably visible, perhaps as a belated recognition by the factory that a car's ID might later be of importance to the owner.

Engine number: The engines were largely unchanged for the Mark V, as were the style and position of the stamped-in engine numbers. The prefixes however were revised to H for the 2½

TABLE 10.7 – MARK V CHASSIS NUMBERS

	Chs no.s from	In	Chs no.s to	In
2½ litre sal RHD	520001	Apr 1949	521481	May 1951
2½ litre sal LHD	527001	Apr 1949	527190	Oct 1950
2½ litre DHC RHD	540001	Feb 1950	540017	May 1951
2½ litre DHC LHD	547001	Apr 1950	547012	Nov 1950
3½ litre sal RHD	620001	Dec 1948	625926	May 1951
3½ litre sal LHD	627001	Mar 1949	628905	Jan 1951
3½ litre DHC RHD	640001	Jan 1949 (Nov-Dec 1949)	640395	Jul 1951
3½ litre DHC LHD	647001	Jan 1949 (Nov-Dec 1949)	647577	May 1951

TABLE 10.8 – MARK V ENGINE NUMBERS

	Eng no.s from	In	Eng no.s to	In
2½ litre	H 2001	Apr 1949	H 3727	May 1951
3½ litre	T 5001	Dec 1948	T 9999	May 1950 *
3½ litre	Z 1501	May 1950	Z 5378	Jul 1951

* about 200-plus left-over T engines continued to be used through to Jun 1951

TABLE 10.9 – MARK V BODY NUMBERS

	Body no.s from	In	Body no.s to	In
Saloons	G 1001	Dec 1948	G 10428	May 1951
Saloons, CKD	PP 1051	Oct 1949	PP 1145 *	Feb 1951
Drophead coupes (prototypes)	C 3001	Jan 1949	C 3003	Jan 1949
Drophead coupes	DH 1101	Sep 1949	DH 2097	Jul 1951

* some CKD body numbers issued were out of sequence and/or duplicated

TABLE 10.10 – MARK V GEARBOX NUMBERS

	Gearbox no.s from	In	Gearbox no.s to	In	Quantity
SH series	approx. SH 3000 (and some lower no.s)	Jan 1949	SH 10000	Jun 1951	6119
JH series	JH 11	Jan 1949	JH 6899	Jul 1951	3858
SH "A" series	SH 1 A	Jan 1951	SH 1416 A	Jul 1951	403
Not recorded					123

Gearbox numbers are widely spread as the same types of gearboxes were also used on other Jaguars in production at the same time, the six-cylinder Mark IVs, the XK 120, and later the Mark VII.

avoid the risk of damaging the braking system. It also avoided the possibility of confusion with the Lockheed brakes which were fitted on the XK 120.

Since the sides of the bonnet were now fixed in place, the commission plates would no longer be visible if fixed to the side of the bulkhead as on the Mark IV, so they were relocated to sit on the top of the bulkhead on the right-hand side, and the body number plates were moved to the top surface of the bulkhead on the left-hand side.

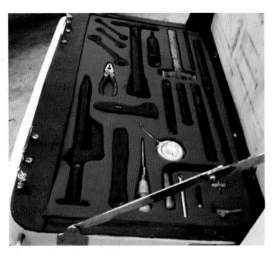

1936 1½ litre Saloon.

Tool kits

With the exception of the SS 100, all the SS Jaguar and Jaguar cars had full tool kits, stowed in tool trays in their boot lids. The contents of the tool kits are listed in the Spare Parts Catalogues for the 1936-37 saloons, the pre- and post-war all steel SS Jaguar and Mark IV cars, and the Mark V cars, but no similar record exists of the tools for the SS 100 and the SS Jaguar Tourer.

The 1936-37 lists only gave descriptions of the tools; no part or drawing numbers were quoted, no doubt because none existed. The first drawing numbers of tools appeared in the Spares Parts Catalogue covering the cars from 1938 onwards, but these are almost all C-prefixed numbers which were only drawn up post-war and with few exceptions do not name the suppliers, as they only define the sizes and shapes of the tools. Still, this was enough detail to ensure that the tools would fit into their allocated recesses in the tool tray, and for ordering a tool as a spare part if required.

For each year and for most models there is a photograph of a representative tool kit and tray, with most of the tools presumed to be of the type that the factory would have supplied, though there are some that are obviously incorrect, but the accompanying photograph has been included as a guide to the layout of the tray.

The SS Jaguar Tourer tool kit was housed within the boot lid, which is hinged at the bottom. Compared to the tool kit on the 1935 S.S.I Tourer, where the jack and starting handle were under the bonnet, the jack is a slimmer type fitted in the tool tray, and the starting handle is also in this area. The SS 100 just had a lidded cavity under the passenger's seat for the jack, the jack handle and the starting handle, all specific to the SS 100, and no doubt other tools such as spanners, a screwdriver, a hammer with a soft, probably lead, head for the wheel hub nuts, and maybe tyre levers and a pump.

1936-37 Saloons

The important special large flat ring spanners needed to remove and secure the cover for the side-mounted spare wheel on both the 1½ and 2½ litre saloons are not listed, and has been added only to the kit of the 1937 2½ litre and perhaps that of the 1936 car too, if an example could be found. The 1½ tool kit has a valve lifter for use on the side-valve engine. Both cars have three tappet spanners according to the list, but these are not evident in surviving tool kits.

1937 1½ litre Saloon.

1937 2½ litre Saloon.

1936 Tourer

This kit is similar to or the same as that on the 1935 S.S.I Tourer, and is housed within the boot lid, which is hinged at the bottom and opens rearwards.

1936 SS Jaguar Tourer.

SS 100 under-seat tool locker.

1938/39 1½ litre DHC.

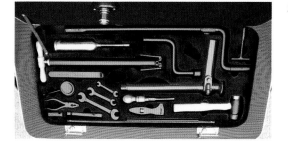

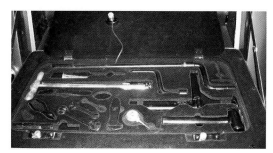

1938/39 2½ litre DHC.

1940 2½ litre Saloon.

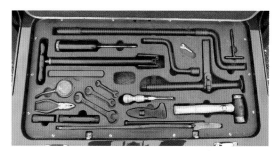

A very complete and correct 1948 2½ litre Mark IV tool kit.

1949 3½ litre Mark V tool tray and tools.

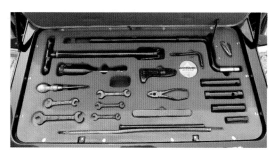

1949 tools in the spare wheel compartment.

SS 100

This shows the location of the tool storage area and the jack specific to the SS 100, with the folding extension, and the wedge that is needed when the jack is used.

1938 to 1940 Models, and Mark IV

These have similar tool trays, although some time in 1938 the finish of the tray changed from black to green. The 1938-39 2½ litre tray does not have a recess for a screwdriver, though one is listed as being in the kit, but there is one for the smaller car apparently.

The grease gun was changed on the Mark IV from the thin steel-bodied gun to a larger Bakelite-bodied, gun with the addition of a nozzle to use in place of the pressure cap when using the gun as an oil gun for filling the differential.

Mark V

The Mark V tool kit was expanded to include the A/F spanners and the kit needed for the newly adopted hydraulic braking system. The grease gun nozzle was omitted, presumably to give more space for the added items, since the Mark V had the same back axle as the Mark IV.

Appendix 1:
Production and Sales Figures

1.1: PRODUCTION FIGURES FOR ALL CARS, WITH NUMBER OF KNOWN SURVIVORS

1.11: SS Jaguar 1936 to 1940 – cars made by model year, and known survivors

	1936	1937	1938	1939	1940	Total	Number surviving	Percentage surviving
1½ litre								
SV Saloon coachbuilt	700	1492	56			2248	41	1.82%
SV Saloon coachbuilt CKD		2				2	0	0.00%
OHV Saloon all-steel			600	3147	430	4177	41	0.98%
OHV Saloon all-steel SE					224	224	3	1.34%
OHV Saloon all-steel CKD				5		5	0	0.00%
Chassis only				2		2	0	0.00%
DHC			33	610	23	666	18	2.70%
DHC SE					11	11	0	0.00%
Total for 1½ litre	700	1494	689	3764	688	7335	103	1.40%
2½ litre								
Saloon coachbuilt	1448	1978				3426	80	2.34%
Saloon coachbuilt CKD		1				1	1	100.00%
Saloon all-steel			665	776	128	1569	40	2.55%
Saloon all-steel CKD			3	1		4	0	0.00%
Chassis only		16	1	4	1	22	4	18.18%
Tourer	60	45				105	34	32.38%
DHC		1	51	222	6	280	20	7.14%
Total for 2½ litre	1508	2041	720	1003	135	5407	179	3.31%
3½ litre								
Saloon			542	449	65	1056	28	2.65%
Chassis only			3	8		11	2	18.18%
DHC			76	162	3	241	22	9.13%
Total for 3½ litre			621	619	68	1308	52	3.98%
SS 100								
2½ litre OTS	33	93	50	13	1	190	166	87.37%
2½ litre chassis only				1		1	1	100.00%
3½ litre OTS			81	31		112	106	94.64%
3½ litre FHC				1		1	1	100.00%
3½ litre chassis only			1	4		5	5	100.00%
Total for SS 100	33	93	132	50	1	309	279	90.29%
Grand total all models	2241	3628	2162	5436	892	14,359	613	4.27%

1.12: Jaguar Mark IV 1945 to 1949 – cars made by calendar year, and known survivors

	1945	1946	1947	1948	1949	Total	Number surviving	Percentage surviving
1½ litre								
1½ RHD	141	798	436	93		1468	60	4.09%
1½ RHD SE		967	1581	1396	34	3978	124	3.12%
1½ RHD SE CKD				4		4	1	25.00%
1½ LHD				14		14	4	28.57%
1½ LHD SE			134	163		297	11	3.70%
Total for 1½ litre	141	1765	2151	1670	34	5761	200	3.47%
2½ litre								
2½ sal RHD		426	587	616	40	1669	107	6.41%
2½ sal RHD CKD				11		11		0.00%
2½ RHD chs only			2			2	1	50.00%
2½ sal LHD			14	52		66	1	1.52%
2½ DHC RHD				73		73	26	35.62%
2½ DHC LHD				28		28	4	31.80%
Total for 2½ litre		426	603	780	40	1849	139	7.52%

3½ litre

3½ sal RHD		737	1483	1138	237	3595	218	6.06%
3½ RHD chs only			11			11	2	18.18%
3½ sal LHD			56	106		162	35	21.60%
3½ LHD chs only				2		2	0	0.00%
3½ sal LHD CKD			41	49		90	5	5.56%
3½ DHC RHD				184		184	46	25.00%
3½ DHC LHD			13	253		266	116	43.61%
3½ DHC LHD CKD				49		49	5	10.20%
Total for 3½ litre		737	1604	1781	237	4359	427	9.80%
Grand total all models	141	2928	4358	4231	311	11,969	766	6.40%

Note: 1948 and total figures are the final figures after conversion of some cars from LHD to RHD.

1.13: Jaguar Mark V 1948 to 1951 – cars made by calendar year, and known survivors

	1948	1949	1950	1951	Total	Number surviving	Percentage surviving
2½ litre							
2½ sal RHD		626	816	5	1447	69	4.77%
2½ sal RHD CKD		14	20		34	3	8.82%
2½ sal LHD		120	68		188	5	2.66%
2½ LHD chs only			2		2	0	0.00%
2½ DHC RHD			16	1	17	2	11.76%
2½ DHC LHD			12		12	3	25.00%
Total for 2½ litre		760	934	6	1700	82	4.82%
3½ litre							
3½ sal RHD	2	2273	2874	719	5868	310	5.28%
3½ sal RHD CKD		39	12	4	55	16	29.09%
3½ RHD chs only	1	1			2	0	0.00%
3½ sal LHD		704	1190	8	1902	217	11.40%
3½ LHD chs only			1		1	0	0.00%
3½ DHC RHD		4	139	251	394	108	27.34%
3½ DHC LHD		6	528	43	577	188	32.58%
Total for 3½ litre	3	3027	4744	1025	8799	839	9.53%
Grand total all models	3	3787	5678	1031	10,499	921	8.77%

Note: The Mark V figures are final figures after conversions of four cars in 1948-49.

The total number of all cars made from 1936 to 1951 was 36,827, and the number of known survivors at the end of 2012 was 2300, giving an average survival rate of 6.24 per cent.

1.2 HOME VERSUS EXPORT SALES

1.21: SS Jaguar, 1936 to 1940 by model year

		1936	1937	1938	1939	1940	Total, all years	Export percentage by model
1½ litre	Home	682	1445	659	3681	645	7112	
	Export	18	49	30	83	43	223	3.0%
	Total	700	1494	689	3764	688	7335	
2½ litre	Home	1415	1870	648	919	109	4961	
	Export	93	171	72	84	26	446	8.2%
	Total	1508	2041	720	1003	135	5407	
3½ litre	Home			578	575	61	1214	
	Export			43	44	7	94	7.2%
	Total			621	619	68	1308	
SS 100 2½ litre	Home	29	80	41	11	1	162	
	Export	4	13	9	3		29	15.2%
	Total	33	93	50	14	1	191	
SS 100 3½ litre	Home			69	30		99	
	Export			13	6		19	16.1%
	Total			82	36		118	
All models	Home	2126	3395	1995	5216	816	13,548	
	Export	115	233	167	220	76	811	5.65%
	Total	2241	3628	2162	5436	892	14,359	
Export percentage by year		5.1%	6.4%	7.7%	4.0%	8.5%	5.65%	

1.22: Mark IV, 1945 to 1949, by calendar year

		1945	1946	1947	1948	1949	Total, all years	Export percentage by model
1½ litre	Home	100	1283	1547	1230	34	4194	
	Export	41	482	604	440		1567	27.2%
	Total	141	1765	2151	1670	34	5761	
2½ litre	Home		359	384	429	39	1211	
	Export		67	219	351	1	638	34.5%
	Total		426	603	780	40	1849	
3½ litre	Home		571	1015	910	236	2732	
	Export		166	589	871	1	1627	37.3%
	Total		737	1604	1781	237	4359	
All models	Home	100	2213	2946	2569	309	8137	
	Export	41	715	1412	1662	2	3832	32.0%
	Total	141	2928	4358	4231	311	11,969	
Export percentage by year		29.0%	24.4%	32.4%	39.3%	0.6%	32.0%	

1.23: Mark V, 1948 to 1951, by calendar year

		1948	1949	1950	1951	Total	Export percentage by model
2½ litre	Home		480	626	6	1112	
	Export		280	308		588	34.6%
	Total		760	934	6	1700	
3½ litre	Home	2	1321	1416	503	3242	
	Export		1707	3328	522	5557	63.2%
	Total	2	3028	4744	1025	8799	
All cars	Home	2	1801	2042	509	4354	
	Export		1987	3636	522	6145	58.5%
	Total	2	3788	5678	1031	10,499	
Export percentage by year		0.0%	52.5%	64.0%	50.6%	58.5%	

1.3 SALES BY DISTRIBUTOR

1.31: Pre-war home sales by distributor in order of volume

		1½ litre	2½ litre	3½ litre	SS 100	All cars
Henlys	London	2882	2448	623	126	6079
Henlys	Manchester	665	379	81	15	1140
Appleyard	Leeds	437	286	70	17	810
Parkers	Bolton	441	208	59	8	716
PJ Evans	Birmingham	366	251	61	16	694
Rossleigh	Edinburgh, Newcastle	377	248	47	6	678
Glovers of Ripon	Harrogate	272	203	41	13	529
Ritchies	Glasgow	267	143	21	4	435
Ernest W Hatfield	Sheffield	163	85	23	1	272
Tom Norton	Cardiff	183	57	14	1	255
Charles Attwood	Wolverhampton	147	76	22	9	254
CH Truman	Nottingham	100	76	22	6	204
Roland C Bellamy	Grimsby	95	81	17	3	196
SH Newsome	Coventry	95	69	22	8	194
HA Browett	Leicester	93	76	14	0	183
Loxhams	Lancaster	89	39	10	5	143
SS Cars Limited	Coventry	47	44	25	15	131
Byatts of Fenton	Stoke on Trent	78	35	10	2	125
Victor	Belfast	87	22	2	0	111
W L Thompson	Hull	57	25	5	2	89
Scottish Motor Traction	Carlisle	63	17	7	1	88
Sanderson & Holmes	Derby	33	14	5	1	53
St Helier Garage	Jersey	22	24	2		48
Wales & Edwards	Shrewsbury	20	16	3	1	40
Atkey & Co	Derby	14	21			35
WH Shimmin	Douglas, Isle of Man	7	3	1		11
F Guyver	Stratford-upon-Avon	7	3			10

Standard Motor Co	Coventry		2	4	6
Stouts Garage	Whitehaven	1	4		5
Athol Garage	Douglas, Isle of Man	1	1		2
Various agents		3	5	3	1	12
		7112	4961	1214	261	13,548

1.32: Pre-war export sales by territory

		1½ litre	2½ litre	3½ litre	SS 100	All cars
Europe						
Georg Hans Koch	Austria	3	5	1	2	11
WE Du Vivier	Belgium		23	9	3	35
Jaguar Car Distributors *	Belgium				1	1
Klika	Czechoslovakia	1	10	2	6	19
Bohnstedt-Petersen	Denmark		1			1
John Freybach	Estonia	1	2			3
Saar & Co	Estonia	1				1
Automobiles Marboeuf	France		6			6
Charles Delecroix	France		3			3
Neumann Automobile	Germany		12	1	2	15
Von Carnap & Franck	Germany				1	1
Lagerwijs	Holland	2	23	2	3	30
Bolgar Motors	Hungary			1		1
Frank Cavey	Ireland	13	7	1		21
Joyce & Brady	Ireland		1			1
McEntagart	Ireland	3	2			5
R W Archer	Ireland		1			1
Godwin E Muscat	Malta	4	1			5
Mizzi Bros	Malta		1			1
Standard Autos	Norway (?)		3			3
Kupfermann	Poland	1				1
Leon Leszczynski	Poland	1				1
Polchem	Poland	5			1	6
Auto Omnia	Portugal	6	9		1	16
WC Ennor	Portugal		2		1	3
Anglo Cars	Romania		6	1	2	9
Drawyl & Litman	Romania		2			2
Georges Herascu	Romania		1			1
C de Salamanca	Spain	4	3			7
Emil Frey	Switzerland	15	66	25	4	110
Garage Place Claparede	Switzerland	16	53	12	1	82
Stevo R Lemaic	Yugoslavia		3			3
British India						
Govan Bros	Baluchistan	1	1			2
Automobile Co, Woolley	Bombay	1	3			4
Garware	Bombay	1		1		2
Hendry Bros (Garware)	Bombay		1	1		2
Volkart Bros	Bombay	1	3	2		6
French Motor Car Co	Calcutta	12	19	1	1	33
Pearey Lal	Delhi	1		2		3
Fonseca & Co	Delhi		1			1
Sanghi Bros	Jodhpur		2			2
Girdharilal & Co	Karachi		1			1
Paris Motors	Lahore	3	1	2		6
Rest of Asia						
Alexander Young, Ensign	Burma	8	1			9
AF Dom	Dutch East Indies		5	1	2	8
KV Brockdorff	Dutch East Indies			1		1
Gilman	Hong Kong	4	5	2	1	12
Paul Braga	Hong Kong	2				2
Mitsui	Japan		1			1
Nosawa	Japan	1	1			2
Thompsons Agencies	Malaya		1			1
JI Thornycroft	Singapore	41	15	5	2	63

Banque R Sabbag	Syria			1		1
Butler & Webster	Thailand	6	1			7
MacKinlay & Co	Palestine			1	1	2
Africa						
Automobile Imports	Egypt	1	3			4
Gollin & Co	Mauritius	1				1
JA Ewing	Nyasaland	3				3
Hays Garage	Nyasaland				1	1
JR Martin, Fishers Garage	South Africa		4			4
Garlick	South Africa		1			1
Americas						
Ehlert Nash	Argentina		16	2	2	20
Brice Pinder	Bahamas		1			1
British Motor Agency	Canada	1	8			9
British Motors	USA		13		1	14
Parrish Ellis	Venezuela		1			1
Australia, New Zealand						
Tozer Kemsley & Millbourn	various	54	84	17	9	164
Not located or PED						
Claridge Holt, London	Export shippers	2	3			5
SS Cars Limited	PED	1	2			3
Walkers Bros	PED	1	1			2
Gordon Richards	PED (?)	1				1
Maira Bros, Lahore, India (?)	PED (?)		1			1
Total		**223**	**446**	**94**	**48**	**811**

* The SS 100 sent to Jaguar Car Distributors (in chassis form) was only despatched in 1947.

1.33: Post-war home sales by distributor in order of volume

		Mark IV 1½	Mark IV 2½	Mark IV 3½	Mark IV total	Mark V 2½	Mark V 3½	Mark V total	All cars
Henlys	London	1977	570	1206	**3753**	532	1462	**1994**	5747
Henlys	Manchester	309	111	200	**620**	95	207	**302**	922
PJ Evans	Birmingham	207	66	135	**408**	46	195	**241**	649
Rossleigh	Edinburgh, Newcastle	206	53	139	**398**	58	172	**230**	628
Appleyard	Leeds	174	52	139	**365**	36	149	**185**	550
Parkers	Bolton	170	42	128	**340**	55	135	**190**	530
Ritchies	Glasgow	132	35	94	**261**	32	123	**155**	416
Glovers of Ripon	Harrogate	126	24	96	**246**	34	104	**138**	384
SH Newsome	Coventry	68	22	57	**147**	15	81	**96**	243
Ernest W Hatfield	Sheffield	73	13	61	**147**	13	73	**86**	233
Charles Attwood	Wolverhampton	68	21	46	**135**	17	58	**75**	210
Exclusive Cars	Cardiff	56	17	48	**121**	31	55	**86**	207
Walter E Sturgess	Leicester	56	20	44	**120**	17	45	**62**	182
Ashton Preston	Preston	57	15	40	**112**	12	54	**66**	178
CH Truman	Nottingham	55	17	40	**112**	16	45	**61**	173
Roland C Bellamy	Grimsby	48	16	39	**103**	27	33	**60**	163
St Helier Garage	Jersey	87	30	22	**139**	7	13	**20**	159
Victor	Belfast	46	12	30	**88**	7	37	**44**	132
Tom Byatt of Fenton	Stoke-on-Trent	35	10	22	**67**	12	31	**43**	110
WL Thompson	Hull	28	4	27	**59**	15	25	**40**	99
Sanderson & Holmes	Derby	25	5	27	**57**	12	28	**40**	97
Scottish Motor Traction	Carlisle	27	5	22	**54**	9	32	**41**	95
Rothwell & Milbourne	Malvern	18	8	12	**38**	5	24	**29**	67
Wales & Edwards	Shrewsbury	18	9	14	**41**	6	20	**26**	67
WH Shimmin	Douglas, Isle of Man	10	4	7	**21**	2	8	**10**	31
Tom Norton	Cardiff	14	3	6	**23**				23
St Peter Port Garage	Guernsey	11			**11**				11
Loxhams Garages	Preston	6	1		**7**				7
Jaguar Cars Ltd	Direct sales,								
Works cars*		87	26	31	**144**	1	33	**34**	178
TOTAL home sales		**4194**	**1211**	**2732**	**8137**	**1112**	**3242**	**4354**	**12,491**

* including 2 cars destroyed in the factory fire in 1947

1.34: Post-war export sales by territory

		Mk IV 1½	Mk IV 2½	Mk IV 3½	Mk IV total	Mk V 2½	Mk V 3½	Mk V total	All cars
Europe									
Georg Hans Koch	Austria					3	25	28	28
Jaguar Car Distributors	Belgium	338	8	212	558	23	96	119	677
PM Tseriotis	Cyprus	6		1	7	1		1	8
Klika	Czechoslovakia		1	1	2				2
Sommer	Denmark	30	2		32	19	5	24	56
SM Kauppa	Finland					8	6	14	14
Delecroix	France	17	6	28	51	5	97	102	153
Fendler & Luedemann	Germany						6	6	6
RM Overseas	Germany		1		1		42	42	43
Alfred Bassadone	Gibraltar	26	5	10	41	12	7	19	60
Coulentianos	Greece					4	3	7	7
Lagerwij's	Holland	19	2	5	26	6	42	48	74
Frank Cavey	Ireland	15	67	45	127	31	27	58	185
CGA	Italy						3	3	3
Leacock e Cia Ltda	Madeira	1	1	2	4				4
Madeira Supply Co	Madeira		1	4	5		1	1	6
Godwin E Muscat	Malta	7	4		11	2	2	4	15
Standard Autos	Norway	1			1		5	5	6
Auto Omnia	Portugal	38	11	24	73	1	19	20	93
ATASA	Spain	2	2	2	6	2	2	4	10
C de Salamanca	Spain	9	2	9	20				20
Fredlunds	Sweden	34	2	10	46	7	223	230	276
Emil Frey	Switzerland	116	51	115	282	37	108	145	427
Garage Claparede	Switzerland	64	40	61	165	18	63	81	246
Otokar Tiaret	Turkey						16	16	16
British India									
BD Garware	Bombay	62	22	14	98	2	34	36	134
French Car Co	Calcutta	38	3	4	45		15	15	60
Pearey Lal	Delhi	2		2	4		2	2	6
Sanghi Bros	Jodhpur	8		1	9				9
Reliance Motor Co	Madras	3	1	1	5	1	4	5	10
Wallace Cartwright	Madras						9	9	9
Girdharilal & Co	Karachi	6	1	1	8				8
Polad & Co	Karachi					5	2	7	7
Rest of Asia									
Peacocks	Burma					1	2	3	3
Brown & Co	Ceylon	19	1	4	24	5	1	6	30
Gilman & Co	Hong Kong	25	3	8	36	7	38	45	81
Neil Buchanan	Japan						6	6	6
Stanley Shashoua	Iran	12		1	13				13
Boutagy & Sons	Lebanon					1		1	1
MA Chiek	Lebanon	6			6				6
Palestine Motors	Palestine	19	4	4	27				27
Brinkman	Singapore	40	2	3	45	17	17	34	79
Cycle & Carriage	Singapore					25	69	94	94
Hilterman	Singapore	3			3		2	2	5
ASSIA	Thailand	4	3	2	9	11	6	17	26
South Africa									
Robb Motors	Cape Town	15	3	31	49		9	9	58
Fishers' Garage	Durban	9	1	13	23		2	2	25
JB Clarke's Garage	Johannesburg	40	5	37	82		15	15	97
Rest of Africa									
Universal Motor Co	Egypt	17	30	45	92	6	24	30	122
Berberi Freres	Gold Coast						9	9	9
Thomas Armah & Co	Gold Coast						1	1	1
Lowis & Hodgkiss	Kenya	1	1	3	5		45	45	50
Adam & Co	Mauritius					1		1	1
Biddle Sawyer	Mauritius (?)	4	1		5	1		1	6
Hain S Bendelac	Morocco	5	2		7	3	2	5	12
Moto Maroc	Morocco	1	1		2	2	19	21	23
Teixeira de Rocha	Mozambique		1		1				1

		Mk IV 1½	Mk IV 2½	Mk IV 3½	Mk IV total	Mk V 2½	Mk V 3½	Mk V total	All cars
British West Africa Corp	Nigeria			1	1		1	1	2
Hays Garage	Nyasaland					3	1	4	4
Ranares	Portuguese Guinea						2	2	2
Sagers Motors	Rhodesia	1			1		105	105	106
Marston Motor Co	Tanganyika					2	11	13	13
USA									
British Motor Car Co	San Francisco			1	1				1
Clayrich Motors	St Louis			6	6				6
Fergus Motors	New York			9	9				9
Foreign Motors	Santa Barbara			1	1				1
Hoffman	New York	2		191	193		574	574	767
Hornburg	Los Angeles			21	21		358	358	379
International Car Dist.	Seattle			3	3				3
International Motors	Los Angeles			58	58				58
James Baird	Seattle			6	6				6
Los Angeles Distributors	Los Angeles			2	2				2
SH Lynch & Co	Texas			6	6				6
Qvale Motors	San Bruno			2	2				2
British Motor Imports	Hawaii						2	2	2
Canada									
Budd & Dyer	Montreal						54	54	54
James L Cooke	Toronto						126	126	126
Murch Motors	Halifax						3	3	3
Thomas Plimley	Vancouver						103	103	103
Waverley Motors	Ottawa						13	13	13
Rest of Americas									
Ehlert Nash	Argentina	36	4	30	70	2	3	5	75
Commission Merchants	Bahamas			1	1		3	3	4
Goodwin Cocozza	Brazil	107	38	38	183	64	493	557	740
Willens Co	British Guyana					1	1	1	1
Importadora Fisk	Chile		2		2		1	1	3
Frank Seiglie	Cuba						18	18	18
Kusters	Curacao					3	3	6	6
PH Traynor	Jamaica	1	2		3				3
Daytona Sales	Jamaica						7	7	7
Jorge Barranco	Mexico	1			1		1	1	2
Prod. Auto. Britanicos	Mexico	7		4	11				11
Fenix	Peru						22	22	22
Esteve	Puerto Rico						4	4	4
HJ Miller	Trinidad	2	1		3	5	5	10	13
Pablo Aicardi	Uruguay	20		4	24	28	5	33	57
CAMAV	Venezuela			11	11		63	63	74
Australia									
Andersons Agencies	Brisbane	21	24	24	69	23	156	179	248
Brooking	Perth		29	13	42	53	91	144	186
Brylaw	Sydney/Melbourne	151	153	389	693	73	1638	1711	2404
Dominion Motors	Adelaide	39	30	34	103	38	220	258	361
Standard Cars	Sydney/Melbourne	15	5		20				20
New Zealand									
Amuri Motors	various	8	5	2	15				15
Arcihbalds Garage	Christchurch						29	29	29
Independent Motor Sales	Wellington	11	4	5	20	1	41	42	62
Reilly's	Dunedin	3			3				3
Shorters Garage	Auckland	7	19	14	40	14	84	98	138
Various									
Tozer Kemsley & Millbourn	Australia, Far East	54	11	10	75		1	1	76
The Shaska Trading Co	unknown	3			3				3
PED cars ordered in UK									
Henlys PED	London etc	10	8	14	32	2	80	82	114
Jaguar Cars Ltd PED	Coventry	6	11	24	41	8	101	109	150
Parkers PED	Bolton		1		1		1	1	2
Rossleigh PED	Edinburgh						2	2	2
CH Truman PED	Nottingham						1	1	1
Victor PED	Belfast					1		1	1
TOTAL export sales		1567	638	1627	3832	588	5557	6145	9977

Appendix 2:
Chassis Deliveries

2.1: CHASSIS DELIVERIES, ALL MODELS 1936-1950

Date man	Chs no	Home/ export	Distributor	Coachbuilder, type of bodywork	Date desp
SS Jaguar1½ litre					
Sep 38	50800	Home	Henlys, London	Maltby DHC	15 Sep 1938
Sep 38	50801	Home	Henlys, London	Maltby DHC	15 Sep 1938
SS Jaguar 2½ litre					
Oct 36	11797	Export	Emil Frey, Switzerland	Gurney Nutting Saloon	5 Oct 1936
Dec 36	12290	Home	Henlys, London	Salmons DHC	11 Jan 1937
Jan 37	12496	Export	Garage Claparede, Switzerland	Worblaufen DHC	13 Jan 1937
Feb 37	12637	Export	Emil Frey, Switzerland	Tüscher DHC	10 Feb 1937
Feb 37	12660	Export	Emil Frey, Switzerland	Tüscher DHC	10 Feb 1937
Feb 37	12675	Export	Emil Frey, Switzerland	Tüscher DHC	10 Feb 1937
Feb 37	12690	Export	Emil Frey, Switzerland	Tüscher DHC	9 Feb 1937
Feb 37	12691	Export	Emil Frey, Switzerland	Tüscher DHC	10 Feb 1937
Feb 37	12697	Export	Emil Frey, Switzerland	Tüscher DHC	9 Feb 1937
Feb 37	12706	Export	Garage Claparede, Switzerland	Graber DHC	21 May 1937
May 37	13280	Export	Emil Frey, Switzerland	Tüscher DHC	26 May 1937
May 37	13285	Export	Emil Frey, Switzerland	Tüscher DHC	26 May 1937
May 37	13286	Export	Emil Frey, Switzerland	Tüscher DHC	26 May 1937
May 37	13310	Export	Emil Frey, Switzerland	Tüscher DHC	26 May 1937
May 37	13311	Export	Emil Frey, Switzerland	Tüscher DHC	26 May 1937
May 37	13312	Export	Emil Frey, Switzerland	Tüscher DHC	26 May 1937
25 Jul 38	40655	Export	Garage Claparede, Switzerland	Not known	29 Jul 1938
24 Aug 38	40734	Export	Garage Claparede, Switzerland	Not known	1 Sep 1938
29 Aug 38	40763	Home	Henlys, London	Maltby DHC	14 Sep 1938
14 Nov 38	40966	Home	Henlys, London	Not known	18 Nov 1938
14 Nov 38	40967	Home	Henlys, London	Maltby DHC	22 Nov 1938
22 Aug 39	80048	Home	Henlys, London	Not known	1 Sep 1939
SS Jaguar 3½ litre					
29 Mar 38	30180	Home	Henlys, London	Freestone & Webb saloon	5 Apr 1938
29 Mar 38	30181	Export	Garage Claparede, Switzerland	Not known	6 Apr 1938
25 Mar 38	30182	Export	Garage Claparede, Switzerland	Graber FHC	6 Apr 1938
Oct 38	30669	Export	Emil Frey, Switzerland	Worblaufen DHC	18 Oct 1938
28 Oct 38	30698	Export	Emil Frey, Switzerland	Graber DHC	12 Dec 1938
14 Dec 38	30793	Export	Emil Frey, Switzerland	Worblaufen DHC	3 Jan 1939
09 Jan 39	30857	Export	Emil Frey, Switzerland	Tüscher DHC	2 Feb 1939
18 Mar 39	30947	Export	Garage Claparede, Switzerland	Not known	28 Mar 1939
18 Mar 39	30948	Home	Standard Motor Company, Coventry	Mulliners Limousine	31 Mar 1939
15 Jun 39	30998	Home	Henlys, London	Maltby DHC	28 Jun 1939
21 Jun 39	31002	Home	Standard Motor Company, Coventry	Mulliners Limousine	27 Jun 1939
SS 100					
12 May 38	39070	Export	Anglo Cars, Romania	Leonida OTS	2 Jun 1938
Dec 38	39092	Export	Emil Frey, Switzerland	Worblaufen DHC	12 Dec 1938
Mar 39	39109	Home	SH Newsome, Coventry	Avon DHC	7 Mar 1939
Apr 39	39113	Export	Emil Frey, Switzerland	Worblaufen DHC	28 Apr 1939
Jun 39	39115	Home	SH Newsome, Coventry	Avon DHC	30 Jun 1939
Jun 39	49064	Export	Jaguar Car Distributors, Belgium	Vanden Plas OTS	20 Jun 1947

Mark IV

22 Jan 47	510451	Export	Garage Claparede, Switzerland	Worblaufen DHC	15 Feb 1947
22 Jan 47	510455	Export	Emil Frey, Switzerland	Worblaufen DHC	15 Feb 1947
20 Jan 47	610812	Export	Emil Frey, Switzerland	Not known	14 Feb 1947
20 Jan 47	610813	Export	Garage Claparede, Switzerland	Worblaufen DHC	14 Feb 1947
28 Mar 47	611053	Export	Emil Frey, Switzerland	Not known	2 May 1947
28 Mar 47	611054	Export	Emil Frey, Switzerland	Not known	2 May 1947
28 Mar 47	611055	Export	Emil Frey, Switzerland	Worblaufen DHC	2 May 1947
28 Mar 47	611056	Export	Emil Frey, Switzerland	Not known	2 May 1947
4 Apr 47	611107	Export	n/r; Emil Frey, Switzerland	Not known	2 May 1947
4 Apr 47	611108	Export	n/r; Emil Frey, Switzerland	Not known	2 May 1947
4 Apr 47	611109	Export	n/r; Emil Frey, Switzerland	Not known	2 May 1947
4 Apr 47	611110	Export	n/r; Emil Frey, Switzerland	Not known	2 May 1947
5 Jun 47	611423	Export	Jaguar Car Distributors, Belgium	Vanden Plas DHC	12 Jun 47
1 Feb 48	630123	Export	Jaguar Car Distributors, Belgium	Probably Vanden Plas DHC	6 Feb 48

Mark V

23 May 50	527160	Export	Coulentianos, Greece		13 Jun 1950
23 May 50	527161	Export	Coulentianos, Greece		13 Jun 1950
1 Dec 48	620005	Home	Ritchies, Glasgow; show chassis for 1949 Scottish Motor Show (?)		7 Dec 1948
1 Jan 49	620007	Home	Jaguar Cars Ltd		
10 May 50	628019	Export	Coulentianos, Greece		13 Jun 1950

Appendix 3:
Colour Schemes

With the Jaguar models, SS acquired a new-found respectability in the market which had never been enjoyed by the slightly oddball S.S.I and S.S.II cars. As part of the work-over of the image of the brand, bright colours such as Apple Green, Carnation Red, and Nile Blue, together with two-tone schemes, were replaced by a much more muted palette. Inevitably, Black was the most popular colour, accounting for anything up to half of all cars depending on model year and model, and often as not combined with Brown trim. When an increased range of colours was introduced for the all-steel 1938 models, the new Gunmetal – a very attractive dark grey metallic finish – quickly became the second-most popular choice, usually with Red or Silver (i.e. Grey) trim.

Despite the wide choice of paint and trim colours on offer, there were still surprisingly many customers who wanted something different, and in the pre-war period 325 saloons, tourers, and dropheads were finished in non-standard colours, as were 37 SS 100 cars. There were also apparently 235 cars with special trim colours, but it should be pointed out that the entries for trim colours (and quite possibly for some paint colours) often appear inconsistent in the original ledgers and can therefore be confusing. The statistics below are probably the best that can be compiled.

3.1: 1936 MODELS (EXCLUDING SS 100)

The 1936 and 1937 paint colour ranges were the same, but there were some differences in the trim colours.

| Paint colours | Trim colours | | | | | | | | | | | |
	Blue	Brown	Green	Maroon	Olive Green	Pigskin	Red *	Silver (grey)	Suede Green	n/r	Special trim	Total
Black	4	514	51	141	78	166	13	178	6	2	24	1177
Cream	24	2	11	33	17	4	4				10	105
Dark Blue	66					1				19	7	93
Lavender Grey	133		31	62	16	2	4	3	6		18	275
Maroon				123		2					3	128
Olive Green		1			45					17	1	64
Suede Green						2			176	70		248
Special colours	45	4	3	5	2	6	9	2	1	18	23	118
Total	272	521	96	364	158	183	30	183	189	129	83	2208

*Red trim was mainly found on the tourer model

3.2: 1937 MODELS (EXCLUDING SS 100)

Paint colours	Trim colours										
	Beige	Blue	Brown	Maroon	Olive Green	Pigskin	Silver Special Silver	Suede Green	n/r	Special trim	Total
Black	241	2	600	187	204	258	183	17	4	39	1735
Cream	2	48	2	66	49	1		4		8	180
Dark Blue	5	55	4	2		4	3		82	3	158
Lavender Grey	1	192	2	82	71			7		14	369
Maroon	3		1	22		2			214		242
Olive Green	1			2	1	2		2	97	2	107
Suede Green	2				2			2	601		607
Special colours	17	14	1	6	5	5	13	3	26	28	118
Chassis only									16		16
CKD									3		3
Total	272	311	610	367	332	272	199	35	1043	94	3535

* Where the trim colour is not recorded (n/r) it is most likely that the trim colour was the same as the paint colour

3.3: 1938 MODELS (EXCLUDING SS 100)

The 1938 paint colour range had several new colours including Jaguar's first standard metallic colour, Gunmetal. This range was kept through the 1940 model year and most of the colours were used post-war as well. Honeysuckle and Mountain Ash Green, though rare, were quoted as standard colours.

Paint colours	Trim colours											
	Beige	Blue	Brown	Maroon	Olive Green	Pigskin	Red	Silver (Grey)	Suede Green	n/r	Special trim	Total
Battleship Grey	2	1					13	19				35
Birch Grey		1					30	24		1		56
Black	145	3	356	3	55	126	104	119	7	2	9	929
Cream **				4								4
Dark Blue	10	5					2			37	1	55
Gunmetal	5	3		1	1	2	129	276	2	1	1	421
Honeysuckle	11						3					14
Ivory	16	4		1	1	5	27	3	10		1	68
Lavender Grey	3	42	2	1			27	2	25		1	103
Maroon	10			20			1			26		57
Mountain Ash Green							1		22			23
Olive Green	6				7	1				20		34
Suede Green									2	192	1	195
Special colours	1	9	3	1		4	1	3	1	1	4	28
Not recorded										1		1
Chassis only										4		4
CKD										3		3
Total	209	68	361	31	64	138	338	446	70	287	18	2030

* Where the trim colour is not recorded (n/r) it is most likely that the trim colour was the same as the paint colour
** Cream, a 1936-37 paint colour, with Maroon trim was found only on four 1½ litre 12hp side-valve models

3.31: 1938 DHC hood colours

There were basically four standard hood colours, Black, Dark Sand (or Sand), French Grey (or Grey), and Gunmetal. Some of the pre-war dropheads had special hood colours including Beige, Blue, Green, Maroon, and Red, some times to match paint or trim colour, chosen no doubt by fussy clients, and probably charged extra.

Paint colours	Hood colours						
	Black	Dark Sand	French Grey	Gunmetal	n/r	Special hoods	Total
Battleship Grey			1	3	2		6
Birch Grey	1		7	1			9
Black	31	11	12	2	1	3	60

Dark Blue	1		3			1	5
Gunmetal	3	1	7	30			41
Honeysuckle		3					3
Ivory	1	10				1	12
Lavender Grey			6				6
Maroon			1	2			3
Mountain Ash Green			2				2
Olive Green	1					1	2
Suede Green	1		6			1	8
Special colours	1					2	3
Total	40	25	45	38	3	9	160

3.4: 1939 MODELS (EXCLUDING SS 100)

Paint colours	Trim colours											
	Beige	Blue	Brown	Maroon	Olive Green	Pigskin	Red	Silver (Grey)	Suede Green	n/r	Special trim	Total
Battleship Grey	1	1				5	30	63		1		101
Birch Grey	1	4				1	63	61	1		2	133
Black	296	7	759	6	128	323	304	349	15	1	16	2204
Dark Blue	28	60				1	3			17	2	111
Gunmetal	4	1	2		1	6	521	951	8		4	1498
Honeysuckle	27						9				1	37
Ivory	59	3	4			11	104	1	47		1	230
Lavender Grey	1	65	1	2		2	55		67	1	1	195
Maroon	51	1	104			1	1	1		26		185
Mountain Ash Green	3						2	1	94			100
Olive Green	26				57		2			14		99
Suede Green	2		1				2		316	96		417
Special colours	10	12			1	2	10	7	3		9	54
Not recorded		1								1		2
Chassis only										14		14
CKD										6		6
Total	509	154	768	112	187	358	1100	1434	551	177	36	5386

* Where the trim colour is not recorded (n/r) it is most likely that the trim colour was the same as the paint colour

3.41: 1939 DHC hood colours

Paint colours	Hood colours						
	Black	Dark Sand New Dark Sand Sand	French Grey Grey	Gunmetal	n/r	Special hoods	Total
Battleship Grey	5		20	9			34
Birch Grey	3		35	9			47
Black	185	94	52	4	3	3	341
Dark Blue	7	1	16	2	1	1	28
Gunmetal	24		29	221	3	4	281
Honeysuckle	1	6					7
Ivory	16	53			3	7	79
Lavender Grey	3	2	35		1	1	42
Maroon	5	1	18	11			35
Mountain Ash Green	4		13	1			18
Olive Green	6	1	16		1		24
Suede Green	3		38				41
Special colours	5	1	6	2		3	17
Total	267	159	278	259	12	19	994

3.5: 1940 MODELS (EXCLUDING SS 100)

Paint colours	Trim colours											
	Beige	Blue	Brown	Maroon	Olive Green	Pigskin	Red	Silver (Grey)	Suede Green	n/r	Special trim	Total
Battleship Grey		1		1			5	8				15
Birch Grey		2					9	8				19
Black	50		167	1	15	76	44	81		1	2	437
Dark Blue	2	11						1				14
Gunmetal		4	1				71	169			1	246
Honeysuckle	1						3					4
Ivory	6						12		8			26
Lavender Grey		3		1			10		3			17
Maroon	2			11								13
Mountain Ash Green									5	1		6
Olive Green	4				13							17
Suede Green	1								68			69
Special colours		2		1		1	1	1			1	7
Chassis only										1		1
Total	66	23	168	14	29	77	155	268	85	2	4	891

3.51: 1940 DHC hood colours

Paint colours	Hood colours					
	Black	Dark Sand	French Grey	Gunmetal	n/r	Total
Battleship Grey			1			1
Birch Grey			1			1
Black	5	5	4			14
Gunmetal	3		3	14	1	21
Ivory		1				1
Lavender Grey	1					1
Maroon			1	1		2
Suede Green			1			1
Special colours		1				1
Total	9	7	11	15	1	43

3.6: SPECIAL COLOURS ON PRE-WAR CARS, EXCLUDING SS 100 (SEE BELOW)

No less than 113 different special colours or colour schemes have been found in the records, accounting altogether for 325 cars (apart from the SS 100s). Clearly there were individualistic owners who were prepared to pay the extra amount usually required for painting a car in a special colour, although some non-standard paint finishes were probably the company's own try-outs of a new colour. Whether even SS Jaguar drew the line somewhere is uncertain, but it is of interest that the 8 cars finished in primer are not the CKD cars (discussed in chapter 7) but all seem to have been supplied as complete cars for a variety of home and export destinations, presumably to be painted to very specific requirements from particularly demanding customers. The most popular non-standard colours were Blue (unspecified) on 40 cars, "Blue Sheen" on 39 cars, Silver on 25 cars, and Metallic Grey on 16 cars. Non-standard colours were in greatest demand during the two first years of production of the coachbuilt cars, less so for the all-steel cars which followed.

	1935-36 model year	1936-37 model year	1937-38 model year	1938-39 model year	1939-40 model year	Total
Beige, Browns: 14 cars						
Beige	2	3	1	1		7
Brown	1		2			3
Chocolate		1				1
Cinnamon		1				1
Dockers's Nigger Brown		1				1
Tobacco Brown		1				1
Blues: 131 cars						
Air Force Blue				1	1	2
Austin Light Blue				1		1
Blue	18	4	7	10	1	40
Blue-Grey	2					2
Blue Sheen	4	29	2	3	1	39

Colour							Total
Blue, Special				1	1		2
Blue Steel	7						7
Belco Silver Blue				1			1
Colonial Blue					1		1
Humber Aero Blue				1			1
Light Blue	1		1	1	1		4
Light Powder Blue			1				1
Metallic Blue	1		1		3		5
Ming Blue					1		1
Nile Blue	5		2		1		8
Pale Blue			1				1
Royal Blue	2						2
Sea Blue	4						4
Smoke Blue					1		1
Snow Shadow (blue)	1						1
Special Blue	1						1
Steel Blue	3						3
Tekaloid Blue			1				1
Union Jack Blue			1				1
Wedgwood Blue			1				1
Greens: 20 cars							
Apple Green	2			1			3
Beaufort Green	1						1
Belco Chrome Green			1				1
Bradite Green Sheen					1		1
Green			3				3
Green, special					1		1
Green Grey			1	1	1		3
Lugano Green					1		1
Marcelle Green					1		1
Metallic Green	1						1
Pale Green			1				1
Quaker Green	1						1
Special Green			1				1
Special Light Green			1				1
Greys: 89 cars							
"B Grey"					1		1
Beaufort Grey	1						1
Birch Grey	5		2				7
Bradite Grey Sheen					1		1
Dark Grey			1				1
Dove Grey	3						3
Dreadnought Grey			1				1
Duck Egg Grey			1				1
French Grey	1						1
Grey	4		5				9
Grey metallic			1				1
Grey, special					4	2	6
Gunmetal	1		1				2
Lavender, special					1		1
Light French Grey			1				1
Light Grey	1		1				2
Metallic Grey			16				16
"No. 1/2/3" Grey			3				3
Silver	13		5	2	5		25
Silver Grey				1			1
Smoke Grey			1				1
Special Grey				1			1
Special Light Grey					1		1
War Office Grey						1	1
Zofelac Grey	1						1

Reds: 13 cars

Burgundy				1		1
Carnation Red	2	1		1		4
Lake	4					4
Red	1					1
Panhard Red				1		1
Special Red		1				1
Vermillion				1		1

Violet, purple: 4 cars

Light Violet		1				1
Royal Purple		1				1
Violet	1	1				2

Yellows, Whites etc.: 9 cars

Dockers Drag Yellow				1		1
Special Yellow			1			1
White	3		1	1		5
Honeysuckle metallic		2				2

Two-tone: 33 cars

Birch Grey and Black	1					1
Black and Cream	2					2
Black and Silver			1			1
Black with Red wings			1			1
Cream and Black	1					1
Cream with Blue wings		1				1
Cream with Maroon wings		2				2
Dark Blue with Black wings		1	1	1		3
Dark Blue with White wings		1				1
Grey and Blue	1					1
Grey and Black	1					1
Ivory and Black	2					2
Ivory and Green	2					2
Ivory with Lavender Grey wings			1			1
Ivory with Red wings				1	1	2
Lake and Black	1					1
Lavender Grey with Blue wings		1				1
Maroon with Black wings		1	1			2
Olive Green with Black Wings		1				1
Opaline Green with Opaline Grey wings		1				1
Pale Apricot with Gull Grey wings		1				1
Red with Black wings		1				1
Silver and Blue	2					2
White with Dark Blue wings		1				1

Not identified: 12 cars

Belco (?)	1					1
Nobels Almond		1				1
Primer	4	2	1	1		8
Thornley & Knight	1					1
Jewelescence	1					1
Total for model year	118	118	28	54	7	325

3.7: SS 100, ALL MODEL YEARS

The SS 100 shared the standard colour range of the saloons, and Black and later Gunmetal were the most popular paint colours, but the preferred trim colour was Red, as was appropriate for a sports car, There is very little information on hood colours, presumably the hood colours were the same as for the dropheads, and SS 100 hoods were probably mostly Black. For the few cars where the hood colour was recorded, these were clearly special orders, with hoods in Grey, Lavender Grey, Maroon, or Crimson.

Paint colours	Trim colours												
	Beige	Blue	Brown	Green	Maroon	Olive Green	Pigskin	Red	Silver	Suede Green	n/r	Special trim	Total
Battleship Grey						1		4	4				9
Birch Grey		2						5					7
Black	1	1	8	4	3	13	7	39	11	1		1	89

	1	2	3	4	5	6	7	8	9	10	11	12	Total
Cream		3						5					8
Dark Blue		3									3		6
Gunmetal		2						36	42		1		81
Ivory							1	10	1				12
Lavender Grey		11				1		13	3	2			30
Maroon					3						5		8
Mountain Ash Green										3	1		4
Olive Green						2					2		4
Suede Green										2	5		7
Special colours		4		2			1	10	14		2	4	37
n/r (metallic finish)								1					1
Chassis										6			6
Total	1	26	8	6	6	16	10	123	75	8	25	5	309

3.71: SS 100 cars in special paint colours (37) or with special trim colours (5)

Paint and trim colours	No.
Black (standard colour), with special Black trim	1
Blue Sheen, with Blue trim	1
Blue metallic, with Silver trim	1
Carnation Red, with Silver trim	1
Green, special, with Green trim	1
Grey, metallic, with Silver trim	9
Mephisto Red, with special Mephisto Red trim	1
Nile Blue, with Blue trim (1) or not recorded (1)	2
Pillar Box Red, with Red trim	1
Red Sheen, with Red trim	1
Red, bright, with Pigskin trim	1
Red, special, with Red (2) or special Black trim (1)	3
Rust Red metallic, with Red trim	2
Silver, with Blue (1), Green (1), or Red (2) trim	4
Silver Blue, with special Powder Blue trim (1) or nor recorded (1)	2
Silver, metallic, with special Powder Blue trim	1
Snow Shadow Blue, with Blue trim	1
Steel Dust, with Silver trim	2
White, with Red (2) or Silver (1) trim	3

3.8: MARK IV

The post-war range of paint and trim colours was sensibly slightly reduced and rationalised, even so the Jaguars of this period were available in a wider choice than probably almost any other British make of car, in an era where "black with brown trim" was often the only colour scheme on offer.

| Paint colours | Trim colours | | | | | | | | | Total |
	Beige	Brown	Cloth	Pigskin	Red	Silver Black	Suede Green	n/r	Special trim	
Battleship Grey	3	1		55	249	265	1			574
Birch Grey	1		1	1	270	260	2		4	539
Black	320	2366	490	1070	1177	258	8	1	3	5693
Gunmetal	3	2		3	1031	1183	1		2	2225
Ivory	16	1		6	77	1	13			114
Lavender Grey	2	1		10	401	3	536		1	954
Suede Green	2		1				1800			1803
Special colours	3			1	3		2		7	16
Primer				6	16	1	8	2		33
Chassis only								14		14
Not recorded								4		4
Total	350	2371	492	1152	3224	1971	2371	21	17	11,969

3.81: Mark IV cars in special paint colours

Paint and trim colours	No.
Blue, with Pigskin and Red trim respectively	2
Cream, with special Tan trim	1
Dark Fawn, with Red trim	1
Dark Grey, with special Powder Blue trim	1
Dove Grey, with special Blue trim	1
Honeysuckle, with Beige trim	1
Light Blue, with special Biscuit trim	1
Light Grey, with special Powder Blue trim	1
Mist (grey?), with Red trim	1
Mountain Ash Green, with Suede Green trim	2
Novo Blue, with special Blue trim	1
Olive Green, with Beige trim	2
Slate Grey, with special Powder Blue trim	1

3.82: Mark IV with special trim colours

Note that 7 cars had both special paint and special trim and are included both in this table and in the table above:

Paint and trim colours	No.
Birch Grey, with Blue trim	4
Black, with Tan trim	3
Cream (special), with Tan trim	1
Dark Grey (special), with Powder Blue trim	1
Dove Grey (special), with Blue trim	1
Gunmetal, with Blue and Moquette cloth trim respectively	2
Lavender Grey, with Maroon trim	1
Light Blue (special), with Biscuit trim	1
Light Grey (special), with Powder Blue trim	1
Novo Blue (special), with Blue trim	1
Slate Grey (special), with Powder Blue trim	1

3.83: Mark IV DHC hood colours

The hood colours were the same as before the war, but interestingly with the addition of Maroon and Suede Green. These two hood colours were short-lived and were not used on the Mark V dropheads.

Paint colours	Hood colours							
	Black	Dark Sand	French Grey Grey	Gunmetal	Maroon	Suede Green	n/r	Total
Battleship Grey	6		17	23	2			48
Birch Grey	7		30	9	2			48
Black	58	140	48	3			2	251
Gunmetal	6		16	47	3		2	74
Ivory	11	10	2	1	2	6	1	33
Lavender Grey	7	2	45		2	16		72
Suede Green	3		19			50	2	74
Total	98	152	177	83	11	72	7	600

3.9: MARK V

The Mark V was available in the same colours as the Mark IV range, but also Cream and Dove Grey, and with the unusual addition of some new lighter metallic colours, Pastel Blue, Pastel Green, and Silver. These were probably primarily intended for the XK 120 and were most commonly found on the DHC models. The Mark V and XK 120 colour ranges were however not quite the same, thus neither Bronze nor Red were offered on the Mark V, and the two-tone interior trim found on many XK 120s was used only on a handful of Mark Vs.

Paint colours	Trim colours									
	Biscuit	Blue	Grey	Pigskin	Red	Suede Green	Tan	n/r	Special trim	Total
Battleship Grey	132	4	213	42	308	2	3			704
Birch Grey		478	244	2	294		4			1022
Black	635	6	187	908	755	22	1440		37	3990

Cream	4	48		1	114	5		3	175
Dove Grey	62			19			409		490
Gunmetal	13	743	366	1	618	6	1		1748
Ivory	2	9			18	2		3	34
Lavender Grey	4	168	1	8	322	260	15		778
Pastel Blue		310	11	1	2			3	327
Pastel Green		3	44		1	296			344
Silver		6	2		7				15
Suede Green	31			1	3	701	1		737
Special colours	6	8	1	2	9	4	1	3	34
CKD finish	30				47	4	4		85
Primer	1	1		3	2	2			9
Chassis only								5	5
Not recorded								2	5
Total	920	1784	1069	988	2500	1304	1878	7	49	10,499

3.91: Mark V cars in special paint colours

Paint and trim colours	No.
Battalion Beige, with Biscuit trim	2
Blue Sheen, with Blue trim	1
Bronze Sheen, with Tan trim	1
Bronze, with Biscuit trim	2
Canary Yellow, with special Maroon trim	1
Dark Blue, with Red trim	1
Dark Grey, with Biscuit trim	1
Dark Metallic Green, with Suede Green trim	1
French Grey, with Blue trim	1
Green Sheen, with Suede Green trim	1
Light Coffee, with Red trim	1
Light Green Sheen, with Grey trim	1
Maroon, with Pigskin trim	1
Mist Grey, with Red trim	1
Mountain Ash Green, with special Beige trim	1
Mountain Blue, with Blue trim	4
Navy Blue, with Red trim	1
Nebular Grey, with Red trim	1
Olive Green, with Biscuit, Pigskin, and special Beige trim respectively	3
Red and White, with Red trim	1
Sage Metallic Green, with Suede Green trim	1
Suede Green with Black wings, with Suede Green trim	1
Sun Beetle Green, with Blue trim	1
Twilight Blue, with Blue trim	1
White, with Red trim	2
Woodland Brown, with Red trim	1

3.92: Mark V with special trim colours

Of the 49 cars with special trim, 35 were in Black with cloth trim. The other 14 were in the following paint and trim combinations: (note that 3 cars had both special paint and special trim and are included both in this table and in the table above)

Paint and trim colours	No.
Black, with Biscuit and Tan trim	1
Black, with Rust trim	1
Canary Yellow (special), with Maroon trim	1
Cream, with Biscuit and Red trim	3
Ivory, with Pale Blue trim	3
Mountain Ash Green (special), with Beige trim	1
Olive Green (special), with Beige trim	1
Pastel Blue, with Duo-blue trim	3

3.93: Mark V DHC hood colours

Paint colours	Hood colours						
	Black	Dark Sand Sand	Fawn	French Grey Grey	Gunmetal	n/r	Total
Battleship Grey	15		2	33	39	4	93
Birch Grey	18		10	56	10	9	103
Black	91	127	30	24	6	14	292
Cream	57	24		11		5	97
Dove Grey		30	3	2			35
Gunmetal	24	2	5	28	103	10	172
Ivory	5						5
Lavender Grey	14	2	5	30	2	3	56
Pastel Blue	15		3	15	9	1	43
Pastel Green	2	4	1	20		2	29
Silver					3		3
Suede Green	7	1	2	52		2	64
Special colours	2		1		2	3	8
	250	190	62	271	174	53	1000

Appendix 4:
Rally Entries

MONTE CARLO RALLY

Entrant	Model	Chassis no.	Reg no.	Rally no.	Result
1936 15th Rally					
Hon B Lewis	2½ litre sal	10088	BHP 7		70th overall; 2nd in Concours de Confort
W Zwerts de Jong	SS I 20hp sal	248196	Dutch	62	57th overall
1937 16th Rally					
J Harrop	SS 100 2½ litre	18050	CVU 2	46	30th overall; RSAC Cup
Miss G Booth, Miss Peter				51	non-starter
AJE Howey	2½ litre sal	12419	CDU 122	63	45th overall
JFC Wellings	SS 100 2½ litre	18051	EPJ 460	122	32nd overall; 2nd for Open Cars over 1500cc
1938 17th Rally					
JOH Willing	3½ litre sal	30004(?)	ELN 789	45	42nd overall; Grand Prix d'Honneur, Concours de Confort
R Eccles				66	non-starter
1939 18th Rally					
T Edward-Moss, Miss RE-Moss	3½ litre sal	30708		15	95th overall
Sir WEF Carmichael-Anstruther	3½ litre sal	30496	MG 6130	54	20th overall
Major DEM Douglas-Morris	1½ litre sal		MJ 9283	67	71st overall
J Harrop, G Mangoletsi, WE Currie	3½ litre sal	30797	DKV 101	95	10th overall; Barclays Bank Cup
PRB Haggie	3½ litre DHC		FXW 586	101	45th overall
GA Apour	2½ litre sal			133	98th overall
1949 19th Rally					
JC Rockman	Mark IV 3½ litre	612571		14	75th overall
L Ponsard, J Felix				58	retired
1950 20th Rally					
JC Rockman, Pulver	Mark IV 3½ litre	612571		70	122nd overall
D, F, and A Warwick	Mark V 3½ litre	621962	LJH 866	72	
Donald Penman	2½ litre			88	
Van Herk, Prins	Mark IV 1½ litre		H-30460	209	retired
1951 21st Rally					
Sandgren, Bergendahl	Mark V 3½ litre			50	176th overall
Descals Juncosa, Roque Rivero	Mark V 3½ litre			121	224th overall

C Vard, A Young, Jolley	Mark V 3½ litre	624890	ZE 7445	211	3rd overall; Barclays Bank Cup; RSAC Cup
Bailey, Cavey, Keogh	Mark V 2½ litre	520682	ZJ 8726	213	170th overall
KW Hole, Zetter	Mark V 3½ litre		FNV 205	227	122nd overall
Tongue, Warr, Royce	Mark V 3½ litre	622796	KYP 935	241	31st overall
S Barslay, J Dudgeon	Mark V 3½ litre	622601		242	retired
Waring, Wadham, Sharp	Mark V 3½ litre	624424	JAA 915	254	9th overall; Public Schools Trophy; 2nd Concours de Confort (over 1,500 cc)

1952 22nd Rally

DG & FM Warwick	Mark V 3½ litre	621962	LJH 866	90	retired
JRJ Mansbridge, P Taylor	Mark V 3½ litre		RVW 330	118	94th overall

1953 23rd Rally

Harrop, Saxon, Handsforth	Mark V 2½ litre		LTD 933	136	335th overall
C Vard, Jolley, Biggar	Mark V 3½ litre	624890	ZE 7445	339	5th overall; L'Equipe Challenge Trophy for best 3 cars of one make with two Mark VII cars

1954 24th Rally

LS Norman, DJ Farquharson	Mark V		GRY 21	187	186th overall
J Lucas, LH Handley	Mark V		JUE 794	232	89th overall

Notes:

1952 start of entries for Mark VII; 1953 Ian and Pat Appleyard 2nd overall in Mark VII; 1956 won for the first time by Ronnie Adams and Frank Bigger in a Mark VII

TULIP RALLY

Entrant	Model	Chassis no.	Reg no.	Rally no.	Result
1949 1st					
Ian Appleyard, CA Stuart	SS 100 3½ litre	49010	LNW 100	4	2nd overall, 1st in Category 1
F Edwards, F Barker, JW Brocklehurst	Probably Mark IV			77	result not known
1950 2nd					
DL Jowett, H Lang	Mark V			22	retired (?)
S Barslay, I Moyell, M Barsley	Mark V	622601		31	22nd in Category 1
Mrs NEH Foster, Miss A Buckle	Mark V	622504	JWK 15	48	85th in Category 1
Hora Siccama, Bloem	Mark V (?)				20th in Category 1
1951 3rd					
WA & Mrs J Herrmann, L Schnackenborg	Mark V 3½ litre	628508	KDU 917 *	56	30th in Category 1
C Lohmander, A Hemmingsson	Mark V (?)		Swedish	58	non-starter
CEL Powell, J Caton	Mark V (?)			89	71st in Category 1
S Barslay, RW Cookson	Mark V 3½ litre	622601		139	not placed
E Ainsworth, NB Ainsworth, J Beckett	Mark V			222	15th overall, 9th in Category 1
HG Arndt, S Salmagne	SS 100 (?)			299	not placed
1952 4th					
WA & Mrs J Herrmann, J Schnackenborg	Mark V 3½ litre	628508	KDU 917 *	74	98th overall, 11th in Category 1
E Ainsworth, W Loakes, Mrs B Ainsworth	Mark V			153	not placed

* KDU 917 was the UK Registration before going to Denmark

RAC RALLY

Entrant	Model	Chassis no.	Reg no.	Rally no.	Result
1936 Torquay 24-28 March					
W Roberts	SS 90	249497	BUO 159	188	
Hon Brian Lewis	SS 100 2½ litre	18001	BHP 800	202	
FGT Prunty	SS I 16hp DHC			204	
J Eaves	2½ litre sal			217	
W Hetherington	2½ litre sal	10964	AXJ 58	219	

CL Bembridge	2½ litre sal	10438		229	
IDK Stuart	2½ litre sal	10103		233	
H Bolton	2½ litre sal	10197		234	
SA Bell	SS I 16hp sal			235	
B Sleath	2½ litre sal	10435	AHP 161	239	
ES Harris	SS I 20hp sal	248705		240	
B Hickman	2½ litre sal	10029	UN 9317	241	
DS Hand	2½ litre sal	10443		242	Coachwork 2nd in Class 4c
Miss MC Smith	2½ litre sal			248	Coachwork 1st in Class 4c

1937 Hastings 9-13 March

W Lambert	1½ litre SV sal			63	32 of 33
Miss AL Butler	1½ litre SV sal	21360		111	12 of 27
J Harrop	SS 100 2½ litre	18050	CVU 2	123	1 of 33; Hastings Corporation Trophy; Buxton Starting Control Prize
IWH Thomson	2½ litre tourer	19088	CDU 886	125	11 of 33
TH Wisdom	SS 100 2½ litre	18008	BWK 77	142	2 of 33; 1st Manufacturer's Team Prize; Leamington Starting Control Prize
Hon Brian Lewis	SS 100 2½ litre	18069	CHP402	143	25 of 33; 1st Manufacturer's Team Prize
W Vaughan (E Rankin, E Jacob)	SS 100 2½ litre	18080	CHP 295	144	4 of 33; 1st Manufacturer's Team Prize; 2nd in Class (4 door closed)
Miss BJN Streather	SS 100 2½ litre	18004	BRW 776	146	23 of 33
P Smith	2½ litre tourer			161	10 of 48
AP Smith	2½ litre sal	11666		162	13 of 48
W Hetherington	2½ litre sal	10964		163	41 of 48
CL Bembridge	2½ litre sal	10438		165	24 of 48
J Willing	2½ litre sal	11410		202	8 of 48
ES Coppen, DA Rice	2½ litre sal			204	42 of 48
GH Tudhope	2½ litre sal	11852		211	12 of 48

1938 Blackpool 26-30 April

JM Archer	SS 100 3½ litre	39010		150	non-starter
AGH Rimmel	Open			156	
IWH Thomson	Open			157	non-starter
J Harrop *	SS 100 3½ litre	39055	DHP 736	158	1 of 38 in Group 5 for Open Cars over 15hp Harrogate Starting Control Yorkshire Post Trophy
HE Bradley	SS 100 3½ litre	39035		159	5 of 38
KT Wild	SS 100 2½ litre	49001		163	9 of 38
OKR Freeman	Open			164	non-starter
CE Truett	SS 100 2½ litre	18105	DYL 469	165	14 of 38
EH Jacob *	SS 100 2½ litre	18070	CHP 295	167	30 of 38
Miss AL Adda	SS 100 2½ litre	49004	DYA 273	169	24 of 38
SH Newsome	SS 100 3½ litre	39050	DDU 822	170	4 of 38
Miss BJM Streather	SS 100 3½ litre	39053	DHP 734	172	13 of 38
W Hetherington	SS 100 2½ litre	18086	CRW 7	182	11 of 38
J Willing	SS 100 2½ litre	18092	DYL 475	184	35 of 38
GE Matthews	SS 100 2½ litre		ELK 38	188	35 of 38
TH Wisdom*	SS 100 2½ litre			190	17 of 38
BD Matthews	SS 100 2½ litre	18096	GMP 8	192	15 of 38
AP Smith	2½ litre sal			203	retired
J Hammond	3½ litre DHC	36018	CKU 515	209	48 of 62
CJ Jay	2½ litre sal			213	30 of 62
Mrs P Collinge	2½ litre DHC			244	38 of 62
Mrs EM Wisdom	3½ litre sal		DHP 941	245	33 of 62, 1st in coachwork, Closed car class £351 - £600

* entered by SS Cars

1939 Brighton 25-29 April

S Hince	1½ litre OHV DHC	56358	EDU 238	81	17of 20, Coachwork 1st in Class 2d
RM Procter	1½ litre OHV DHC	56416	DAK 157	96	13 of 20, Coachwork 2nd in Class 2d
WJ Knight	1½ litre OHV sal	52627		101	18 of 25, Coachwork 2nd in Class 2c
Dr AR Gray	1½ litre OHV sal	51293		111	14 of 25
D Wood	1½ litre SV sal	21959		112	20 of 25
ADC Gordon	SS 100 2½ litre	18048	CXJ 363	129	9 of 35, 2nd in Team Prize, SS Car Club
Miss BJM Streather, Miss A Adda	SS 100 3½ litre	39052	DHP 492	130	retired

Entrant	Model	Chassis no.	Reg no.	Rally no.	Result
T Frame Thomson	SS 100 3½ litre			131	non-starter
TH Bridgewater	2½ litre DHC		FLO 721	134	25 of 35, Coachwork 1st in Class 3d
Mrs IW McLennan	SS 100 2½ litre	49016	EUL 525	135	34 of 35
CJ Gibson	SS 100 3½ litre	39015	FVW 100	145	4 of 35, 2nd in Team Prize, SS Car Club; Torquay Starting Control Prize
TH Wisdom *	SS 100 3½ litre	39112	EHP 203	146	22 of 35
J Harrop *	SS 100 3½ litre	39111	EHP 202	158	6 of 35
SH Newsome *	SS 100 3½ litre	39110	EHP 201	169	2 of 35
C Mann	SS 100 3½ litre	39062	EYF 376	160	7 of 35, 2nd in Team Prize, SS Car Club
Miss EV Watson	SS 100 3½ litre	39100	DDV 777	161	11 of 35
W Gilling	3½ litre sal			172	did not complete tests
C Johnson Jay	2½ litre sal			193	Retired
AP Smith	2½ litre DHC			207	39 of 42
J Hammond	3½ litre sal			211	25 of 42
Mrs EM Wisdom, Mrs G Lyons	3½ litre sal	30935	EDU 615	223	15 of 42, Coachwork 1st in class 3c
A Bryde	3½ litre sal	30558		225	7 of 42

* Works Team

1951 Bournemouth 4-9 June

Entrant	Model	Chassis no.	Reg no.	Rally no.	Result
WH Waring	Mark V 3½ litre	624424		93	
Denis G Warwick	Mark V 3½ litre	621962			13th overall
P Herbert	Mark V 3½ litre		GCO 329		25th overall
JC Smith	Mark V 3½ litre	622614	JWY 529		retired
S Oakes	Mark V 3½ litre	625788	KVC 516		12th overall
HW Ede	Mark V 3½ litre	620347			
HD London	Mark V 3½ litre	624880	HYS 780		Reg uncertain
RA Pierson	Mark V 3½ litre	624202			
F Runton	Mark IV 3½ litre				retired
HJ Verden					
JH Mathew	Mark V 3½ litre				
WA Merifield	uncertain				
LT Rogers					
JF Montgomery	uncertain				

There were 50 Jaguars entered in 1951

1952 Scarborough 31 March-4 April

Entrant	Model	Chassis no.	Reg no.	Rally no.	Result
JC Smith	Mark V 3½ litre	622614	JWY 529	27	3rd in Class 3, over 2500cc (closed cars)

Scottish Rally (Royal Scottish Automobile Club)

Entrant	Model	Chassis no.	Reg no.	Rally no.	Result (in class)
1936 1 June; 5th Rally					
Peter Press	SS 90			22	
A Douglas Clease	SS 90	249476	AVC 277	41	14/22
SH Newsome	SS 100 2½ litre	18008	BWK 77	42	22/22
Miss Jessie Sleigh	2½ litre sal		WS 9391	53	5/33
W Hetherington	2½ litre sal		CNC 553	62	22/33
WG Vaughan	SS I 20 hp tourer	248123		63	19/22
RD Hunnam	2½ litre sal		CKX 77	64	32/33
Denis Hand	2½ litre sal			89	6/33
Miss Louise Mitchell	SS II 12hp sal	301172		118	35/36
CL Bembridge	2½ litre sal		TL 5050	132	3/33
10 entrants					
1937 17 May; 6th Rally					
Coronation Rally					
Mrs Jessie Agnew	SS 100 2½ litre	18019	CS 4100	13	25/27
Miss Eileen Smith	SS 100 2½ litre			17	
A Douglas Clease (Team A)	SS 100 2½ litre	18069	CHP 402	32	15/27
SH Newsome (Team A)	SS 100 2½ litre	18008	BWK 77	33	12/27
Hon Brian Lewis (Team A)	SS 100 2½ litre			34	
CL Bembridge	2½ litre sal	10438		45	10/32
Harold Goozee (Team C)	2½ litre sal	11013	xxx 924	53	23/32
WGV Vaughan (Team B)	SS 100 2½ litre	18097	FPE 299	56	7/27
R Donaldson Hunnam (Team B)	SS 100 2½ litre	18077	SS 4690	57	13/27

Entrant	Model	Chassis no.	Reg no.	Rally no.	Result
EH Jacob (Team B)	SS 100 2½ litre	18046	ATM 700	58	4/27
GE Matthews (Team C)	SS 100 2½ litre	18085	CRW 300	59	8/27
Norman Jackman	2½ litre sal	12694	CWM 22	60	8/32
BD Matthews (Team C)	SS 100 2½ litre	18096	GMH 8	61	6/27
Miss Alice Butler	1½ litre SV sal	21360		70	
Mrs V Hetherington (Team D)	SS 100 2½ litre	18086	AVM 1	71	24/27
W Hetherington (Team D)	SS 100 2½ litre		CRW 7	72	16/27
Miss Sheila Thompson	1½ litre SV sal	20920	CS 4745	73	29/32
Miss Jessie Sleigh	SS 100 2½ litre			76	3/27
HF Dixon	2½ litre sal	10980		107	3/32
FW Hamlet	2½ litre sal	12618		131	
Denis Hand	2½ litre sal	10443	CKX 77	141	24/32
Dr Olive Gimson			CND 902	159	23/32
William Munro	2½ litre sal	12438		164	

Teams referred to are from the SS Car Club; 23 entrants

1938 6 June; 7th Rally
Empire Exhibition Rally

Entrant	Model	Chassis no.	Reg no.	Rally no.	Result
Norman Jackman	1½ litre OHV sal			3	20/43
Mrs Jessie Agnew	SS 100 2½ litre	18019	CS 4100	13	17/32
Miss Eileen Smith	SS 100 3½ litre			19	13/32
Miss Jessie Sleigh	SS 100 3½ litre			40	29/32
Mrs Violet Hetherington	SS 100 3½ litre	39051	AVM 1	56	25/32
Ian DK Stuart	SS 100 3½ litre	39037	BGG 52	70	16/32
Robert Hunnam	SS 100 2½ litre	40148		72	
BD Matthews	SS 100 2½ litre	18096	GMH 8	73	3/32
Harold Goozee	SS 100 3½ litre	39039	HMX 87	83	26/32
William Crawford	1½ litre OHV sal	50170		90	6/43
Alexander Grant	1½ litre OHV sal			93	non-starter
Harold Bradley	SS 100 3½ litre	39035	HG 6247	108	14/32
Douglas Grant	1½ litre OHV DHC	56007		116	14/43
John M Archer	SS 100 3½ litre	39010		117	non-starter
SH Newsome	SS 100 3½ litre			119	4/32
Harry Botton	SS 100 3½ litre			143	6/32
Miss L Hunt	2½ litre sal	40123		173	33/33
AS Pearce	2½ litre sal		BKW 207	174	8/33
James Martin	SS 100 3½ litre	39058		183	11/32
Arthur P Smith	2½ litre sal			195	10/33
Mrs Ila Willing	SS 100 2½ litre	18092	DYL 475	201	non-starter
James Hammond	3½ litre DHC	36016		203	non-starter

22 entrants

1939 29 May; 8th Rally

Entrant	Model	Chassis no.	Reg no.	Rally no.	Result
Miss E Violet Watson	SS 100 3½ litre	39100	DDV 777	4	16/20
Miss Jessie Sleigh	SS 100 3½ litre	39111	EHP 202	28	4/20
Mrs Violet Hetherington	SS 100 3½ litre	39051	AVM 1	46	19/20
Harold Goozee	SS 100 3½ litre	39039	HMX 87	48	14/20
RM Hardaker	SS 100 2½ litre	49027	CAK 497	53	6/20
James Martin	SS 100 3½ litre	39058	GS 8040	85	non-starter
Dennis Patterson	SS 100 2½ litre	49062	FOC 170	95	17/20
John McCubbin	2½ litre sal	41287		96	18/24
Walter Norton	SS 100 3½ litre	39110	EHP 201	109	18/20
JF Montgomery	SS 100 2½ litre	18109	AUK 634	114	2/20
George Pyman	SS 100 3½ litre	39029	EXT 207	136	15/20

11 entrants

Welsh Rally

Entrant	Model	Chassis no.	Reg no.	Rally no.	Result
1936 14-17 July					
AG Grimmond	2½ litre sal	11337		49	retired
GE Matthews	2½ litre sal	10204	DEV 207	50	
EH Jacob	2½ litre sal			51	2nd in closed cars over 16hp
DS Hand	2½ litre sal	10443		53	1st in closed cars over 16hp

RS Sandland	1½ litre SV sal			66	1st closed car 10-16hp; 1st in coachwork 4-door closed cars from £251-£350
WA Atkinson	2½ litre sal	10645		83	non-starter
W Hetherington	2½ litre sal	10964	CNC 553	84	non-starter
7 entrants					
1937 30 June-2 July					
SG Davies	2½ litre sal		ABO 562	5	
DS Hand	2½ litre sal	10443	CKX 77	16	
BA Hickman	2½ litre sal	10029	ACA 947	19	
RHA Adam	SS 100 2½ litre	18087		30	
EH Jacob	SS 100 2½ litre	18046	ATM 700	33	Premier Award; Eliminating prize; 1st Manufacturers' Team prize; 1st Team Club prize SS Car Club
EW Rankin	SS 100 2½ litre	18091	CRW 809	34	1st Manufacturers' Team prize; 1st Team Club prize SS Car Club
BD Matthews	SS 100 2½ litre	18096	GMH 8	35	
GE Matthews	SS 100 2½ litre	18085	CRW 300	37	Starting Control prize – London; 1st Manufacturers' Team prize; 1st Team Club prize SS Car Club
W Hetherington	SS 100 2½ litre	18086	CRW 7	39	1st coachwork open car £351-£500
Mrs V Hetherington	SS 100 2½ litre		AVM 1	40	
HT Lewis	2½ litre sal		DXT 135	49	
N Howfield	2½ litre sal		HB 5316	52	
C Ryall	1½ litre SV sal		DGT 646	65	
13 entrants					
1938 20-23 July					
H Ripley	2½ litre sal			14	
R Shakespeare	2½ litre sal		YJ 4853	15	
C Johnson-Jay	2½ litre sal		DHW 60	23	
H Munday	SS 100 2½ litre			27	
A Clarke	SS 100 2½ litre			29	
H Bradley	SS 100 3½ litre	39035	HG 6247	31	
Mrs V Hetherington	SS 100 3½ litre	39051	AVM 1	32	1st open car class over 15hp; Supporters' prize
I Stuart	SS 100 3½ litre	39037	BGG 52	37	
Miss B Streather	SS 100 3½ litre	39053	DHP 734	38	2nd open car class over 15hp
G Matthews	SS 100 3½ litre			42	
Mrs E McLennan	SS 100 2½ litre	49016	EUL 525	44	
ADC Gordon	SS 100 2½ litre	18048	CXJ 363	45	
Tim Davies	SS 100 3½ litre			46	
B Matthews	SS 100 2½ litre	18096	GMH 8	49	
D Bryden	1½ litre OHV DHC	56007		61	1st in coachwork class DHC
WNKN Crawford	1½ litre OHV sal	50170		66	
Miss Betty Rogers	1½ litre SV sal	22238		79	
17 entrants					
1939 18-21 July					
David Rowland	DHC over 15hp			2	retired
C Johnson-Jay	Sal over 15hp		DHW 60	11	
RW Shakespeare	Sal over 15hp			25	non-starter
H Munday	SS 100			27	
Miss EV Watson	SS 100 3½ litre	39100	DDV 777	31	Starting prize, Chester
Miss Jessie S Sleigh	SS 100 3½ litre	39111	EHP 202	35	retired
Miss BJM Streather	SS 100 3½ litre		BHP 792	36	
CJ Gibson	SS 100			38	non-starter
WCN Norton	SS 100 3½ litre	39110	EHP 201	41	1st open car class over 15hp
ADC Gordon	SS 100 3½ litre	39066	JFB 437	43	Starting prize, London; Supporters' prize
HC Goozee	SS 100 3½ litre	39039	HMX 87	46	non-starter
Mrs E McLennan	SS 100 2½ litre	49016	EUL 525	48	
12 entrants					